PRENTICE
HALL
POCKET
ENCYCLOPEDIA

VEGETARIAN
COOKERY

PRENTICE
HALL
POCKET
ENCYCLOPEDIA
VEGETARIAN
COOKERY

Contributing editor
Sarah Brown

PRENTICE HALL CANADA, INC.
SCARBOROUGH, ONTARIO

A Dorling Kindersley Book

First published in Canada in 1991 by
Prentice Hall Canada, Inc.
Scarborough, Ontario

First published in Great Britain in 1991
by Dorling Kindersley Limited,
9 Henrietta Street, London WC2E 8PS

Designed and edited by Swallow Books,
260 Pentonville Road, London N1 9JY

Canadian Cataloguing in Publication Data
Main entry under title:

Prentice Hall pocket encyclopedia of
vegetarian cookery

ISBN 0-13-722125-8

1. Vegetarian cookery. I. Brown, Sarah
II. Title: Pocket encyclopedia of
vegetarian cookery.

TX837.P74 1991 641.5'636 C91-094223-4

Typeset by Bournetype, Bournemouth
Reproduced by Colourscan, Singapore
Printed in Singapore by Kyodo Printing (Co) Pte Ltd.

CONTENTS

INTRODUCTION

Throughout the 1980s we were bombarded with contradictory information about what food we should be including in our daily diet. We were told facts such as: saturated fat is bad for you, but polyunsaturated fats lower our cholesterol levels; eat plenty of fresh vegetables, but cut down on bananas – they're fattening; avoid eggs, they could contain salmonella. We became more aware of health and diet, but it became harder to sort out the facts from all the advice and differing opinions. When is something really good for you and when is it just a fad or a clever piece of marketing? This confusion extends to the foods themselves: are they really "full of natural goodness", "wholesome" or "energy building", and are they nutritionally sound?

This book explains which foods the body needs in order to remain healthy when eating a vegetarian diet, and how to buy the right balance of ingredients, and cook them with care to retain all the nutrients. A true vegetarian does not eat any fish, meat, or poultry and may or may not eat dairy products and eggs.

From the health point of view, the case for vegetarianism is a strong one. Most of the so-called diseases of civilization such as cancer, heart disease, high blood pressure, obesity, and diverticulitis are becoming increasingly linked with diet – more specifically diets that are high in refined sugar, fat and salt, and low in fibre. As long ago as 1916, studies comparing the low-fat diets of the Japanese to the cholesterol-rich diets of northern Europe and America found a definite correlation between high-fat, low-fibre Western diets and cancer and heart disease. A vegetarian diet not only replaces animal fats with vegetable ones, but often cuts down on the

total fat intake, since in the average diet a third of the fats come from meat and another third from dairy products. Eating cereals, pulses, fruit, and vegetables will ensure an adequate fibre intake, and if you eat sufficient amounts of whole foods, you will avoid the high levels of added salt and sugar that many processed foods contain.

A healthier approach

Finding out how the body can get all the nutrients it needs in a vegetarian diet is an important issue, especially if you've just decided to give up meat. The early chapters of the book tell you about the main sources of protein, fibre, vitamins, minerals, fats, and carbohydrates in foods. They tell you what the recommended daily intakes for the average adult are, and give helpful hints on how you can cut down on saturated fats, salt, and sugar, as well as suggesting appetizing alternatives.

If you walk into a health food shop you can be overwhelmed by the variety of goods that are available on the shelves, and be confused as to what to buy. *The Store Cupboard* (*see pages 44–99*) helps you to find out what grains, pulses, nuts, fruit, and vegetables you need to keep regular stocks of, and also gives you some useful information on how to prepare and cook them.

Once your cupboards are full to the brim, you'll want to start learning some vegetarian cookery techniques and it won't be long before you're getting the satisfaction of seeing people enjoy your own home-made yogurt (*see page 105*) or eating your hot, fresh home-baked wholewheat bread (*see page 102*) straight from the oven.

Cooking vegetarian meals for family and friends might seem a bit unusual at first, but they will soon be amazed at the variety of ingredients that can be used, and the delicious meals that can be concocted. The main recipe section (*see pages 122–81*) is divided into course order – soups, starters, salads, vegetable dishes, rice and pasta dishes, casseroles and roasts, desserts and puddings – so that you can easily find the dish you are looking for. Each recipe is based on the high-fibre, high-protein, low-fat principle, and has a nutritional profile to help you understand exactly which nutrients are contained in each dish, and in what quantity.

To help you plan how to put meals together, and cater for those special occasions when you want to produce a meal that is just that bit different, there are nine interesting, and well-balanced menus (*see pages 182–219*). Once again each menu and recipe has a nutritional profile. The menus are all high in fibre and protein, low in saturated fat, and provide a good source of vitamins and minerals.

Once you start using this book you soon realize that the days of gourmet dinner parties have not gone, and that food can be both good for you and taste delicious. The variety of recipes included means that you do not have to miss out on any of the pleasure of well-cooked, interestingly seasoned food. What is more, your concept of what is delicious will eventually change so that if you used to enjoy sweet, sugary things they will come to taste sickly, while rich, high-fat foods will seem heavy and indigestible.

Follow the principles outlined in the book and see how you start to enjoy your food more, whilst knowing that you're also improving your overall diet and general health.

Shopping for a healthier diet

You will soon begin to enjoy spending more time at the fruit and vegetable stall, making your selection of ingredients for the week's meals.

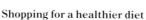

CHAPTER ONE

SOURCES OF NUTRIENTS

Which foods are essential to our bodies, and what are we better off not eating at all? The answer to these questions needs to be fully understood before you can see whether or not your normal daily diet is a well-balanced and truly healthy and nutritious one.

Proteins, fats, carbohydrates, vitamins, and minerals are all essential to life. This part of the book explains why they are so necessary to us, which foods supply them (including complementary proteins), and the recommended daily allowance of each one.

On the following pages is an easy-to-use photographic guide to the commonly available foods that are the best sources of essential nutrients. Divided by nutrient type, each food item illustrated is shown with the quantity of protein, vitamin, mineral, fat, or carbohydrate per 100g (3½oz).

Nutritious foods
A healthy diet needs to include a good, overall mix of foods such as fresh vegetables, fruit, pulses, and dairy produce.

Protein

Proteins have two main functions. Firstly, they promote growth and form the basic framework of different body structures such as skin, nails, and hair. A constant supply of protein is needed for the maintenance of body structures and to repair worn-out tissues. Secondly, proteins maintain supplies of enzymes, hormones, and antibodies. These regulate many of the body's most important functions, such as the ability to digest food. Excess protein is either changed to fat and stored, or used to produce heat and energy.

Proteins are made up of amino acids, which consist of carbon, hydrogen, and oxygen groups, together with nitrogen, which enables the amino acids to string together forming long, complex molecules. Some 20 or so amino acids act like building blocks, combining in different ways to produce a wide variety of proteins. Eight are called essential, because the body cannot do without them and cannot synthesize them for itself. These are leucine, isoleucine, lysine, methionine, phenylalanine, threonine, tryptophan, and valine. Growing children also need arginine and histidine.

Proteins from animal sources – meat, milk, and eggs – contain all the essential amino acids in roughly the proportions that the body needs, hence they are called first class proteins. No single vegetable food contains amino acids in the proportions the body needs, so they are referred to as second class proteins. A mixture of vegetable proteins is needed to provide an adequate level of the essential amino acids in the total diet. For example, wheat is low in lysine but contains adequate methionine; beans are low in methionine but contain adequate lysine. Eat the two foods together and the body's amino acid requirements are met – the combination of the protein sources gives a high-quality protein supply. The ability of different proteins to make up for each other's deficiencies is known as their supplementary or complementary value. Most traditional cuisines have recipes based on protein's ability to do this. For example, rice and dhal (lentils) are combined, and pasta (wheat) and chick peas.

We are currently advised to eat fewer saturated fats and increase our intake of dietary fibre. Meat and dairy products, although good sources of protein, are also high in saturated fats and lacking in fibre. Plant proteins can easily be combined to provide good proteins while containing little fat (in the case of pulses and grains), and plenty of fibre. The soya bean is exceptional in being a source of high-quality protein in itself, since it contains good proportions of all eight essential amino acids. Good sources of protein are illustrated on these pages. The recommended daily intake is 65–90g (2¼–3¼oz) for men and 55–63g (2–2¼oz) for women.

Extracts and grains

Yeast extract
Protein per 100g (3½oz): 39.7g (1²⁄₅₀z)

Soya flour
Protein per 100g (3½oz): 36.8g (1²⁄₇oz)

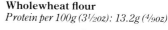

Wholewheat flour
Protein per 100g (3½oz): 13.2g (⁴⁄₉oz)

Oatmeal
Protein per 100g (3½oz): 12.4g (⁴⁄₉oz)

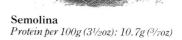

Semolina
Protein per 100g (3½oz): 10.7g (³⁄₇oz)

Wheatgerm
Protein per 100g (3¹/₂oz): 26.5g (⁹/₁₀oz)

Rye flour
Protein per 100g (3¹/₂oz): 8.2g (²/₇oz)

Wholewheat bread
Protein per 100g (3¹/₂oz): 8.8g (¹/₃oz)

Bran
Protein per 100g (3¹/₂oz): 14.1g (¹/₂oz)

Dairy products and eggs

Double Gloucester
Protein per 100g (3¹/₂oz): 26g (⁹/₁₀oz)

Coulommiers
Protein per 100g (3¹/₂oz): 22.8g (⁴/₅oz)

Cottage cheese
Protein per 100g (3¹/₂oz): 13.6g (¹/₂oz)

Parmesan
Protein per 100g (3¹/₂oz): 35.1g (1¹/₈oz)

Eggs
Protein per 100g (3¹/₂oz): 12.3g (⁴/₉oz)

Cheddar
Protein per 100g (3¹/₂oz): 26g (⁹/₁₀oz)

Brie
Protein per 100g (3¹/₂oz): 22.8g (⁴/₅oz)

Whole goat's milk
Protein per 100g (3½oz): 3.3g (1/9oz)

Skimmed milk
Protein per 100g (3½oz): 3.4g (1/8oz)

Soya milk
Protein per 100g (3½oz): 3.6g (1/8oz)

Whole cow's milk
Protein per 100g (3½oz): 3.3g (1/9oz)

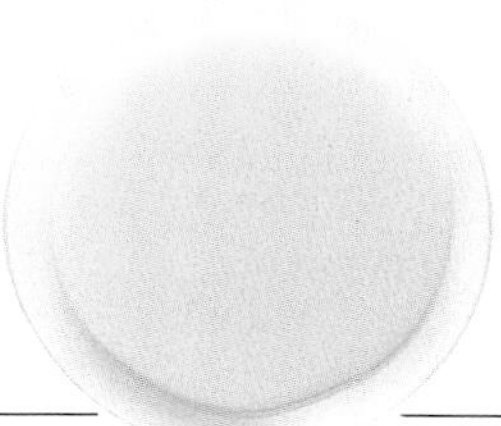

Yogurt
Protein per 100g (3½oz): 5g (1/6oz)

Nuts

Pistachios
Protein per 100g (3½oz): 19.3g (2/3oz)

Peanuts
Protein per 100g (3½oz): 24.3g (6/7oz)

Brazil nuts
Protein per 100g (3½oz): 12g (3/7oz)

Almonds
Protein per 100g (3½oz): 16.9g (3/5oz)

Walnuts
Protein per 100g (3½oz): 20.5g (5/7oz)

Pulses

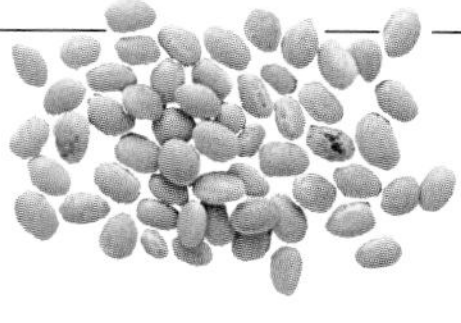

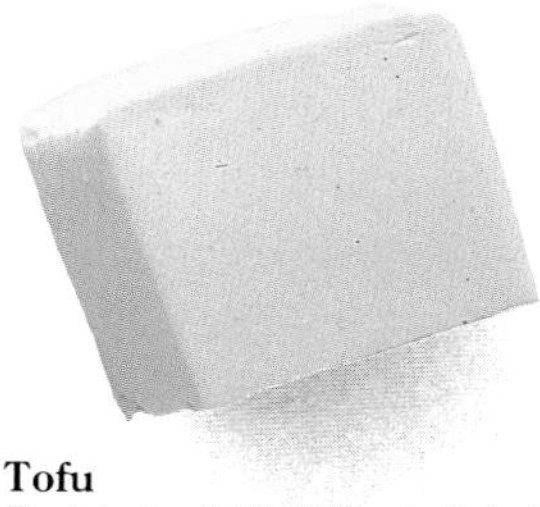

Haricot beans
Protein per 100g (3½oz): 6.6g (2/9oz)

Split peas
Protein per 100g (3½oz): 7.1g (1/4oz)

Lentils
Protein per 100g (3½oz): 7.6g (1/4oz)

Chick peas
Protein per 100g (3½oz): 8g (2/7oz)

Tofu
Protein per 100g (3½oz): 7.4g (1/4oz)

Fibre

Dietary fibre is the term used to describe a group of substances that are not broken down by the digestive enzymes. Fibre, which makes up the cell walls of plants, is a form of carbohydrate. It is essential for the efficient working of the digestive system, although it is not actually digested by the body.

All fibres make food chewy, so that you eat less, and more slowly. This is good exercise for the jaws and stimulates saliva production, which helps neutralize acid formed on the teeth, reducing dental decay. Fibre also swells up in your stomach, making you feel more satisfied after eating.

There are five kinds of fibre: pectin, gum, cellulose, hemicellulose, and lignin. Each plays a different role in improving health and preventing disease.

Pectins

These are found in the cell walls of fruits, and in the form of pectose, in the soft tissues of unripe fruits. In the gut they bind some of the bile salts produced by the gall bladder. This may reduce the digestion and absorption of fats and cholesterol, which may in turn help to prevent heart disease.

Gums

These are sticky substances exuded by plants. Like pectin, gum reduces cholesterol uptake. Gums also line the stomach and slow down the absorption of sugar, which is especially useful for people suffering from diabetes.

Cellulose

This comes from the tough outer walls of plant cells. In the gut it takes up water and increases the bulk of partly digested foods. Bulkier food moves more quickly through the body, and takes with it toxins that may have accumulated in the lower intestine.

Hemicelluloses

These come from the cell walls of plants. They also help to bulk out food, making it pass more quickly through the body.

Lignin

This is a woody substance, found mainly in root vegetables. Like cellulose, it adds bulk to stools, making them easier to pass, and may help to prevent haemorrhoids, varicose veins, and possibly cancer of the rectum.

Good sources of fibre

For a range of fibre intake you should eat beans, whole grains, fresh fruit, and vegetables. Meat and dairy products contain no fibre. Sprinkling bran on top of other food is not the best way to increase fibre intake. An acid in bran combines with minerals, reducing their absorption. Eat fibre as part of a complete food, as this contains a greater quantity of minerals than is found in refined grains.

Among the best sources of fibre are bran, apricots, prunes, and wholewheat bread. The recommended daily intake for both men and women is 25–30g (⅞–1oz).

Grains and pulses

Soya flour
Fibre per 100g (3½oz): 11.9g (³/₇oz)

Wholewheat flour
Fibre per 100g (3½oz): 9.6g (⅓oz)

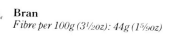

Bran
Fibre per 100g (3½oz): 44g (1⁵/₉oz)

Wholewheat bread
Fibre per 100g (3½oz): 8.5g (³/₁₀oz)

Oatmeal
Fibre per 100g (3¹/₂oz): 7g (¹/₄oz)

Haricot beans
Fibre per 100g (3¹/₂oz): 7.4g (¹/₄oz)

Chickpeas
Fibre per 100g (3¹/₂oz): 6g (¹/₅oz)

Pot barley
Fibre per 100g (3¹/₂oz): 6.5g (²/₉oz)

Fruit

Dried peaches
Fibre per 100g (3¹/₂oz): 14.3g (¹/₂oz)

Blackberries
Fibre per 100g (3¹/₂oz): 7.3g (¹/₄oz)

Prunes
Fibre per 100g (3¹/₂oz): 16.1g (⁴/₇oz)

Dried apricots
Fibre per 100g (3¹/₂oz): 24g (⁶/₇oz)

Dried figs
Fibre per 100g (3¹/₂oz): 18.5g (²/₃oz)

Currants
Fibre per 100g (3¹/₂oz): 6.5g (²/₉oz)

Plantain
Fibre per 100g (3¹/₂oz): 6.4g (²/₉oz)

Blackcurrants
Fibre per 100g (3¹/₂oz): 8.7g (³/₁₀oz)

Dates
Fibre per 100g (3¹/₂oz): 8.7g (³/₁₀oz)

Passion fruit
Fibre per 100g (3¹/₂oz): 6.7g (²/₉oz)

Raisins
Fibre per 100g (3¹/₂oz): 6.4g (²/₉oz)

Raspberries
Fibre per 100g (3¹/₂oz): 7.4g (¹/₄oz)

Sultanas
Fibre per 100g (3¹/₂oz): 7g (¹/₄oz)

Nuts

Peanuts
Fibre per 100g (3¹/₂oz): 8.1g (²/₇oz)

Fresh coconut
Fibre per 100g (3¹/₂oz): 13.6g (¹/₂oz)

Brazil nuts
Fibre per 100g (3¹/₂oz): 9g (¹/₃oz)

Almonds
Fibre per 100g (3¹/₂oz): 14.3g (¹/₂oz)

Desiccated coconut
Fibre per 100g (3¹/₂oz): 23.5g (⁵/₆oz)

Vegetables

Spinach
Fibre per 100g (3¹/₂oz): 6.3g (²/₉oz)

Sweetcorn
Fibre per 100g (3¹/₂oz): 5.7g (¹/₅oz)

Parsley
Fibre per 100g (3¹/₂oz): 9.1g (¹/₃oz)
Peas
Fibre per 100g (3¹/₂oz): 12g (³/₇oz)

Celery
Fibre per 100g (3¹/₂oz): 4.9g (¹/₆oz)

Vitamins

Vitamins are essential chemicals, required by the body in very small quantities. Since the body cannot produce them, they must be supplied by external means, i.e. in food.

Vitamins fall into two distinct groups: water-soluble (the Vitamin B group, Vitamin C and folic acid), and fat-soluble (Vitamins A, D, E, and K). Water-soluble vitamins dissolve in the blood and tissue fluids; they cannot be stored in the body for long. Any excess is excreted in the urine. Fat-soluble vitamins can be stored by the body in the liver and fatty tissues.

The amount of any vitamin required each day varies according to age, sex, and occupation. Growing children, pregnant women, and lactating mothers all need more vitamins, as do the elderly, and those recovering from illness.

Other factors, such as diet or lifestyle, also influence the body's vitamin requirements. Some chemicals contained in many widely consumed substances – alcohol, cigarettes, coffee, aspirins, the Pill – use up much of the body's vitamin resources, so people who smoke, drink, or take regular medication need to be sure that their food is rich in vitamins.

Vitamins can be destroyed during the storing, processing, or cooking of food. Refined foods such as white flour have relatively few vitamins compared to brown or wholemeal flour. Water-soluble vitamins are vulnerable to heat; a large amount can be destroyed during cooking, especially in water, since the vitamins escape into the cooking liquid and are thrown away with it. Fat-soluble vitamins are generally more stable but can be sensitive to light and air. Freezing does little damage to most vitamins.

Vitamin A

This keeps skin and mucous membranes (linings of the stomach, intestines, bladder, nose, throat, and respiratory passageways) healthy. It is essential for vision in dim light.

The B group vitamins

These are important in the metabolism of carbohydrates, fats, and proteins in the body. They keep the hair, skin, eyes, mouth, and liver healthy. They are needed for the proper functioning of the brain, nervous and circulatory systems, and for red blood cell formation.

Vitamin C

This is necessary for healthy connective tissues such as bone cartilage and collagen. It promotes the healing of wounds, helps the body to fight against infection, and increases the absorption of iron.

Vitamin D

This is essential for maintaining normal levels of calcium and phosphorus in the blood, and enhances the absorption of calcium, ensuring sound formation of bones and teeth. Vitamin D is especially important for pregnant women and young children.

Vitamin E

This is a component of all cell membranes. It acts in a similar way to antioxidants (used to prevent food from going rancid), and so prevents damage to the components of the cell membranes. It protects unsaturated fats in the body from damage and protects Vitamin A from destruction.

Vitamin K

This vitamin is needed to prevent the body from haemorrhaging.

Folic Acid

This, along with Vitamin B_{12}, is needed for the successful formation of genetic material in the DNA molecules contained in cells (which is why it is important in early pregnancy). It also helps in the formation of proteins.

Recommended amounts

The recommended daily intake for each of these vitamins is as follows: Vitamin A $750\mu g$; Vitamin B_1 0.9–1.4mg; Vitamin B_2 1.3–1.7mg; Vitamin B_3 15–18mg; Vitamin B_6 2mg; Vitamin B_{12} 1–2μg; Vitamin C 30mg; Vitamin D 2.5μg; Vitamin E 11mg; Vitamin K 70–104μg; folic acid 200μg.

Vitamin A

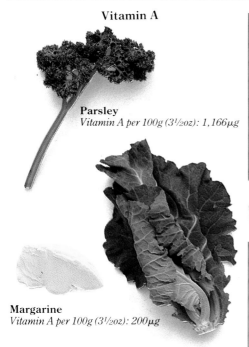

Parsley
Vitamin A per 100g (3½oz): 1,166μg

Margarine
Vitamin A per 100g (3½oz): 200μg

Spring cabbage
Vitamin A per 100g (3½oz): 83μg

Sorrel
Vitamin A per 100g (3½oz): 2,150μg

Carrots
Vitamin A per 100g (3½oz): 2,000μg

Vitamin B₁

Peanuts
Vitamin B₁ per 100g (3½oz): 0.90mg

Yeast extract
Vitamin B₁ per 100g (3½oz): 3.10mg

Brazil nuts
Vitamin B₁ per 100g (3½oz): 1mg

Millet
Vitamin B₁ per 100g (3½oz): 0.73mg

Soya flour
Vitamin B₁ per 100g (3½oz): 0.75mg

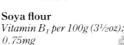

Bran
Vitamin B₁ per 100g (3½oz): 0.89mg
Wheatgerm
Vitamin B₁ per 100g (3½oz): 1.45mg

Yeast extract
Vitamin B₂ per 100g (3¹/₂oz): 11mg

Vitamin B₂

Almonds
Vitamin B₂ per 100g (3¹/₂oz): 0.92mg

Wheatgerm
Vitamin B₂ per 100g (3¹/₂oz): 0.61mg

Brie
Vitamin B₂ per 100g (3¹/₂oz): 0.60mg

Cheddar
Vitamin B₂ per 100g (3¹/₂oz): 0.50mg

Egg yolk
Vitamin B₂ per 100g (3¹/₂oz): 0.47mg

Parmesan
Vitamin B₂ per 100g (3¹/₂oz): 0.50mg

Vitamin B₃

Yeast extract
Vitamin B₃ per 100g (3¹/₂oz): 58mg

Wheatgerm
Vitamin B₃ per 100g (3¹/₂oz): 5.8mg

Peanuts
Vitamin B₃ per 100g (3¹/₂oz): 16mg

Dried peaches
Vitamin B₃ per 100g (3¹/₂oz): 5.3mg

Button mushrooms
Vitamin B₃ per 100g (3¹/₂oz): 4mg

Wholewheat flour
Vitamin B₃ per 100g (3¹/₂oz): 5.6mg

Bran
Vitamin B₃ per 100g (3¹/₂oz): 29.6mg

Vitamin B$_6$

Soya flour
Vitamin B$_6$ per 100g (3^1/$_2$oz): 0.57mg

Walnuts
Vitamin B$_6$ per 100g (3^1/$_2$oz): 0.73mg

Wheatgerm
Vitamin B$_6$ per 100g (3^1/$_2$oz): 0.93mg

Banana
Vitamin B$_6$ per 100g (3^1/$_2$oz): 0.51mg

Hazelnuts
Vitamin B$_6$ per 100g (3^1/$_2$oz): 0.55mg

Bran
Vitamin B$_6$ per 100g (3^1/$_2$oz): 1.38mg

Yeast extract
Vitamin B$_6$ per 100g (3^1/$_2$oz): 1.30mg

Vitamin B$_{12}$

Cheddar
Vitamin B$_{12}$ per 100g (3^1/$_2$oz): 1.7µg

Cottage cheese
Vitamin B$_{12}$ per 100g (3^1/$_2$oz): 0.5µg

Egg yolk
Vitamin B$_{12}$ per 100g (3^1/$_2$oz): 4.9µg

Yeast extract
Vitamin B$_{12}$ per 100g (3^1/$_2$oz): 0.5µg

Brie
Vitamin B$_{12}$ per 100g (3^1/$_2$oz): 1.2µg

Parmesan
Vitamin B$_{12}$ per 100g (3^1/$_2$oz): 1.5µg

Vitamin C

Lemon
Vitamin C per 100g (3¹/₂oz): 80mg

Sorrel
Vitamin C per 100g (3¹/₂oz): 119mg

Red pepper
Vitamin C per 100g (3¹/₂oz): 204mg

Blackcurrants
Vitamin C per 100g (3¹/₂oz): 200mg

Parsley
Vitamin C per 100g (3¹/₂oz): 150mg

Green pepper
Vitamin C per 100g (3¹/₂oz): 100mg

Vitamin D

Egg yolk
Vitamin D per 100g (3¹/₂oz): 5.00µg

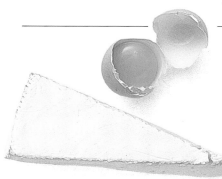

Margarine
Vitamin D per 100g (3¹/₂oz): 7.94µg

Cheddar
Vitamin D per 100g (3¹/₂oz): 0.26µg

Brie
Vitamin D per 100g (3¹/₂oz): 0.18µg

Vitamin E

Peanuts
Vitamin E per 100g (3¹/₂oz): 8.1mg

Almonds
Vitamin E per 100g (3¹/₂oz): 20mg

Hazelnuts
Vitamin E per 100g (3¹/₂oz): 21mg

Brazil nuts
Vitamin E per 100g (3¹/₂oz): 6.5mg

Egg yolk
Vitamin E per 100g (3¹/₂oz): 4.6mg

Margarine
Vitamin E per 100g (3¹/₂oz): 8mg

Vitamin K

Soya beans
Vitamin K per 100g (3¹/₂oz): 190µg

Cauliflower
Vitamin K per 100g (3¹/₂oz): 150µg

Lettuce
Vitamin K per 100g (3¹/₂oz): 200µg
Cabbage
Vitamin K per 100g (3¹/₂oz): 100µg

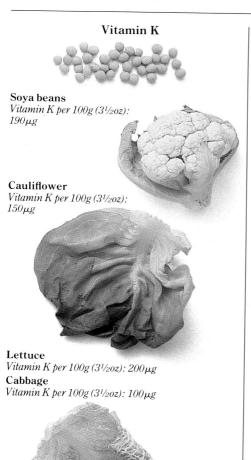

Folic Acid

Watercress
Folic acid per 100g (3¹/₂oz): 200µg

Bran
Folic acid per 100g (3¹/₂oz): 130µg

Wheatgerm
Folic acid per 100g (3¹/₂oz): 62µg

Yeast extract
Folic acid per 100g (3¹/₂oz): 83µg

Minerals

Four per cent of our body is made up of 100 or so different minerals, of which about 20 are known or suspected to be essential. Six are present in the body in large quantities: sodium, potassium, chlorine, calcium, phosphorus, and magnesium. A sufficient supply of sodium and phosphorus is obtainable from most foods. The other 14 are called trace elements, making up less than 1/10,000th part of our body.

Plants are the main source of minerals, as they absorb them from the soil. Minerals are part of the structural framework of the body, being present in bones and teeth, as well as in muscle fibres and nerve cells. They enable muscles to contract and relax, and impulses to be transmitted through the nerves. As soluble salts, they contribute to the composition and balance of body fluids. Minerals are constituents of enzymes, vitamins, and hormones. They enable many chemical reactions to take place which break down and utilize food.

Apart from their individual functions, minerals also work in groups. A balanced relationship is important. Taking supplements of only one mineral may cause a deficiency of another. Balance is the key, and the relationship between minerals can be easily upset.

Modern agricultural and food processing techniques can distort the mineral balance. For example, phosphates are used extensively as fertilizers. A high intake of phosphorus increases the body's need for calcium. Another example is salt. Our intake of sodium is some eight to ten times our requirement due to the salt contained in processed foods and added in cooking; this may upset the sodium/potassium balance. Pollution from car exhausts, cigarette smoke, drugs such as the Pill, alcohol, and caffeine all affect our mineral needs.

A varied diet of wholefoods, fresh fruit, vegetables, and nuts should provide an ample supply of all the essential elements, particularly if the food is grown on healthy, composted soil.

Sodium, potassium, and chlorine
These are responsible in different ways for the mechanisms that ensure a constant volume of body fluids. Chlorine (in the form of chloride) is necessary for making hydrochloric acid in the gastric juices of the stomach. This is required for the digestion of proteins. Potassium is required for muscle cells and blood corpuscles. Sodium is essential for balancing the quantities of fluids inside and outside each cell.

Calcium, phosphorus, and magnesium
Calcium is a major component of the bones and teeth and is necessary for their maintenance. It is also needed for blood clotting, maintenance of cell membranes, and for proper functioning of the nervous system. Phosphorus teams up with calcium to maintain healthy bones and is also important for energy release. Magnesium is necessary for the utilization of calcium and potassium by the body, and for the correct functioning of the nervous system.

Iron, zinc, and copper
Iron is necessary for the formation in the body of haemoglobin, which carries oxygen in the blood. Vitamin C enhances iron absorption, and a trace of copper is needed for the correct functioning of iron in the body. Zinc is essential for growth and for the synthesis of proteins. It is necessary for wound healing, sexual maturation, and the maintenance of skin, hair, nails, and mucous membranes. An adequate supply of iron, zinc, and copper is particularly important for those who eat little or no meat, since a supply of these minerals is usually obtained from liver and other meat.

Iodine
Very small quantities of iodine are required for the normal functioning of the thyroid gland, which regulates the body's metabolic rate.

Recommended daily intake
The following pages illustrate some good sources of the different minerals described here. Recommended daily intakes for the different minerals are: potassium 3mg, calcium 500mg, magnesium 250mg, iron 10–12mg, zinc 12mg, and copper 2–3mg. There are no recommended daily intakes of sodium, chlorine, and phosphorus in the UK.

Magnesium

Bran
Magnesium per 100g (3¹/₂oz): 520mg

Brazil nuts
Magnesium per 100g (3¹/₂oz): 410mg

Wheatgerm
Magnesium per 100g (3¹/₂oz): 300mg

Almonds
Magnesium per 100g (3¹/₂oz): 260mg

Soya flour
Magnesium per 100g (3¹/₂oz): 240mg

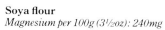

Millet
Magnesium per 100g (3¹/₂oz): 162mg

Oatmeal
Magnesium per 100g (3¹/₂oz): 110mg

Peanuts
Magnesium per 100g (3¹/₂oz): 180mg

Walnuts
Magnesium per 100g (3¹/₂oz): 130mg

Wholewheat flour
Magnesium per 100g (3¹/₂oz): 140mg

Calcium

Parmesan
Calcium per 100g (3¹/₂oz): 1,200mg

Cheddar
Calcium per 100g (3¹/₂oz): 800mg

Dried figs
Calcium per 100g (3½oz): 280mg

Almonds
Calcium per 100g (3½oz): 250mg

Spinach
Calcium per 100g (3½oz): 600mg

Parsley
Calcium per 100g (3½oz): 330mg

Brazil nuts
Calcium per 100g (3½oz): 180mg

Watercress
Calcium per 100g (3½oz): 220mg

Brie
Calcium per 100g (3½oz): 380mg

Soya flour
Calcium per 100g (3½oz): 210mg

Potassium

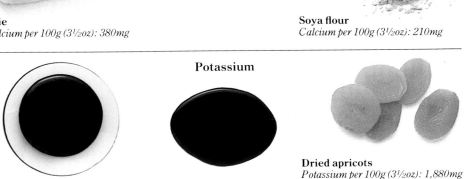

Dried apricots
Potassium per 100g (3½oz): 1,880mg

Blackstrap molasses
Potassium per 100g (3½oz): 2,927mg

Yeast extract
Potassium per 100g (3½oz): 2,600mg

Dried peaches
Potassium per 100g (3½oz): 1,100mg

Soya flour
Potassium per 100g (3½oz): 1,660mg

Wheatgerm
Potassium per 100g (3½oz): 1,000mg

Dried figs
Potassium per 100g (3½oz): 1,010mg

Parsley
Potassium per 100g (3½oz): 1,080mg

Bran
Potassium per 100g (3½oz): 1,160mg

Sultanas
Potassium per 100g (3½oz): 860mg

Iron

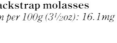

Wheatgerm
Iron per 100g (3½oz): 10mg

Blackstrap molasses
Iron per 100g (3½oz): 16.1mg

Parsley
Iron per 100g (3½oz): 8mg

Bran
Iron per 100g (3½oz): 12.9mg

Soya flour
Iron per 100g (3¹/₂oz): 6.9mg

Dried peaches
Iron per 100g (3¹/₂oz): 6.8mg

Millet
Iron per 100g (3¹/₂oz): 6.8mg

Egg yolk
Iron per 100g (3¹/₂oz): 6.1mg

Fresh yeast
Iron per 100g (3¹/₂oz): 5mg

Dried figs
Iron per 100g (3¹/₂oz): 4.2mg

Zinc

Bran
Zinc per 100g (3¹/₂oz): 16.2mg

Brazil nuts
Zinc per 100g (3¹/₂oz): 4.2mg

Parmesan
Zinc per 100g (3¹/₂oz): 4mg

Almonds
Zinc per 100g (3¹/₂oz): 3.1mg

Cheddar
Zinc per 100g (3¹/₂oz): 4mg

Walnuts
Zinc per 100g (3¹/₂oz): 3mg

Peanuts
Zinc per 100g (3¹/₂oz): 3mg

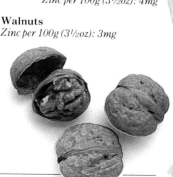

Wholewheat flour
Zinc per 100g (3¹/₂oz): 3mg

Oatmeal
Zinc per 100g (3¹/₂oz): 3mg

Brie
Zinc per 100g (3¹/₂oz): 3mg

Fresh yeast
Copper per 100g (3¹/₂oz): 5mg

Copper

Bran
Copper per 100g (3¹/₂oz): 1.3mg

Brazil nuts
Copper per 100g (3¹/₂oz): 1.1mg

Whole egg
Copper per 100g (3¹/₂oz): 1mg

Desiccated coconut
Copper per 100g (3¹/₂oz): 0.6mg

Dried peaches
Copper per 100g (3¹/₂oz): 0.6mg

Broad beans
Copper per 100g (3¹/₂oz): 0.4mg

Parsley
Copper per 100g (3¹/₂oz): 0.5mg

Wholewheat flour
Copper per 100g (3¹/₂oz): 0.4mg

Currants
Copper per 100g (3¹/₂oz): 0.5mg

Fats

There are three main types of fat; they are known as saturated, monounsaturated, and polyunsaturated. The type is determined by the number of free "links" in the chemical structure. Saturated fats have hydrogen atoms attached to all of their links, monounsaturated fats have a few links free, and polyunsaturated fats have many free links.

Saturated fats are generally of animal origin, with the exceptions of coconut and palm oil, and hydrogenated (artificially hardened) vegetable fats. Polyunsaturated fats (PUFA) tend to be liquid at room temperature, and are found mainly in plants and in fish. Monounsaturated fats are found particularly in nuts and fruit. No single food contains only one sort of fat; what distinguishes foods is the proportions in which different fats are present.

Apart from being a concentrated source of energy, fat has several other functions. Food containing fat is more palatable, since fats help the flavours to mingle and facilitate swallowing.

Fats satisfy the appetite, not only because they are high in calories, but also because they slow down digestion, keeping the stomach full for a longer period. The fatty tissues store the fat-soluble Vitamins A, D, E, and K. Fat is stored in layers under the skin to help keep the body warm, and it cushions the vital organs to protect them against impact and hold them in place. Stored fat can be used for fuel if the body is deprived of food for any length of time.

Polyunsaturated fats provide essential fatty acids (EFA) – these are linoleic, linolenic, and arachidonic. They are vital constituents of the capillaries and membranes, and are used to regulate blood flow. Linoleic acid needs to come from the food we eat; the other EFAs can be synthesized by the body, but this process is slow and it is better to obtain them directly from food.

For more about the different types of fat and their effect on health, see pp. 36–7. There is no recommended daily intake of fats in the UK.

Polyunsaturated fats

Safflower seed oil
PUFA per 100g (3¹/₂oz): 72.11g (2¹/₂oz)

Sunflower seed oil
PUFA per 100g (3¹/₂oz): 49.95g (1³/₄oz)

Soya bean oil
PUFA per 100g (3¹/₂oz): 56.73g (2oz)

Walnuts
PUFA per 100g (3¹/₂oz): 35.15g (1¹/₄oz)

Brazil nuts
PUFA per 100g (3¹/₂oz): 22.93g (⁴/₅oz)

Peanuts
PUFA per 100g (3¹/₂oz): 13.95g (¹/₂oz)

Soya flour
PUFA per 100g (3¹/₂oz): 13.34g (⁴/₉oz)

Carbohydrates

Carbohydrates are compounds of carbon, hydrogen, and oxygen. The two main types of digestible carbohydrates are sugars (simple carbohydrates) and starches (complex carbohydrates); they are our most important source of energy.

The chief sugars are simple sugars or monosaccharides, consisting of glucose, fructose, and galactose, or double sugars, or disaccharides, comprising sucrose, maltose, and lactose. Sucrose is the most commonly eaten sugar, yet it provides no nutrients at all.

Starches are an example of polysaccharides, or complex carbohydrates. It is recommended that we should eat more starches (contained in potatoes, wholewheat bread, and flour products) and fewer simple carbohydrates.

Before being used by the body, carbohydrates must be broken down into simple sugars, which can then be absorbed through the walls of the small intestine into the bloodstream. They are then either broken down to produce energy, or stored in the liver as glycogen. This forms a reserve to help maintain blood sugar levels between meals or during exercise. Excess carbohydrate is stored as fat.

Apart from giving us energy, carbohydrates are needed to metabolize protein so that it can be used to build and repair body tissues. The central nervous system also requires a steady supply of carbohydrates.

To release the energy that is stored in carbohydrates, the body requires sufficient quantities of vitamins. Especially important in this respect are vitamins in the B complex group, used to regulate the production of energy from glucose.

The best sources of carbohydrates are illustrated here. There is no recommended daily intake of carbohydrates in the UK.

Grains and pulses

Rice
Carbohydrate per 100g (3½oz):
86.8g (3oz)

Pot barley
Carbohydrate per 100g (3½oz):
83.6g (2⁹/₁₀oz)

Rye flour
Carbohydrate per 100g (3½oz):
75.9g (2²/₃oz)

Oatmeal
Carbohydrate per 100g (3½oz):
72.8g (2⁴/₇oz)

Split peas
Carbohydrate per 100g (3½oz):
54.7g (1⁹/₁₀oz)

Lentils
Carbohydrate per 100g (3½oz):
50.8g (1⁴/₅oz)

Butter beans
Carbohydrate per 100g (3½oz):
46.2g (1⁵/₈oz)

Wholewheat flour
Carbohydrate per 100g (3½oz):
63.5g (2¼ oz)

· CHAPTER TWO ·

HEALTHY EATING

"Eat less fat, less salt, and less, if any, sugar. Eat more fibre and complex carbohydrate, especially from whole grains, pulses, fresh fruit, and vegetables." This is the message from nutritionists. These guidelines sound straightforward, but if it were simple to follow them, no doubt we would all be healthier tomorrow. Change is not easy. People become rooted in their eating habits, and cannot believe that what is being suggested can really improve their health and general well-being. However, if you approach change gradually, the transition to good health can be relatively painless! It will also give you time to change to a new shopping and cooking routine. Remember, while it is important to aim for meals that reflect the low fat, low salt, low sugar, high protein, high fibre principle, do not worry if every dish does not contain the perfect balance. What counts is your average intake of nutrients over a week. This chapter shows you how to change to a well-balanced diet.

The right choice
By combining well-chosen ingredients for starters: Top left: Papaya and lime salad (see p.190); main courses: Bottom left: Celebration roast (see p.186); Top right: Radicchio salad (see p.213); and desserts: Bottom right: Mango and orange sorbet (see p.211), you can create perfectly-balanced meals for friends and family.

Changing to a healthy diet

Look carefully at your present diet. Ask yourself: Do I eat enough fresh fruit? Do I eat a lot of fats? Do I eat too much tinned or processed food? Only you can decide what changes need to take place. Then think about which of the foods that you normally buy could be replaced with something more healthy.

Foods for a healthy diet should be wholesome and nutritious, but containing no dangerous chemicals or additives. The term "wholefoods" applies to foods to which nothing has been added and nothing taken away. The benefit of these types of food is that they retain nutrients that would be lost in refining or food processing.

Nowadays, wholefoods are not restricted to healthfood shops. Many supermarkets produce a range of products that are largely additive-free, using good-quality, natural ingredients. There is a range of wholewheat products – flours, breads, pastas, biscuits, and cereals – as well as preservative-free yogurts and fruit juices, and unrefined oils.

Next, start looking at the labels on any processed food that you buy – look particularly for the sugar, salt, and fat content. Start buying sugar-free breakfast cereals, watch out for sugar in savoury products such as canned soups and baked beans, and note the salt content in canned vegetables – and some frozen ones. In fact, try to cut down on canned food altogether. Think about some of the processed foods that you buy, and consider making them yourself. Mayonnaise, sweet and savoury sauces, muesli, and soups can all be made quite easily at home and by doing this you can be sure there are no unwanted additives.

Consider the quality of the fresh food you are eating. If you are able to grow your own fruit and vegetables, you can eat really fresh produce that has been cultivated without chemical sprays and pesticides. (Advice on organic growing methods is given in the *DK Pocket Encyclopedia of Organic Gardening.*) If you cannot grow your own fruit and vegetables, do choose quality produce; go to a reputable shop, preferably one supplying organic fruit and vegetables.

Think about your meals

Once you have the correct ingredients, small changes to your menus can make huge differences to your diet.

Breakfast: Make your own muesli or choose a sugar- or fat-free cereal. If you prefer a hot breakfast, try porridge, home-made muffins, or home-made baked beans, grilled tomatoes, or mushrooms on wholewheat or rye bread. Drink unsweetened fruit juices, and coffee substitutes or herbal teas (see *Drinks*, p. 43).

Lunch and supper: There is a wide range of staple foods for you to draw from. Cereals and pulses should be eaten for their carbohydrate, fibre, protein, vitamin, and mineral content; nuts and seeds for proteins and fats (remember they have a high fat content); vegetables and fruit for their fibre, vitamins, and minerals. Within these groups different foods have different nutritional values (see pp. 12–31).

Change the emphasis so that the main part of your meals is unrefined carbohydrate, which is satisfying, and provides energy – do not rely on high calorie, low nutrient processed foods to fill you up. Alter the way you cook your meals: grill or bake instead of frying, and steam or stir-fry your vegetables.

Try to include some raw fruit or vegetables in at least one of your main meals to obtain maximum nutritional benefit. This could be a salad starter or main course – there are plenty of ideas in the book to choose from that are a far cry from lettuce and tomato. You could also serve a fresh fruit salad instead of a sticky pudding – just as satisfying and nutritionally far better for you.

Snacks: Fresh vegetables and fresh fruit make nourishing snacks. Replace sweets with dried fruit, and savoury nibbles with nuts and seeds. Eat sugar-free or low-sugar biscuits or cakes until you can give up sweet snacks, and try wholewheat bread spread with a savoury spread such as miso for a savoury snack.

Eating out

Healthfood restaurants are burgeoning, and they generally have a good range of dishes to choose from. Eating in a conventional

Unusual salads
Fresh salads of vegetables and pulses make light nourishing meals, such as sweetcorn salad (see p.191), and green bean julienne (see p.199). Alternatively, for a more exotic flavour, mix dried apricots with bulgar wheat and pumpkin seeds, or chopped Brussels sprouts with nuts, and fruit.

restaurant is sometimes more difficult. I find the starters more imaginative than the main courses and order several plus a salad. Select steamed rather than fried vegetables.

Eating in other people's houses is often more difficult because you will rarely be given a choice of dishes or meals to eat. Just remember that no food is completely forbidden in a healthy diet; it is really up to you to balance your diet on a weekly basis.

Meals for children
If your children have always eaten wholefoods at home, problems start only when they go out or go to school. It is up to you to make sure that the rest of their diet is balanced. If you are changing to a wholefood diet yourselves, your children may be more resistant to change, but again it is a question of introducing new foods gradually. Remember to let them have the odd treat occasionally as well.

Main courses are relatively easy because most children like pizzas, pastas, and grain dishes, particularly rice and millet. For puddings try the trifle (see p.176), cranachan (see p.177), or just yogurt with fresh fruit.

If you are making packed lunches for school or picnics, vary the type of bread you use, and fill sandwiches with imaginative spreads such as quark, golden tofu pâté (see p.138), or a sweet tahini spread. The latter two are especially good for children because they are high in protein, which is essential for their growth and development. Make pasties with a light yeasted pastry or use a shortcrust wholewheat pastry for flans and tartlets.

Snacks are a particular problem with children because raw fruit and vegetables do not have the same appeal as a bar of chocolate or a sticky cake. However, dried fruit can make a good substitute for sweets, and there are several recipes in the book for sugar-free cakes and biscuits, for example, carob biscuits (see p.180) and fruit and nut bars (see p.181). Avoid giving very young children small nuts and seeds because they can easily choke, and avoid fruit squash, which is high in additives – offer fruit juices mixed with sparkling mineral water as an alternative.

Healthy alternatives

This section is intended as a guide to the foods to avoid or cut down on, with suggestions for alternatives to help you ease into a new and healthier way of eating, without really missing the old way. First steps might be to reduce your fat intake by replacing whole milk with skimmed milk, and butter with polyunsaturated margarine, to eat wholewheat bread and pasta, and brown rice instead of polished white rice.

Fats

Most fatty foods were once afforded only by the rich. Fats are now the cheapest form of calories available. This is because weight for weight they contain almost twice as many calories as both carbohydrates and proteins. Estimates suggest in 1800 fat accounted for about 10 per cent of the calories in our diet. Now it accounts for 40 per cent.

Variety salads
Try mixing fresh fruit and nuts in your salads for added vitamins and protein, and for variety. The mixtures featured here are beetroot with apple, courgette with an orange and tahini dressing, strawberry with cucumber, orange with olive, and coleslaw with apricots or with fennel.

Fats and disease
There are now clear links between fat and various so-called Western diseases. Too much fat can make you fat, leading to obesity. This brings a greater likelihood of illness such as diabetes, arthritis, gall bladder disease, high blood pressure, and heart trouble. Even without obesity there are clear links between fat consumption and heart disease, and because high-fat diets tend to be low-fibre diets, they are thought to be a contributory factor in cancer of the bowel.

Reduce consumption
We urgently need to cut down our consumption of fats to less than 30 per cent of our total calorie intake. Although we need some fat in our diet for energy, and to supply essential fatty acids and fat-soluble vitamins, on average an adult needs to eat less than 85g (3oz) per day.

Saturated v. unsaturated fats
It is not just a matter of how much fat we eat but also the type of fat (see p.30). Saturated fats can cause fatty deposits on artery walls. These fatty deposits are largely cholesterol, a normal component of most body tissues, supplied only by animal and dairy fats. The deposits may build up and block the arteries, thus obstructing the flow of blood, a process called atherosclerosis. If this occurs in a heart artery it can cause a heart attack. Blockage in other regions can cause strokes, angina, or other circulatory problems. Low blood cholesterol levels reduce the risk of heart attacks, it is known that cholesterol levels fall when less saturated fat is eaten. Unsaturated fats are thought to offer some protection against atherosclerosis by lowering blood cholesterol levels. However, the best protection is to eat less fat altogether – particularly saturated fats.

Avoiding fats

In practical terms, this means cutting down on animal-derived products such as lard, eggs, butter, hard cheese, cream, and full-fat milk. This can be very hard to do unless you make everything you eat so that you can see exactly what goes into things. Processed foods may be loaded with unsuspected fats and the only way to tell is by reading the labels: they should give the fat content, if not the type. Generally, ingredients are listed in descending order of weight, so it should be possible to get some idea of the proportion of fat. This particularly applies to oils and margarines.

The percentage of fat on a label is given by weight, sometimes wet weight. Thus, in sausage, for example, which is fatty meats, cereals, and water, the overall fat content may appear to be only 25 per cent. Because water has no energy value however, the percentage of calories coming from the fat is actually nearer 70 per cent.

Blended oils should be avoided as they may well be made from a mixture of palm or coconut oil (both containing saturated fats) and an unsaturated oil such as sunflower. Buy the unmixed, unsaturated oils such as corn, sunflower, and safflower, and get them cold-pressed if possible because the heat used in other methods of processing can destroy some of the important nutrients they contain, such as lecithin and Vitamin E.

HOW TO CUT DOWN ON FAT

- Eat more vegetarian meals.
- Have fresh fruit salads, fruit compotes, or yogurt instead of puddings.
- Use yogurt as a salad dressing instead of oil.
- Grill or bake rather than fry.
- Use non-stick pans so that you use less oil.
- Use gentle heat when cooking, because high temperatures change unsaturated fats into saturated fats.
- Use polyunsaturated oil and margarine in place of butter and lard.
- Use fresh herbs on food instead of butter.
- Change from full-fat milk to skimmed milk.
- Moisten sandwiches or crispbreads with salad or savoury spread rather than butter.
- Avoid blended oils made partly with saturated fats; use cold-pressed oils instead.
- Have cakes, pastries, chocolate, crisps, biscuits, and ice-cream rarely, even home-made low-fat ones.
- Avoid food where fat is high on the label.

Many margarine manufacturers start with cheap ingredients such as beef suet and whale oil and rely on extensive processing, colouring, and additives to produce palatable results. Moreover, they use the process of hydrogenation to solidify the fat, thus turning unsaturated fats into saturated fats. The best margarines are made with cold-pressed, unsaturated oils that have not been hydrogenated, and can be found in healthfood shops.

Dairy products

About a third of our fat intake comes from meat and a third from dairy products. Together, these make up about 40 per cent of our saturated fat intake, so it makes sense to cut down on these products or to use less fatty alternatives. Although dairy products contain high proportions of proteins, vitamins, and minerals, we can in fact make do with less butter, milk, cream, and cheese because all these nutrients can be found in other sources (see *Sources of Nutrients*, pp. 10–31).

There are, however, other reasons, apart from a high fat content, for cutting down on dairy products. Milk contributes to a number of complaints, and milk allergies are common. There are two types of milk allergy: some people are allergic to milk protein, which can result in breathing difficulties, catarrh, or eczema; others have an enzyme deficiency known as lactose intolerance that hinders the breaking down of milk sugars in the body. Lactose is one of the milk sugars and it is broken down by an enzyme called lactase. If lactase is not present, the lactose accumulates in the intestine, ferments, and causes cramps and diarrhoea.

After chocolate, the most likely causes of migraine headaches are cheese and other dairy products. They also cause the formation of mucus and may contribute to various sinus problems and bronchitis.

Baked potatoes
Potatoes are a good source of protein and fibre, and are not especially fattening, except when filled with butter or full-fat cheese. Try serving them with a sauce made from smetana and chopped chives, or chillis and beans. Alternatively, scoop out the inside and mix it with another vegetable such as spinach or broccoli.

Alternatives to dairy products

There are many ways in which you can cut down on your consumption of dairy products. Start by using skimmed milk. If you cannot drink cow's milk, try goat's milk or soya milk.

Skimmed milk: Whole, full-fat milk is about 3.8 per cent fat; skimmed milk is only 0.1 per cent. Semi-skimmed milk contains about half as much fat as whole milk. The advantage of skimmed milk is that only the fat and fat-soluble vitamins are removed. Skimmed milk does taste different and it can take time to get used to it, but when you become adjusted, whole milk will seem too rich.

Goat's milk and soya milk: Those allergic to cow's milk can substitute goat's milk or soya milk. Goat's milk has a higher phosphate, copper, and magnesium content than cow's milk but beware, because it also has a much higher fat content and it is very difficult to obtain low-fat goat's milk. Soya milk also has a higher fat content than skimmed milk. Both soya and goat's milk are available in powdered form.

Low-fat milk products: It is easy enough to cut down on fatty dairy products. I have listed some of the low-fat ones below. Some of the products have high-fat versions, or versions containing water and salt, so it is important to check the labels carefully.

Cottage cheese is similar to curd cheese but made from skimmed milk so it is low in fat, yielding about 30 calories per 25g (1oz). Some varieties contain salt and preservatives, so

check the label carefully. Curd cheese is made from the separated curd of whole cow's or goat's milk, so it is about 11 per cent fat and gives 40–45 calories per 25g (1oz). Quark is another soft, white cheese, but it is made from semi-skimmed milk and does not contain salt. The fat content is generally low but can be up to 40 per cent, so it is wise to check the label.

Smetana looks like cream and tastes similar to sour cream but is made from low-fat dairy products. Its fat content varies from 5 to 10 per cent. Check the label if you buy it or make your own (see *Making smetana*, p. 107). Yogurt can be made from skimmed or whole milk but is acidic enough to break down milk protein into a more easily digested form. You can make your own (see *Making yogurt*, pp. 105–6).

HOW TO CUT DOWN ON HIGH-FAT DAIRY PRODUCTS

- Use skimmed milk instead of whole milk.
- Serve yogurt as a pudding.
- Use yogurt or smetana instead of cream when you are cooking creamy dishes.
- Make yogurt-based dressings for salads.
- Soak muesli in fruit juice instead of milk.
- Try herbal teas instead of milky drinks.
- Sprinkle cooked vegetables with herbs such as parsley instead of butter.
- Use a good-quality margarine made from polyunsaturated fats instead of butter.
- Avoid butter in sandwiches; moisten the bread with tahini, yeast extract, or a similar savoury spread.

Salt

We need less than 4g (¹/₇oz) of salt per day and we can get this from whole, fresh foods, yet we add salt to our food and take in about ten to twelve times as much as we need. There are links between intake of salt and high blood pressure, a condition which can lead to other circulatory problems, such as heart disease and strokes.

Salt is sodium chloride. Sodium and potassium together help to regulate the body fluids, and the balance is a delicate one (see *Minerals*, p. 24). Too much salt can upset the balance and cause fluid to be retained in the body. The kidneys also have to work harder to get rid of the excess salt.

Avoiding salt

Most of the salt we eat comes from processed foods. Canned vegetables, for example, may have as much as 200 per cent more sodium than fresh ones, so it is not just obvious things like crisps that you have to watch. High-salt foods include many canned and packet soups, pickles, sauces, butter, and margarine, as well as plenty of unexpected ones, such as breakfast cereals. Many of the additives contained in processed foods are sodium-based.

The best strategy is to cut out all processed foods and, when cooking, simply leave salt out of a recipe, or use one of the alternatives given right. Give your taste buds a chance to get the flavour of a dish. Adding salt at the table is often just a habit, sometimes an addiction; you will probably find it easier to give up salt if you reduce the amount you add gradually.

HOW TO CUT DOWN ON SALT

- Use a low-sodium salt.
- Use gomasio or herb salt instead of ordinary, unmixed salt.
- Use miso as a savoury spread.
- Sprinkle vegetables with fresh herbs, spices, or lemon juice instead of adding salt during cooking.
- Use miso, shoyu, or tamari instead of salt to flavour soups and stews.

Alternatives

There are several flavourings that can be used instead of salt, and there is even a way to make a low-salt version of baking soda.

Low-sodium salt: Half sodium salt and half potassium salt, this is helpful in making the transition between using salt and not using it.

Herb salt: This is salt with herbs. While it is just as salty, it has more flavour and will therefore help you to use less salt.

Gomasio: A mixture of toasted, crushed sesame seeds and salt.

Miso: A seasoning made from soya beans fermented with salt and wheat or barley, which has the consistency of a dense spread. There are several varieties available (see p. 89). It can be stored for several months but should not be subjected to extremes of temperature.

Shoyu and tamari: Dark liquids with a salty taste (see *Seasonings and flavourings*, p. 90), these can be added to any savoury dish. Shoyu is made from soya beans, wheat, salt, and water. Tamari should be made without wheat. Shoyu and tamari will keep indefinitely.

Low-sodium baking powder: This is a useful substitute for baking soda, which is high in salt. Mix equal parts of rice flour or arrowroot, cream of tartar, and potassium bicarbonate.

Sugar

We know that refined sugar can make us fat, rot our teeth, and that it is linked with diabetes. So why do we in the Western world eat on average 1kg (2lb) of refined sugar a week each? Is sugar addictive? The culprit is sucrose in the form of white or brown sugar. The way that nature packages sugar, along with fibre, vitamins, minerals, and water – as, for

example, in fresh fruit and vegetables – ensures that we do not eat too much. Refined sugar, on the other hand, gives only calories.

Whatever we eat raises the level of blood glucose (blood sugar). Provided glucose is released slowly and steadily during digestion, the blood sugar level is maintained within normal limits, sustaining mental and physical ability, helping us to concentrate and keeping our emotions balanced. All goes well when unrefined, high-fibre carbohydrates (both

Sugar-free puddings
Many delicious puddings – such as baked millet pudding with stewed apricots, and poached pears with carob sauce – can be made by using honey and other natural sweeteners in place of refined sugar.

starches and sugars) are eaten because these are digested slowly, but a concentrated supply of refined sugar is absorbed quickly and raises blood sugar to high levels. The pancreas sends insulin to lower the sugar level, causing a rapid fall, which leaves a craving for more sugar. It is a vicious circle, causing bursts of energy followed by fatigue and moody ups and downs. If the pancreas cannot cope with so many sudden demands for insulin, this may lead to diabetes. The acid-producing bacteria that attack teeth love sugar, as it reacts with saliva to produce just the right environment.

Sugar is also a drain on nutrients, especially B vitamins and calcium, which are used in metabolizing sugar. Naturally sweet foods like dates often contain enough of the B vitamins to compensate, as do unrefined carbohydrates. Refined sugar, which lacks nutrients, draws more nutrients away from the body's supplies.

There appear to be links between sugar intake and hyperactivity in children and heart disease. Too much sugar also increases the level of triglycerides (fats) in the blood, and increase in fats may be associated with circulatory disorders such as atherosclerosis.

As much as three-quarters of the sugar we eat is found in manufactured foods, and not just obvious ones like fizzy drinks. A surprising number of savoury foods contain sugar, among them soups, sauces, pickles, ready-made salads, and canned vegetables.

Alternatives to sugar

It is possible to avoid packet sugar altogether by using unrefined natural sweeteners.

Honey: This contains fructose and glucose. It has slightly fewer calories than sucrose and is sweeter, so you use less. It contains traces of vitamins and minerals. Honey can be used as a sweetener in drinks, on food such as yogurt, or in cooking.

Molasses: This is the residue left after extracting sugar from cane or beet, which contains minerals, especially calcium and iron, and vitamins. It is sucrose, not fructose, but it has a strong flavour so you will find that you do not need to use very much.

Maple syrup: This is not as sweet as honey and is largely sucrose, but it does contain calcium and potassium.

Malt extract: A product of beer-making, malt extract contains maltose, which is far less sweet than sucrose. It has a strong flavour and contains iron and some of the B vitamins. Other grain syrups have a similar taste.

Fruit juice concentrates: Undiluted, these can be used instead of sugar in cakes and cereals. In the refrigerator they will keep, undiluted, for about 3–5 weeks.

Dried fruit purées: These make excellent sugar substitutes in baking – the sweetest is date purée. To make fruit purée, chop the fruit finely, cover it with water and simmer, for 10–15 minutes, until the fruit is soft enough to mash. Cream it in with the fats as you would sugar. I find that 25–50g (1–2oz) dates is equal to about 25g (1oz) of sugar.

HOW TO CUT DOWN ON SUGAR
• Do without sugar in hot drinks.
• Buy sugar-free breakfast cereals or make your own muesli at home.
• Avoid fruit squash and drink unsweetened fruit juice or mineral water.
• Use less sugar than called for in recipes.
• Eat ice-cream and sweets only rarely.
• Replace puddings with fruit, low-fat cheese, or yogurt, perhaps with an unrefined natural sweetener.
• Eat dried fruit, fresh fruit, and raw vegetables.
• Avoid processed foods as much as possible.
• Buy sugar-free or reduced-sugar jams, or switch to savoury spreads such as miso (see *Seasonings and flavourings*, p.89).
• Check labels on processed foods.

Additives

Nutritionists caution against too much fat, salt and sugar but these are not the only "baddies". High on the list of substances to cut down on or avoid are additives. Mostly non-nutritive substances, additives are added to food to prolong shelf life, assist in processing, and cosmetically improve the taste and appearance of food. They are now so commonplace that it is almost impossible to avoid them.

Additives include flavourings and flavour-enhancers, thickeners, stabilizers, emulsifiers, colourings, preservatives, bases, antioxidants, sweeteners, bleaches, and glazing agents. Different countries have different laws governing the use of additives in food. The general rule is that they must be safe and not used in greater quantities than necessary.

The testing of a new additive is often not necessarily foolproof. Results of tests on animals may or may not be valid on humans, and little is known about the long-term effects. Some additives may cause cancer but it is hard to trace the cause of a disease that takes years to develop. Studies are needed to see if harmful effects are being passed from one generation to another. We know little about how additives interact with other chemicals in food.

When an additive comes into common use, it may be consumed in large quantities from several different sources, so a permitted safety limit set for any one food is irrelevant. We need more information, and unfortunately food labels are not much use. In the UK, flavourings do not have to be listed and, even when additives are listed, they are generally referred to by their "E" numbers, so unless you are a chemist it is like a foreign language.

Avoiding additives

The best way to avoid additives is by eating as many whole, fresh foods as possible. However, it may be difficult to avoid buying some processed foods: even wholewheat bread, for example, may contain emulsifiers.

Antioxidants: Vitamins C and E are natural antioxidants. Artificial antioxidants are substances normally used to keep fats from going rancid and to prolong shelf life. BHA (E320, butylated hydroxyanisole) and BHT (E321, butylated hydroxytoluene), when tested on animals, were found to cause abnormalities and poor growth in the young. BHA affects the intestinal muscles of humans. BHT has caused liver and kidney damage, balding, raised cholesterol levels and altered brain chemistry in animals, while human effects include asthma and other allergies. Both are found in butter, margarine, cooking oils and bakery products containing fats. Other anti-oxidants to avoid are: E310 (propyl gallate), E311 (octyl gallate) and E312 (dodecyl gallate) found in oils, fats and breakfast cereals. They can cause asthma and skin complaints.

Artificial sweeteners: These are used to add sweetening without calories. Saccharine, the best known, is used in ever-increasing amounts. Reported ill-effects include tumours in old animals, and digestive, blood clotting disorders, and skin allergies in humans. Saccharine is banned in several countries.

Bleaching agents: Used to whiten flour, bleaching agents destroy most of the nutrients not already removed in refining, particularly Vitamin E. Chlorine (925) and chlorine dioxide (926) are powerful irritants and their use is banned in every EEC country except the UK. Potassium bromate (924) has been shown to cause nausea and diarrhoea.

Colourings: These are the least justifiable additives, because they are purely cosmetic. They are increasingly used to make cheap food look appealing, although the actual number of permitted colourings is likely to be reduced, due to doubts about their safety. The main ones to watch out for are coal tar dyes, which are made synthetically, and, in particular, azo dyes. Coal tar dyes causing cancer in animals have already been banned. These dyes have been implicated in hyperactivity in children. About a fifth of those sensitive to aspirin also react to azo dyes; other reactions include asthma, rashes, and gastric upsets. Watch out for colourings particularly in soft drinks, packet soups, sweets, canned fruits and vegetables, cake mixes, biscuits, smoked fish, salad cream and jam. The following colourings are azo dyes: E102 (tartrazine), E110 (sunset yellow FCF), E122 (carmoisine), E123 (amaranth), E124 (ponceall 4R), E128 (red 2G), 154 (brown FK), 155 (chocolate brown HT), E151 (black PN), E180 (pigment rubine). The following numbers denote other types of coal tar dyes: E104 (quinoline yellow), E127 (erythrosine BS), E131 (patent blue V), E132 (indigo carmine), and E133 (brilliant blue FCF).

E150 (caramel) is both a colouring and a flavouring additive which, when made with ammonia, can cause Vitamin B_6 deficiency in rats. There are several varieties of caramel and they are found in a wide range of foods.

Flavourings: These comprise the largest group of additives. Few have been tested and there are no permitted lists so manufacturers can use what they like. Glutamates, including monosodium glutamate or MSG (621), enhance flavour. Side-effects of eating food containing them include headaches, dizziness, palpitations, and chest pains. They are banned in baby foods.

Glazing agents: These are used to give food a protective or shiny finish. Mineral oil (905), used on some dried fruits, prevents the body from absorbing fat-soluble vitamins.

Preservatives: These are considered the most justifiable additives because they prevent spoilage and let us enjoy out-of-season foods. E220 (sulphur dioxide), the preservative most commonly used in the UK, is also an antioxidant and a bleach.

Sulphites help to preserve Vitamin C, but in the process destroy Vitamins B_1 and E. They are not supposed to be used in foods that contain significant amounts of Vitamin B_1. They are dangerous to all asthmatics and can cause allergic reactions. Sulphur dioxide is suspected of triggering genetic mutations because it affects nucleic acids, the building blocks that pass our characteristics on to our offspring. You will find sulphites in fruit juices, wine, jam, sugar, dried vegetables, canned fruits, flour, and bakery products.

Other sulphite preservatives used are: E221 (sodium sulphite), E222 (sodium hydrogen sulphite), E223 (sodium metabisulphite), E224 (potassium metabisulphite), E226 (calcium metabisulphite), E227 (calcium hydrogen sulphite), and 513 (sulphuric acid).

Nitrates and nitrites turn meat pink and prevent micro-organisms from growing. In the digestive system nitrates can turn into nitrites, and these can prevent the blood from carrying adequate supplies of oxygen around the body. Allergic reactions, arthritis and an inability to store Vitamin A are other side-effects. Most worrying is evidence that nitrates or nitrites can be turned into nitrosamines during digestion. Some nitrosamines have been shown to cause cancer in animals. They are found in ham, bacon, delicatessen meats, and in some cheeses. E252 (potassium nitrate) is saltpetre but watch out for E250 (sodium nitrite) and E251 (sodium nitrate).

Benzoates preserve food by preventing mould growth. Their presence can cause rashes and other allergic reactions, may numb the mouth, and contribute to hyperactivity in children. The benzoates to avoid are: E210 (benzoic acid), E211 (sodium benzoate), E212 (potassium benzoate), E213 (calcium benzoate), E214 (ethyl 4-hydrobenzoate), E215 (ethyl 4-hydrobenzoate sodium salt), E216 (propyl 4-hydroxybenzoate), E217 (propyl 4-hydroxybenzoate sodium salt), and benzyl peroxide (no number).

Cakes and biscuits
Wholefood cakes and biscuits are full of vitamins and fibre from the fruit and wholewheat flour, as well as being satisfyingly filling and full of flavour.

HOW TO AVOID ADDITIVES

- Avoid all processed foods.
- Wash all fresh fruit and vegetables thoroughly before eating raw or cooking so as to get rid of any chemical sprays or coatings that have been used.

- Look out for new additive-free products in healthfood stores and supermarkets.
- Use wholewheat flour, which, by law, must not contain any additives at all.

- Buy organically produced food where possible.
- Buy bread from shops you know do not use additives, or make your own.
- Read food labels carefully.

Drinks

Drinks are another potential problem area. Fizzy drinks, squashes, and mixers contain additives and sugar, while tea and coffee contain caffeine and tannin.

Caffeine and tannin

Death from too much caffeine is unknown, but the lethal dose is said to be about 10g ($\frac{1}{3}$oz). To take in 250mg, the point at which caffeine qualifies medically as a stimulant, you would need to drink 19 cups of cocoa, four to six cups of tea or instant coffee, three to five 341ml (12fl oz) bottles of Coca-Cola, or only one to two cups of freshly ground coffee. Caffeine makes the heart beat more rapidly and irregularly. It makes you feel more alert when you drink it, but too much can cause anxiety, restlessness, and sleeplessness. It raises blood pressure and levels of fats in the blood. It also makes the pancreas produce more insulin, which lowers blood sugar levels, and makes the stomach more acid.

Sensitivity to coffee and tea varies from one person to another. Caffeine is suspected of preventing iron from being properly used, and of causing deficiencies of certain B vitamins. It may also reduce the absorption of some other vitamins and minerals. Unexplained allergic reactions, including rashes and migraine, sometimes stop when caffeine is excluded from the diet. As well as caffeine, tea contains tannin, which tends to cause constipation.

Alcoholic drinks

A little alcohol may not be a bad thing because it acts as a tranquillizer or relaxant and may lessen the likelihood of heart disease. Alcohol is not, as some people think, a stimulant. Alcohol-tolerance is related to size, so women can take less than men; a recommended safe amount is either two halves of beer, two glasses of wine or sherry, or a double measure of spirits per day. Too much alcohol causes dehydration, puts a strain on the liver, and exhausts supplies of B vitamins. Heavy drinkers can suffer malnutrition because alcohol, like sugar, offers no nourishment, only calories. Pregnant or lactating women should be wary of alcohol because it crosses the placenta and also passes into breast milk.

Alternatives

If you want to cut down on your intake of additives, sugar, caffeine, tannin, or alcohol, try one of the drinks below.

Decaffeinated coffee and low-tannin tea: This coffee is available as beans or instant coffee. It contains minute traces of caffeine – no more than 3mg per 100g (3½oz) jar – but it can cause digestive disorders. Low-tannin tea is made in the same way as ordinary tea but has a lower tannin content.

Cereal coffees: These are made up of roasted grains such as wheat or barley, and sometimes dandelion or chicory, all of which are good for the digestion.

Herbal teas: These come in a vast range and are best drunk without milk or sugar. You can add lemon juice, or sweeten them with fruit juice concentrate or honey if you prefer.

Carob: A cocoa substitute, this makes a good milky drink when flavoured with cinnamon and honey. Make it with skimmed milk.

Yogurt drink: To make a refreshing drink, beat yogurt until it is frothy, then dilute it with water or orange juice and garnish it with mint.

Fruit juices: These are available from a wide variety of fruit. Look out for those made with organically grown fruit, but if you cannot find them, buy pure, unsweetened juices.

Mineral water: This can be bought either carbonated or still, and makes a refreshing drink. Mix it with unsweetened fruit juice.

· CHAPTER THREE ·

THE STORE CUPBOARD

One of the joys of trying out a different style of cookery is undoubtedly discovering a fresh range of dishes with new combinations of tastes and textures. Based as it is on the cuisines of many different countries, vegetarian cookery draws on a wide variety of ingredients, some of which will be familiar, others, such as sea vegetables and soya products, less so. This section is intended as a guide to those ingredients that play a central part in vegetarian cookery, and that feature in the recipes in this book, from the everyday staples such as cereals and pulses, to different seasonings and flavourings.

Naturally, there is no need to buy every type of bean or cereal product shown here – you can gradually add to your stock as you try out different recipes. A selection of fresh foods is also illustrated, including some of the less common vegetables and wholefood or vegetarian substitutes for animal products.

Keeping stock

Once you have changed to a vegetarian diet, it is well worth stocking up on the vegetables, pulses, fruits, herbs, spices and special flavourings that are needed to cook the dishes.

Grains

Wheat, rice, barley, oats, millet, rye, and maize (corn) are the world's major food grains or cereals, and all belong to the immense family of grasses. The other grain of culinary interest, buckwheat, is the seed not of a grass but of a herbaceous plant. Wheat, millet, and oats are the richest sources of protein, but all unrefined grains also provide fibre, carbohydrate, minerals, and vitamins – especially the B vitamins.

For thousands of years cereals have been the staple foods that have kept people alive: wheat, rye, barley, and oats in temperate climates; rice, maize, and millet in the tropics, and subtropics. Most of the world's populations still eat the staple produce that grows in their back yard, but in the affluent countries meat has pushed cereals out of their primary position, and grains have been refined and processed to the point where all of the fibre and many of the essential nutrients have been lost, along with two other very important ingredients: taste and texture.

Unrefined cereals (whole grains) still contain the germ, an important source of oils, proteins, and minerals and bran, a valuable source of fibre. They may be bought whole or cracked, flaked, parboiled, steamed or toasted, all of which help to shorten cooking time and make them easier to digest.

Buying
Most healthfood and wholefood shops sell grains in all their forms from berries to flour, bread, and pasta. Choose a shop where you can rely on the stock being fresh. Supermarkets often stock a range, if not such a wide one. You may find "brown" flour, or bread made from it, that is white flour treated with caramel or other colouring; the nutrients that were milled out of it may be added back as synthetic vitamins and minerals. Do, therefore, read the labels and make sure that you are getting the whole grain or its product, or that you know exactly what proportion of it you are buying. Also, if you care about organically grown food, check where the flour comes from. Today, most of the world's bread wheat comes from North America and is not organically grown. Organically grown flour is likely to be soft, giving a dense-textured but well-flavoured loaf.

Storing
Whole grains keep indefinitely in cool, dry conditions in an airtight container, but the longer they are stored the longer they take to cook. Flakes and flours do not keep so long and are best used within 3–6 months as the milling process exposes the oil contained in the germ, which eventually goes rancid, particularly in oats, and the Vitamin E content is lost. Unstabilized wheatgerm, that is wheatgerm that has not been heat-treated to remove the most volatile oils, should be kept in the refrigerator. Stabilized wheatgerm keeps longer, but should be used within 2–3 weeks.

Cooking
To cook whole grains, first rinse them to remove surface dust. Choose a pan with a close-fitting lid, or use a pressure cooker. Rub a little oil around the pan to prevent the grains from sticking – this will also make the pan easier to clean. One cup – 250ml (8fl oz) – is enough for 2–3 people.

Put some water in the pan (see the table opposite for quantities) and bring to the boil. Put in the grains, bring to the boil again, then cover the pan and simmer very gently until the water is absorbed. Do not stir unnecessarily as this tends to make the grains sticky, and do not toughen the grains by adding any salt until just before the end of the cooking time.

There are simple ways to vary the basic method. Sauté the grain lightly in a little oil or shoyu before adding boiling water (this is good with barley, buckwheat, and millet in particular); add spices and vegetables for flavour, particularly saffron, ginger, coriander, garlic, or onions. Mix different grains – rice with wheat or barley – for more texture and taste.

The softer grains – millet, rice, and buckwheat – make excellent croquettes. Rice, barley, and millet are good for sweet puddings, and buckwheat, wheat, and oats for substantial breakfast porridges. Cracked grains absorb

PREPARATION AND COOKING TIMES FOR WHOLE GRAINS

Type of grain	Preparation before cooking	Amount of liquid per cup of grain	Average cooking time	Pressure cooking
Wheat	soak overnight (8–12 hours)	4 cups	50–60 minutes	20 minutes
Rice long-grain short-grain	can be toasted or lightly fried	1¾–2 cups 1¾–2 cups	25–30 minutes 20–25 minutes	10 minutes 8–10 minutes
Wild rice	–	3 cups	50–60 minutes	20 minutes
Corn	–	plenty of water	5–10 minutes	
Barley	toast	4 cups	50–60 minutes	20 minutes
Oats	can be toasted	3 cups	30–35 minutes	12 minutes
Rye	soak overnight (8–12 hours)	3 cups	50–60 minutes	20 minutes
Millet	can be toasted or lightly fried	2½–3 cups	20 minutes	8 minutes
Buckwheat	toast or lightly fry	2–2½ cups	20 minutes	8 minutes

water more easily and cook quickly. Bulgar wheat, which is steamed, cracked, and toasted, needs soaking but no further cooking. It is ideal in salads such as the Middle Eastern Taboulleh, where it is mixed with herbs, oil, lemon juice, onions, and tomatoes.

Flakes and meals are used in breakfast cereals (muesli or granola) and as versatile toppings for either sweet or savoury dishes. You can vary the proportions of flakes to flour. Substitute granola for the flakes if you want a sweeter tasting crumble.

Muesli is generally a combination of various flakes, mainly oats, with seeds, nuts, and dried fruit. A good version is one nearer to the original Bircher-Benner muesli, with more emphasis on fresh fruit. For one person, soak 30g (2 tbsp) rolled oats in 30ml (2 tbsp) water for 1–2 hours (or overnight). Just before eating, stir in the juice of an orange, 15g (1 tbsp) ground almonds, and a whole unpeeled apple, grated.

Leftover, cooked, grains make excellent salads when mixed with beans or vegetables, or they can be added to soups or casseroles. Cooked grains will keep for two days in the refrigerator and can be successfully frozen. To reheat, first thaw, either overnight in the refrigerator, or for several hours (the exact time depends on how large a portion you are thawing) at room temperature. Turn into an oiled dish, cover with foil, and heat in a moderate oven (gas mark 4, 180°C, 350°F) for 15–20 minutes.

YEAST

Fresh yeast, specified in all the recipes in this book, is usually the easiest for the beginner to work with. Try to buy it in one piece: it should be a pale beige colour, look smooth, and have a pleasant, fresh smell. Yeast that smells stale, or that is crumbly and beginning to dry out will not work as well as fresh yeast. Store it wrapped up, in the refrigerator, for up to 10 days (or freeze it – small pieces, separately wrapped, are convenient; to revive it, put it in tepid water for 15 minutes). It will also keep in cold water.

Dried yeast is usually sold as granules. It gives the same results as fresh yeast if used properly. Use only a third to a half as much as fresh yeast. To reactivate dried yeast, sprinkle it into a cup of hot water with a little sugar, stir well and leave in a warm place for 10–15 minutes until it froths up. It will keep for up to a year if stored in airtight containers in a cool, dry place.

VARIETIES OF WHEAT

The whole grain or berry is by far the most nutritious form of wheat; when cooked, it is chewy and substantial. It retains its outer covering, or bran, which contains valuable vitamins, minerals, and fat, as well as being high in fibre, and the germ, which is only 2 per cent of the grain but contains the bulk of the nutrients. The rest of the grain, some 70 per cent, is the endosperm and consists mostly of the starch used to make flour. When the grain is milled a rich brown flour is obtained.

Bulgar wheat

Wholewheat berries

Wheatgerm

Wheat flakes

Cracked wheat

Semolina

Bran

Wheatmeal flour

Wholewheat flour

Unbleached white flour

Couscous

Wheat

The most universally grown and the most important of all food grains, wheat (*Triticum vulgare*) is available in a wide variety of forms, from the whole berry to flour, and wheat flour is used more than any other for making bread, cakes, pastry, and pasta. Both wheatgerm and bran can be bought separately and added to breakfast cereals, breads, and cakes or just used as toppings.

Cracked or kibbled wheat is produced by cracking whole wheat berries between rollers so that they will cook more quickly, in only 20 minutes, in fact. If they are then hulled, steamed, and roasted they are known as bulgar wheat, or burghul, and need little or no cooking. Wheat flakes are similar, but rolled flatter and often toasted to a golden brown.

All the above are variants on the whole wheat grain, which is often subjected to further milling to produce lighter, more widely appreciated results. During this process, the two valuable constituents of wheatgerm and bran are lost.

Flour is the form in which wheat is most easily available. Most of today's flour is produced by roller-milling, a process that involves high temperatures and consequent loss of vitamins and flavour. For this reason, stone-ground flour is generally considered preferable, although it is more expensive and slightly coarser in texture.

Wholewheat or wholemeal flour is made from the whole grain. Wheatmeal flour retains a lot of the nutrients, but has 15–19 per cent wheat (in practice, the germ and most of the bran) removed to make it lighter. White flour has had all the bran and germ removed; unbleached white flour is preferable as it has not been chemically treated.

Bread is the end product of most of the world's flour. Leavened bread is made mainly from wheat, the only grain high in gluten, a protein that stretches to form an impermeable skin over the thousands of bubbles of gas formed when yeast ferments. Bread made with strong or hard flour has a lighter consistency than bread made with soft flour. Wholewheat flour gives a rather dense loaf, unbleached white flour produces one with a light texture, which has some percentage of the nutrients still intact. Wheatmeal flour is often considered a good compromise.

Semolina is produced from the starchy part of the grain, the endosperm. It is available as medium or coarse meal and used for puddings or gnocchi. Semolina from durum wheat is used for making pasta commercially. Fine semolina grains coated with flour are known as couscous, the basis of the North African dish.

Rice

Rice can be divided into two main categories, long-grain and short-grain. Properly cooked, long-grain rice has dry, separate grains. It goes well with curries, pilafs, stews, and chicken or meat dishes. Short-grain rice has a softer texture and is stickier when cooked, making it particularly suitable for use in Japanese and Chinese cookery.

Brown (whole grain) rice has a chewy texture and nutty flavour that makes white rice seem bland, stripped as it is of the outer layers and germ, and with them most of the nutrients. It contains bran which gives additional protein, iron, calcium, and Vitamin B, but it can take quite a lot longer to cook than white rice.

Rice can also be found in the form of flakes and flour; the flour has a light consistency and small quantities are good in bread and cakes. The bran and germ removed when rice is milled are sold as rice polish, an excellent source of Vitamin B as well as minerals and protein. Small quantities can be added to cakes, biscuits, or be mixed in with crumble or nutty toppings.

Wild rice is not actually a rice but a grain, although it is a member of the grass family. Originating in North America it is grey-brown in colour. It is often served on its own so as not to submerge its characteristic delicate, subtle flavour, a little like that of artichokes. Wild rice can also be served mixed with some brown rice and used as a stuffing for various bakes and roasts.

Basmati rice
This has the finest flavour of any easily available white rice, although, like all white rices, a high proportion of nutrients have been removed by milling.

Oryza sativa
Rice
Brown rice is, like the wheat berry, the whole natural grain, unprocessed. The type most commonly found is long-grain or indica rice, much grown in India.

Rice flour
This is usually made from white rice. Because of its lack of gluten, it is useful for those who have to cope with low-gluten diets.

Rice flakes
These have been processed so that they cook quickly, in about 10 minutes. They can be used to thicken soups, stews, and casseroles.

Zizania aquatica
Wild rice
Wild rice is not a rice, although it looks like one. Its grains are longer and more slender, dark grey-brown when raw, and turning slightly purplish when cooked. It is native to North America.

Japonica
Short-grain rice
As its Latin name indicates, this is popular in Japan as well as in parts of China. Another type of short-grain rice is grown in Italy and is generally used to make delicious risotto dishes.

Corn (maize)

This originated in Central America, where it was the staple grain of the Incas, Mayas, and Aztecs. Its popularity has spread not only to North America but to Europe, where it is used for such national dishes as polenta in Italy and mamaliga in Romania. Unlike other whole grains, it is not usually dried but is eaten fresh. There are three main varieties: dent corn, which supplies commercial cornmeal;

sweetcorn, or corn on the cob, the form in which we know it as a fresh vegetable; and popcorn, the popular snack.

Cornmeal is available finely or coarsely ground. Stone-ground or water-ground is best, as the germ is not removed. It is too low in gluten to make leavened bread, but mixes well with wheat to give muffins and flat breakfast breads a distinctive taste and colour. Other important products of corn are cooking oil (see p.94) and corn syrup, which is used for sweetening (see p.93).

Coarse cornmeal

Fine cornmeal

Zea mays
Corn
Known as maize in Europe, corn originated in Central America. Popcorn is a variety of it with a very hard endosperm, which explodes when heated.

Cornmeal
Another variety of corn is used to produce cornmeal, both coarse and fine: this is sometimes bolted, or sieved. This process removes the bran and some of the fibre but makes little difference to the product nutritionally.

Oats

Still a popular food in Scotland, northern England, and Ireland, oats probably originated in northern Europe. They are made into oatcakes and parkin, or used for soups, as well as for the traditional porridge. They are higher in protein and fats than other grains and rich in B vitamins and iron.

Oats are most often found as flakes or meals, which cook quickly. Flakes can be used for porridge, granola, muesli, and crumble toppings as well as for oatcakes, to which they add a crunchy texture. Oatmeal is used for porridge and oatcakes and as a crunchy coating for croquettes. It is often mixed with wheat flour to improve the taste of bread.

Avena sativa
Oats
The whole oat grain is known as a groat. It is not often used, although it can be made into porridge for instance, as it takes some time to cook.

Rolled oat flakes (oat flakes, rolled oats, porridge oats)
Rolled oat flakes come from groats that have been broken by rolling; heat can also be applied to prevent the oil from going rancid, and thus improve shelf life.

Oatmeal
This is now generally available in three grades: coarse, medium, and fine, but used to be available in far more. A little added to wheat flour gives flavour to bread.

Jumbo oat flakes
These are similar to rolled oats but, as their name implies, larger. They can also be heat-treated.

Rolled oat flakes

Oatmeal

Jumbo oat flakes

Barley

The whole grain is known as pot barley. Pearl barley has been polished and has lost most of the bran, germ, and Vitamin B. Low in gluten, barley flour will not make leavened bread (unless mixed with wheat flour), but the greyish, flat bread made from it is sweet-tasting and delicious to eat. Barley syrup, sometimes known as malt extract, is used as a sweetening agent in cookery.

Hordeum vulgare
Whole barley
Barley is still important for food in some parts of the world, particularly Japan, although elsewhere it has been superseded as a food crop and is used mainly for brewing. It compares well with other grains nutritionally, and is particularly high in niacin. Like other cereals, it is available in flakes and as flour. The inclusion of barley flour adds sweetness to bread. It is an old food crop known to the Greeks and, Romans.

Barley flakes

Barley flour

Millet

Richer than other grains nutritionally, millet is a particularly good source of iron and the B vitamins. Its delicate flavour can seem bland at first, but it amalgamates well with other flavours and makes an excellent alternative to rice in risottos or milk puddings. Millet flour is often used to make flat breads and griddle cakes, and the grains can be mixed with pulses, and used in soups and stews.

Panicum miliaceum
Millet
This grain is prolific and easy to grow but has only recently been considered suitable for growing in the West, although it has long been an important crop in Africa and Asia, especially northern China. It is related to sorghum, a type of millet which is an important crop in Africa, and is the staple food of the Hunzas, the Himalayan tribe who are well known for their longevity.

Millet flakes
These can be used like other flakes in cereals and sprinkled on dishes as toppings.

Buckwheat

This is not a cereal grain at all but the seed of a herbaceous plant related to dock and rhubarb. It is supposed to have originated in China and is now a staple food in Russia and Poland. The iron and mineral content is high and it contains all the B vitamins and rutin. The seeds need to be roasted by stir-frying before they can be cooked and served in the same way as rice. Kasha, the porridge-like cooked cereal, which is popular in many parts of the Soviet Union, is usually made from the roasted seeds.

Buckwheat grains can also be ground into a flour that can be used to make pancakes and crisp, thin cakes. Buckwheat groats (the hulled and crushed grain) are often added to soups to give them more substance.

Fagopyrum esculentum
Whole buckwheat
This is also sometimes called Saracen corn or wheat as it was supposed to have been introduced to Europe by the Crusaders.

Roasted buckwheat
Buckwheat is popular for its delicious flavour; roasting is the usual way of preparing the grains for cooking.

Buckwheat flour
This is strong and savoury, and is often mixed with wheat flour. It is a good flour for making pancakes, and soba, which are a type of Japanese noodles.

Rye

The groats can be treated like rice or wheat berries, or cracked to produce grits or flakes, which cook more quickly. Rye is a good source of B vitamins, especially B_2 and B_3, and the minerals potassium and magnesium. It also contains rutin, once known as Vitamin P, which is good for helping circulatory complaints.

Rye flakes

Secale cereale
Rye
Rye is popular in northern and eastern Europe, and parts of Russia, where its distinctive sour taste is much appreciated, particularly in bread. The groats can be made into dark rye flour, or they can be partially husked and made into light flour. Although rye contains gluten, it is not the same sort as that found in wheat and will not leaven bread, so that most rye bread is in fact made from a mixture of rye and wheat.

Rye flour

Beans, Peas, and Lentils

Collectively known as pulses or legumes, these have the advantage that they are cheap to buy, readily available (although some of the less common ones may not be so easy to find), and keep well. Most tend to be bland in taste, but cooked in combination with other ingredients they have a capacity for amalgamating with them, especially with stronger flavours, and enhancing them: chickpeas with tahini (sesame seed paste), lentils with spices, and butter or haricot beans with onions, tomatoes, and peppers. Cooked dishes generally improve on being left for several hours or overnight for the full development of flavour before reheating. They may not be the answer if you need to prepare a meal or a snack in a hurry, but they are ideal if you prefer to do the preparation beforehand.

Pulses and grains are the meat in a vegetarian diet because, used together, they make high-quality protein. Apart from soya beans, no one pulse or grain has all the amino acids in sufficient amounts to make a high-quality protein by itself, but when grains and pulses are eaten together, what is lacking in one can be made up by what is in the other.

Dried beans and peas are also good sources of protein, fibre, carbohydrate, minerals, and vitamins. They may lack Vitamin C, but that can be obtained by sprouting them. Vitamin content increases dramatically with sprouting (as much as 600 times for Vitamin C) and, depending on the pulse, you can also use bean and pea sprouts as good sources of Vitamins A, B, D, E, and K.

Soya beans are higher in calories than other beans because they have a higher fat content. They also contain some carbohydrates, calcium, and B vitamins. Tofu (bean curd), made from soya beans, is a cheap, nourishing food from the Far East. It is tasteless so it needs to have flavour added. The firmest kind, which is like white cheese, is often eaten like a piece of meat with a tasty sauce over it, or it may be added to main course vegetable dishes. Softer, custard-like kinds are used to enrich and thicken, much as we use cream or yogurt. Tofu keeps for a month in a vacuum pack but, once opened, it should be used within a week. Store it in water (which needs to be changed daily) in the refrigerator.

One common objection to legumes is that they tend to cause wind. The best way to counter this is to accustom yourself to eating them gradually, making sure that they are thoroughly cooked. Lentils and smaller beans are often found to be more digestible.

Buying and storing

It is becoming easier nowadays to find good-quality dried beans and peas. Buy them from somewhere with a good turnover; although pulses do keep well, if they have spent a year sitting on a shelf they will take a very long time to cook. Choose beans or peas that look plump, brightly coloured, and unwrinkled; these will be the freshest. Pulses are worth buying in bulk as they will keep in good condition for up to six months. All legumes keep best in cool, dry, dark conditions in airtight containers. If you have a fairly rapid turnover – say within a month – they can be kept in glass jars, as long as they are not exposed to full sun, which impairs flavour and nutrients.

Preparation

All pulses, but especially lentils, need to be picked over for stones and grit and given a rinse to wash off the surface dust. Lentils and split peas can then be cooked straight away, but beans and whole peas should be soaked overnight before cooking. Use plenty of water, remembering that pulses absorb water and will swell up to between two and three times their original bulk. There is a quick method, which is the equivalent of an overnight soak: bring the beans or peas to the boil in plenty of water, boil hard for 3–5 minutes and leave to stand in the water for an hour.

Cooking

After soaking, drain and rinse again. Some vitamins will be lost in the soaking water, but this is not crucial. Put in a saucepan, cover with plenty of fresh water, and bring to the boil. Skim off any scum. Do not salt the water; salt

SOAKING AND COOKING CHART FOR BEANS, PEAS, AND LENTILS

"Overnight" here means approximately 8–12 hours. All times given are only a rough guide, as cooking times can vary considerably depending on the age and origin of the crop. The first 10 minutes' cooking of all except lentils and split peas should be done at a fast boil, uncovered, to destroy any toxic elements on the outer skin, except soya beans,* which should boil hard for the first hour. Although lentils and split peas need not be soaked overnight, they will cook faster if they are first steeped in boiling water for 15–30 minutes. Drain well before cooking them.

Type of bean	Recommended soak overnight	Average cooking time	Pressure cooking
Aduki beans	yes	45 minutes	15 minutes
Black-eyed beans	yes	45–50 minutes	15 minutes
Black beans	yes	50–60 minutes	20 minutes
Broad beans	yes	1½ hours	40 minutes
Butter or lima beans	yes	60–90 minutes	25–30 minutes
Cannellini	yes	45–50 minutes	15 minutes
Flageolets	yes	45–50 minutes	15 minutes
Haricot beans	yes	50–60 minutes	20 minutes
Mung beans	yes	30–45 minutes	15 minutes
Pinto beans	yes	60–90 minutes	25–30 minutes
Red kidney beans	yes	45–50 minutes	15 minutes
Soya beans	yes	2–2½ hours*	45–50 minutes
Chick peas	yes	60–90 minutes	25–30 minutes
Whole green peas	yes	60–90 minutes	25–30 minutes
Split peas	no	40–45 minutes	–
Whole lentils	no	30–45 minutes	12–15 minutes
Split lentils	no	15–30 minutes	–

toughens the outer skin and cooking will take longer. Vegetables, herbs, spices, or flavourings can be added: onions, garlic, carrots, other root vegetables, black peppercorns, ginger, or chilli peppers. The addition of anise, dill, fennel, or caraway seeds – 1 teaspoon for 225g (8oz) legumes – or a strip of the sea vegetable kombu (see p.92) helps digestion.

Soaking and cooking times vary. Lentils cook quite quickly without any soaking – red lentils cook in about 15 minutes, continental lentils take slightly longer – but kidney beans need an hour or more after soaking. With ordinary cooking, soya beans need to boil hard for the first hour, and all but lentils and split peas need an initial ten minutes of fast boiling to destroy toxins found in the skins. After the preliminary boiling, turn the heat down until the water just simmers and cover the pan, but not too tightly. If you add a little oil this will prevent the beans or peas from boiling over and also give them a smoother texture. The cooking time also depends on how long the legume has been stored, and whether you want it for a salad or a purée: those for salads should be just tender, while those for a purée need longer cooking. Use the times given in the chart as a guide, and test the pulses for tenderness by pressing them lightly. An alternative cooking method is to use a pressure cooker. It cuts the cooking time by about two-thirds, and there is no need to worry about fast boiling as this happens automatically. Do not cook more than about ½kg (1lb) at a time, or they may froth up and block the safety valve. Timing needs to be precise: even a little overcooking may result in a purée, so use an ordinary saucepan if you are making, say, a bean salad, where the appearance is important.

Serving and keeping
All beans, peas, and lentils can be used as a basis for casseroles, and can be served as a simple side dish, perhaps as a purée: aduki beans, flageolets, or mung beans have a subtle taste and are particularly suitable. Haricots, lima or butter beans, and the other kidney beans are often cooked with spices, herbs, and vegetables for a contrast of flavour. For croquettes, the most suitable are aduki beans, lentils, mung beans, and black-eyed beans. All of them can also be used in soups, and this is the most common use for peas, both split and whole. Almost all beans and lentils are good eaten cold in salads, particularly with a

vinaigrette dressing. The only exceptions are broad beans and soya beans, which are better eaten hot.

Once cooked, beans, peas, and lentils will keep well for several days in a covered container in the refrigerator, or they can be frozen – they retain their flavour excellently. Cool and open freeze them, then pack in rigid containers and label. For soups, a handful or two can be removed from the freezer and put straight into the soup near the end of the cooking time. For salads, allow them to thaw for about an hour at room temperature, or overnight in the refrigerator, then mix with the other vegetables or herbs and the dressing. Croquettes, cooked or uncooked, also freeze well: shape into patties, open freeze on trays, and pack in boxes with waxed paper between them. Thaw overnight in the refrigerator, or for 2 hours at room temperature.

The cooking liquid is well worth keeping. Any toxins will have been destroyed, and it makes an excellent base for soups, stews, and sauces. It will keep for 4–5 days in the refrigerator, and can be frozen.

Phaseolus angularis
Aduki beans
Tiny, round, hard, dark red beans, also known as adzuki beans, these are very popular in the Far East, especially Japan. Rich in protein, they can also be made into flour.

Phaseolus vulgaris
Black beans
The shiny black outside contrasts with the white inside. Popular in Latin America, these are not the same as the black bean often used in China, which is a type of soya bean, fermented, salted, and used as flavouring.

Aduki beans

Vigna unguiculata
Black-eyed beans
Also known as cowpeas, these are native to Central Africa, but were taken to the New World in the

sixteenth century. Not only the seeds are eaten: the immature pods can be cooked and the young shoots and leaves can be boiled like spinach or eaten raw in salads.

Black beans

Black-eyed beans

Vicia faba
Broad beans
Once important in Europe, these yielded popularity to the various kidney beans, possibly because broad beans contain substances which, if eaten in quantity, can cause a blood disease which is known as favism.

Phaseolus vulgaris
Flageolet beans
Very popular in both France and Italy, flageolet beans have an unusually delicate, subtle taste and an attractive pale green colour.

Phaseolus vulgaris
Haricot beans
One of the best known varieties, haricot beans are also known as white haricots, navy beans, or Great Northern beans. These are the original beans used to make Boston baked beans.

Lima beans

Whole green peas

Split yellow peas

Split green peas

Pisum sativum
Peas
Common peas are now mostly eaten fresh, although normally canned or frozen. They were formerly valuable as a dried vegetable, and in this form are available split or whole.

Butter beans

Phaseolus lunatus
Lima beans and butter beans
Originating from tropical America, these are very similar, but lima beans tend to be smaller and sweeter and are an ingredient of the traditional American Indian dish called succotash.

Phaseolus vulgaris
Cannellini
This is a variety of haricot or kidney bean which is much appreciated in Italy. A similar bean is widely grown in Argentina.

Lathyrus sativus
Ful medames
These small dark-brown beans are especially popular in Egypt, where they have given their name to a national dish in which they are baked with eggs, cumin, and garlic.

Whole mung beans

Split red lentils

Split mung beans

Phaseolus vulgaris
Pinto beans
Another variety of haricot bean, pinto beans are not unlike the speckled Italian borlotti beans. The name means "coloured". They turn pink when cooked.

Phaseolus aureus
Mung beans
Native to tropical Asia, the mung bean is still one of the most widely grown legumes. The seeds are mainly used as a vegetable but are also popular, especially in China and the USA, as an important source of bean sprouts.

Continental lentils

Brown lentils

Glycine max
Soya beans
These are the most nutritious beans of all, containing all the essential amino acids. Originally from China, where their value has been recognized for nearly 5,000 years. The popular yellow and black beans can be cooked fresh, dried in stews, sprouted for salads, or turned into curd, soy paste and sauce, soya milk, or can be used as a textured meat substitute.

Phaseolus vulgaris
Red kidney beans
Like all kidney beans, these are native to the New World. This variety is particularly popular in Mexican cookery. It is also called the chilli bean.

Lens esculenta
Lentils
One of the oldest crops, cultivated since prehistoric times, lentils are originally from the eastern Mediterranean, but can now be found all over the Middle East and India. They are available whole or split and come in a variety of different colours.

Cicer arietinum
Chick peas
These are highly popular all over the Mediterranean and the Middle East, as well as in India where they are known as Bengal gram (the Indian word "gram" means pulse or legume). They are also known as garbanzos or garbanzo peas. High in protein, they are very nutritious, and can be ground into flour.

Chick peas

Nuts and Seeds

Botanically, nuts and seeds are the same: both have kernels containing the whole future plant in embryo and are a concentrated source of food.

A combination of mixed nuts and cereals with green vegetables makes a nutritionally adequate main course, and nuts give taste and texture to salads, cooked vegetables, and grains. By themselves, or with sunflower, or pumpkin seeds, they make a good, satisfying snack. Watermelon and pomegranate seeds are also edible.

Buying
It is better to buy nuts in their shells: this protects the kernels and keeps them fresh. If you do want them shelled, buy loose nuts, preferably whole, as these tend to be of better quality. Avoid nuts that have already been coated in fat and salted. Seeds should always be bought whole.

Storing
Store in a cool place. Unshelled nuts will keep up to six months. Keep seeds and shelled nuts in an airtight container; whole, they will stay in good condition for up to 3 months, unless kept in a warm place, when their high fat content means they are liable to go rancid quickly. Split, chopped, or ready-ground nuts will go stale more quickly still and should be eaten within a 4–6 week period.

Preparation
Nuts can be blanched to remove the dark skin, roasted or toasted to improve their flavour (although there is a certain amount of nutrient loss), ground, which also makes them easier to digest, or, in the case of coconut, grated. Seeds, especially sunflower and sesame, are also good toasted.

To blanch nuts, except for hazelnuts, put them in a bowl, cover with boiling water, and leave for a few minutes or until they can be popped out of their skins when gently pressed. If you are not using the skinned nuts immediately, drop them in cold water to keep them white. Hazelnuts should be baked in the oven (or toasted under the grill) for 5 or 6 minutes. If they are then rubbed in a cloth, the fibrous skin will easily come away.

To roast nuts or seeds in the oven, spread them out in a single layer on a shallow tray or baking tin. Sprinkle with a very little oil. Put in a moderate oven for about 10 minutes, and shake the tin two or three times to turn them and ensure even browning. You can also fry them, if you prefer. Use a heavy pan and just enough oil – groundnut, for preference – to grease the bottom lightly. Shake or stir the nuts or seeds over gentle heat until evenly browned. If you are prepared to watch them carefully, they will toast under a hot grill in 2–3 minutes, but must be turned before they burn.

To skin sweet chestnuts, slash each one with a sharp knife (take care, as the skins can be tough), drop them in boiling water and leave them for about 10 minutes. At the end of this time both the outer and inner skins should come away easily. If you prefer, use dried chestnuts which do not need shelling.

Nuts are easily ground: use a small grater, a nut mill, or a liquidizer. A coffee mill, kept especially for the purpose, is ideal. Nuts tend to grind unevenly and it is easier to do a few at a time. Walnuts and Brazil nuts have a tendency to be greasy, and you may need to scrape around the sides of the mill once or twice to remove the ground mixture.

Cooking
As well as being eaten raw, nuts and seeds are used in roasts, bakes, croquettes, and casseroles, in cereal mixtures, and crumble toppings. Peanut butter is the best known nut butter, but cashews, hazelnuts, and almonds also make good spreads and dips. Blend them with a little oil and salt to taste. Alternatively, mix equal quantities of nuts and water with a little oil and salt and blend. Nut butters will keep in the refrigerator for 4–6 weeks if made with only oil, for 3–4 days if made with water. They can also be frozen.

Nut creams and milks are easy to make and can form the basis for sauces or substitutes for cream to serve with puddings or cakes.

Almond milk can be made by blending together 1½ tablespoons blanched ground almonds, 175ml (6fl oz) water and 5ml (1 tsp) honey. Cashew cream is made by blending 100g (4oz) cashew nuts, 100g (4oz) cottage cheese, 15–30ml (1–2 tbsp) honey and up to 150ml (¼ pint) water until smooth. Both will keep in the refrigerator for up to 3–4 days.

COCONUT CREAM

To make 300ml (½ pint) coconut cream, grate 75–100g (3–4oz) of the creamed coconut block, cover with boiling water and leave for half an hour (or put in a blender for half a minute). Stir well and strain before using. For coconut milk, use twice the amount of water. Season with a little salt and use with curries and other rice dishes.

Nuts

Whole almond   *Slivered almonds*

Shelled hazelnuts

Whole hazelnuts

Corylus avellana; C. maxima
Hazelnuts, cobs, filberts
Widely grown in Italy, France, and Turkey, these are low in fat and high in Vitamins B and E.

Shelled almond   *Blanched almond*

Prunus amygdalus
Almonds
These are the most popular nuts of all. The sweet variety is the kind normally used: bitter almonds are toxic, but the unpleasant taste is a deterrent. Almonds have the highest protein content of any nut and are also rich in minerals, especially calcium.

Whole pistachios

Shelled pistachios

Ground almonds

Pistacia vera
Pistachios
Native to the Mediterranean and Middle East, where they are eaten as a snack, pistachios are prized for their bright green colour.

Whole (unshelled) peanuts

Shelled peanuts, with and without skin

Arachis hypogaea
Peanuts
Sometimes called groundnuts or monkeynuts, peanuts are not true nuts but underground legumes.

Whole walnut

Anacardium occidentale
Cashews
The unusual fruit looks like an apple with the kidney-shaped nut hanging beneath it. The nutshell contains an acid and is removed before the nuts are sold.

Whole Brazil nut

Shelled Brazil nuts

Bertholletia excelsa
Brazil nuts
From the Amazon basin, the nuts cluster like orange segments inside a woody fruit. They have the highest fat content of any nut and are also rich in minerals.

Shelled walnuts

Juglans regia; J. nigra
Walnuts
These nuts are good sources of protein, vitamins, minerals, and unsaturated fats, especially the black or American walnut. Green or unripe walnuts are rich in Vitamin C; they are delicious in their pickled form.

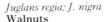

Desiccated coconut

Cocus nucifera
Coconut
The coconut palm is a source of fibre, soap, and animal fodder as well as oil and other edible products. The dried flesh may be compressed into blocks or sold as flakes or powder.

Fresh coconut

Creamed coconut

Whole pecans

Shelled pecans

Whole chestnut

Shelled chestnut

Shelled and peeled chestnut

Carya pecan
Pecans
Related to walnuts, but richer, milder, and subtler in flavour, pecans are much appreciated in their native North America. Hickory and bitternut are also related to them.

Eleocharia tuberosa
Chinese water chestnuts
These are not true nuts, but tubers of a sedge, although with their crisp texture they can be used as nuts.

Castanea sativa
Sweet chestnuts
These are native to southern Europe and unlike most other nuts in that they are very starchy and low in protein. Both the hard shell and the thin inner skin need to be removed. Sweet chestnuts are often also available dried.

Seeds

Pinus pinea
Pine kernels
These are the seeds of various pines, chiefly the stone pine of the Mediterranean, and also known as pignolias or Indian nuts.

Sesamum indicum
Sesame seeds
Of African origin, sesame is now an important crop in the Middle and Far East as well as in Mexico. Sesame seeds are an excellent source of oil.

Cucurbita maxima
Pumpkin seeds
These seeds from a native American plant are eaten roasted. They provide a good source of proteins, fats, and minerals, especially zinc. The seeds are also used as a source of oil.

Helianthus annuus
Sunflower seeds
Rich in proteins and minerals and containing 40 per cent unsaturated oil, they make an excellent snack.

Linum usitatissimum
Linseeds
These are the nutritious and flavoursome seeds of the flax plant. The Greeks and Romans used them as food.

Dried Fruit

Dried fruits are a concentrated form of sugar so they are relatively high in calories, but they are also better for you than sweets because minerals and vitamins are concentrated, too. There is less likelihood of over-indulging because, being full of fibre, they fill you up. Dates are about two-thirds sugar and figs about half, while prunes come out best with about two-thirds the calories of most dried fruits. Prunes and figs are useful natural laxatives, too. Dried fruits can be reconstituted in water and used to make many different types of interesting puddings.

Apples and dessert pears are fairly easy to dry at home. You halve the pears and peel, core, and cut the apples into rings, then put them on racks in a slow oven. Leave for several hours at gas mark 2, 60°C (150°F), or with the door open a little.

Sulphur dioxide is often used as a preservative in dried fruit to slow down browning and prevent spoiling. It helps keep Vitamin C but destroys B_1 and is suspected of being a factor in genetic mutations, a serious cause for alarm (see p. 42). Figs and dates are free of it and some shops carry other dried fruits which have not been sulphured. The pale fruits are very likely to have been sulphured. The shiny appearance of some dried fruit may be due to a coating of mineral oil, something else to avoid if possible. Mineral oil in large quantities can interfere with absorption of calcium and phosphorus in the body; it also picks up oil-soluble vitamins (A, D, E, K) as it passes through the body, which are then excreted. Oestrogen and the adrenal hormones also dissolve in mineral oil and are lost in the faeces.

Buying and storing

Buy plump dried fruit rather than anything that is really hard. It will keep up to a year in an airtight container but after six months it is a good idea to add some orange or lemon peel to keep it moist. Frozen dried fruit also lasts a year but if the fruit has been reconstituted and is then frozen, it will only keep for about two or three months maximum.

Preparation

Much fruit sold these days is already cleaned, but it is still advisable to rinse it again under running water to remove any traces of preservative, and drain well. If it is for a cake mix, where the fruit may sink if damp, clean it by sieving with some flour.

To plump raisins, currants, and sultanas, soak them in hot liquid – water, fruit juice, or wine – for 5 minutes. Drain, pat dry and use at once. Plumped vine fruits give a juicy texture to cakes and puddings. To reconstitute tree fruits, cover with liquid and leave to soak for 8–12 hours. You may need to add more liquid. A quicker method is to put the fruit in a pan, cover it with liquid and bring it to the boil; simmer, covered, for 10–15 minutes and leave for an hour. It may be eaten at this stage or cooked until soft, whichever you prefer.

Cooking

Stew or cook the fruit for 30–40 minutes or until tender: use the soaking liquid, which now contains valuable nutrients, for cooking. It will keep for 3–4 days in the refrigerator.

Cooked fruit can be eaten hot as fruit compote, puréed for use as a sweet pastry filling or in cakes, or it can be added to breakfast cereals, salads, stuffings, and savoury dishes, such as curries.

Apples are unusual in that they do not lose Vitamin C in the drying process. They are mostly used in fruit compôtes.

Apricots are sold whole, halved, or in pieces. The pieces are cheaper and are good for purées and jams. Hunza apricots, from the Himalayas, are small, unsulphured, and pale beige in colour. They are sold whole and unpitted: the stone can be cracked and the delicious kernel, tasting rather like an almond, extracted and eaten.

Bananas have an excellent flavour. Good mixed with dates and figs for rich fruit purées to use in sauces or cakes, they can also be baked in rum or deep-fried.

Dates should be plump and moist with thin skins. Cooking dates are compressed into blocks; break them up before use to check for stones, as it is not uncommon to find some have been left in. These dates can be used to make splendid fruit purées.

Figs are high in calcium and potassium as well as sugar. They can be stuffed: soak them first to reconstitute them and use a cottage cheese stuffing or one based on almonds – figs and almonds go well together and are a traditional combination.

Peaches and *nectarines*, usually available halved, are used in the same way as apricots.

Pears keep their distinctive slightly gritty texture when dried, and are a good addition to fruit dishes such as compôtes.

Prunes (dried plums) are lower in sugar and calories than dates or figs. Ready-made prune purée can also be bought; this is popular in France, where it is used in confectionery, pastries, and cakes.

Raisins, currants, and *sultanas* are all dried grapes, widely used for fruit cakes and mincemeats. Australian sultanas are unsulphured and are sprayed with vegetable rather than mineral oil, so it is worth trying to find them. Lexia raisins from Australia are large, sticky, and very sweet and are sold with the seeds removed. Another variety, the Spanish Muscatel, is not chemically treated.

Dried apple ring

Pyrus communis
Pears
Pears are not peeled before drying. Some Chinese varieties are preserved, like peaches, in sugar or glucose syrup to retain their moisture content.

Dried pear

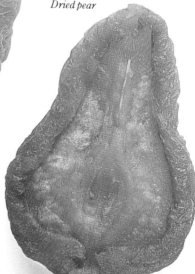

Malus communis
Apples
Apples are usually peeled, cored and cut into rings; occasionally they are cut into segments. The whiter the apple, the more sulphur has been used to preserve it.

Dried peach

Dried nectarine

Prunus persica
Peaches and nectarines
These come mainly from Australia, China, and California. Some Chinese varieties come preserved in sugar: this information will be stated on the box or packet.

Half sun-dried apricot

Half unsulphured apricot

Hunza apricot

Prunus armeniaca
Apricots
Mainly grown in the Far East, North Africa, and California. The best variety is considered to be the Hunza apricots from the Himalayas. Apricots have a higher protein and fibre content than other fruits.

Whole sulphured apricot

Dried Lerida fig

Ficus carica
Figs
Valued according to size, figs should be rich brown with a thin skin. The thinner the skin, the more likelihood of sugaring on the surface: this therefore indicates quality. Lerida figs are the best.

Muscatel raisins

Dried banana

Musa, spp.
Bananas
These dry most successfully when fully ripe with a high sugar content; they may be dried in pieces or slices. Drying helps to concentrate the delicious banana taste.

Phoenix dactylifera
Dates
Dates are very high in sugar (66 per cent) and also contain Vitamin A and some B vitamins. Dessert dates (shown here) are sold unpitted; the best variety is "Deglet Nour". Dried dates for cooking are sold in blocks.

Prunus domestica
Prunes
The type of plum grown for drying is usually late-ripening and black-skinned. Prunes are sold pitted or unpitted. "Tenderized", or partially cooked, prunes need only 8 minutes further cooking.

Vitis vinifera
Sultanas
These come from seedless white grapes. Unlike currants, they are often treated chemically – sulphured to preserve colour and sprayed to give them an attractive gloss.

Vitis vinifera
Currants
These come from small black seedless grapes grown near Corinth (hence their name) and other parts of Greece. They are not chemically treated. Vostizza is considered the best variety.

Vitis vinifera
Raisins
Raisins are not chemically treated and darken naturally in the sun. Dessert raisins (the best known variety is the Lexia raisin from Australia) are larger and juicier.

Thompson's seedless raisins

Lexia raisins

Fresh Fruit

Fresh fruit, preferably eaten raw, is part of any healthy diet. Most fruits contain Vitamin C (which cannot be stored in the body). They also contain a high proportion of natural sugars (fructose), carbohydrates, and fibre as well as minerals and other vitamins.

Buying

Buy fresh, firm, plump fruit that is not shrunken or damaged. Stone fruit, such as peaches, plums, and cherries, should be yielding, neither rock-hard nor too squashy. Melons are ripe when they smell ripe and are a little soft at the stalk end. Pineapples should be more golden than green, with leaves that pull off without much struggle. Mangoes, papayas (pawpaws), kiwi fruit, and figs should be soft, but if you buy them hard they will ripen at room temperature. Ripe passion fruit has wrinkled skin. Kumquats, like tiny oranges, are ripe when they become quite yielding to touch. Lychees are ripe when they turn red. When buying persimmons, check with your greengrocer: some can be eaten straight away, some are far too bitter and must be kept until squashy. Guavas turn a light yellow colour and are very fragrant and soft.

Storing

Fruits with good protective skins, such as citrus fruit, kiwi fruit, apples, and bananas, can be kept at room temperature, but others should go in the refrigerator as soon as they ripen to avoid destruction of Vitamins A, B_2, and C. Lychees keep up to three months in the refrigerator. Once fruit is overripe, and especially if it is bruised, these vitamins quickly disappear. Guavas lose four-fifths of their Vitamin C content in a day when overripe.

Pears in particular have only a day or so when they are at their best, and strawberries, raspberries and other soft fruits are best eaten as soon as possible after picking. Ripe figs and persimmons should also be eaten quickly. Melons, pineapples, mangoes, papayas, and guavas should all be eaten within a few days of ripening; this also applies to grapes and stone fruit, such as peaches and apricots.

Soft fruits like strawberries should go into the refrigerator without washing or stemming because handling can bruise, and bruises increase enzyme action and vitamin losses. If strawberries are handled when well chilled, damage is minimized. Firm fruit, which is less likely to bruise, can be washed before chilling, but avoid soaking and dry it well.

Preparation

Scrub fruit if you think it needs it, but try not to peel unnecessarily. Citrus fruit are often sprayed to give them a healthy shine. This should not affect the fruit inside, but if you are going to use the zest (or eat them whole, as you can with tiny kumquats, the smallest of the family) they will need a scrub.

Fruit salad should be prepared at the last moment because cutting exposes more surface to the harmful effects of air, and discoloration and vitamin losses result. Toss cut fruit in lemon juice to prevent discoloration. Apricots and peaches (and tomatoes) are easy to skin if you pour boiling water over them and leave to soak for 1 minute.

Section oranges and grapefruit by cutting down on either side of the membranes to get skinless segments. For zesting, use a special zester if you have one; otherwise use a potato peeler or a small sharp knife, but as the strips of peel will be a little thicker than true zest, they can be simmered in water for 5–6 minutes to soften them.

A cherry stoner can also be used for olives. Grapes can be halved and the pips hooked out with a hairpin or paperclip.

Melons are usually halved or cut into segments, and pineapples can be halved lengthways, when the flesh can be removed easily. Alternatively, slice pineapples across and remove the peel and core.

Kiwi fruit look prettiest when sliced across. Figs can be halved or sliced. Lychees should be peeled. Persimmons look attractive when sliced across, or the kind that must be allowed to ripen, can have their tops sliced off and the insides scooped out; passion fruit can also be given exactly the same treatment.

Soft fruit needs to be picked over carefully and any mouldy specimens removed; hull, or top and tail, them as necessary. This can be done a few hours in advance and they should then be kept cool. Papayas can be eaten like melons. Guavas are usually peeled and the seeds discarded.

Mangoes are not the most accommodating of fruit to prepare. Remember that the stone is flat and oblong, and examine the fruit to work out how the stone is lying. Cut down on either side of the stone and close to it and you will have two shallow "cheeks"; the flesh can be scooped out and chopped or diced. The mango stone will yield a few more cubes.

Cooking

It seems a shame to do anything to fruit because most of it is so good just as it comes. But if you must, cook it according to the same rules that apply to vegetables, to keep as much of the goodness and flavour as possible. Cook in the shortest possible time and serve in its own liquid to get nutrients that dissolve into the water. Very few need sweetening.

Apple crumble is a basic recipe, and can be varied by using different fruit. Stew peeled, sliced apples in a little water for 5 minutes or until soft with sugar, honey, or dried dates to taste. Add a crumble topping and bake at gas mark 4, 180°C (350°F), for 40 minutes.

Malus, spp.
Apple
The many varieties of apple that are available from Britain and abroad can be divided into two groups: eating and cooking. Crisp, firm and juicy with a sweet taste Cox's Orange Pippin is Britain's most popular eating apple, and is also a good variety to cook.

Cucumis melo
Charentais melon
The Charentais's orange, sugary and fragrant flesh make this fruit popular both as a dessert or first course. It keeps well when stored in a cool, dry place and ripens after several days in a warm room. When ripe, it is fragrant even before being cut. Although best freshly cut, it can be stored in the refrigerator for up to 2 days if covered.

Citrus sinensis
Orange
The best known of the citrus fruits, this is native to China and south-east Asia. There are both bitter and sweet oranges available. Both types are rich in Vitamin C.

Citrus reticulata
Tangerine
Native to southern China and Laos, the tangerine is a small, sweet orange containing numerous pips. These fruits are good eaten on their own or in fruit salads.

Ananas comosus
Pineapple
The pineapple is really a cluster of fruits of the ananas tree, which all combine to form one "multiple fruit". Pineapples can be bought slightly unripe and left to ripen at room temperature.

Prunus, spp.
Nectarine
A smooth-skinned member of the peach family, nectarines have sweet, juicy flesh and are usually served as a dessert fruit. They are normally sold ripe and therefore should always be eaten within a day or two of purchase.

Ficus carica
Fig
There are several varieties of white, purple, and red figs. All are very good eaten fresh. Figs are also excellent in baking and desserts, and good when stewed.

Musa nana
Banana
Bananas are usually eaten raw, either on their own or incorporated in fruit salads, although they can also be gently baked or flambéed with some brown sugar.

Fragaria × ananassa
Strawberry
Native to America, strawberries are available fresh and frozen. They should be handled with care, as they bruise easily, which accelerates enzyme action.

Passiflora edulis
Passion fruit
The fruit of a perennial climbing plant native to Brazil, passion fruit (or purple granadilla) can be eaten fresh when the skins are deeply wrinkled and the fruit is juicy, or be used to make preserves.

Carica papaya
Papaya
The papaya or pawpaw has a fairly sweet taste when ripe (similar to apricots and ginger) and, like melon, makes a good dessert or breakfast fruit.

Williams'

Comice

Pyrus communis
Pear
Pears ripen and are harvested during an extremely short period and, once ripe, go bad very quickly. The stewing varieties keep for a slightly longer period than the dessert pears. The best known English varieties for eating fresh are Williams', in season in late summer, with Comice and Conference becoming available later in the year.

Actinidia sinensis
Kiwi fruit
The kiwi fruit or Chinese gooseberry has a slightly sour taste and a hairy skin, which should be removed before eating. It may be poached and sprinkled with lemon juice, but more commonly is eaten fresh, either on its own or in fruit salads.

Vegetables

Vegetables contain minerals and fibre and are excellent sources of vitamins, particularly Vitamin C. Root vegetables supply starch and natural sugars for energy. They complement beans, grains, and nuts, providing taste and colour, palatability and texture, as well as the vitamins and minerals we need.

If you want vegetables grown organically without artificial fertilizers or sprays, expect to pay a little more. They may be smaller and less perfectly shaped, but that is nothing compared to their superior flavour and nutritional value. For vegetables grown the usual way, find a good greengrocer who will let you select the freshest – go for plumpness and good colour. Nutrients are lost in storage no matter what precautions you take, so it is best to use vegetables as soon as possible.

A growing number of exotic vegetables are available and, if you haven't already tried them, try and sample three in particular. Radicchio rosso, which is a kind of chicory eaten raw as a salad vegetable; Chinese leaves, a cross between celery and greens; and mangetout, young peas in their shells, which are eaten shells and all.

Buying
Freshness is all-important, and being wrapped in polythene does nothing for a vegetable's flavour, so wherever possible buy from a reputable greengrocer. Look for plumpness and a fresh, bright colour: avoid vegetables that are damaged, wrinkled, faded, or limp.

Storing
As soon as you get vegetables home, wash, dry and refrigerate them. This applies to all but salad vegetables and vegetables with skins thick enough to protect against light and air. The point of washing and refrigerating is to stop enzyme action. Enzymes help synthesize vitamins during plant growth but, once the plant is gathered or overripens, enzymes become destroyers. Enzyme action thrives at room temperature but is inhibited by cold or heat, or lack of light, or oxygen. Acid will retard the process but alkali will encourage it.

The following should be eaten as soon as possible: salad vegetables and those to be eaten raw; green vegetables; pods; fruit vegetables such as courgettes, peppers, and aubergines (but tomatoes are often picked unripe and allowed to continue to ripen); shoots; mushrooms; and above all sweetcorn. If any of these vegetables do have to wait, remove any polythene wrappings and keep them in a cool, dark place as light and heat destroy crispness and nutrients, particularly Vitamins B_2 and C. Greens can lose up to 50 per cent of their Vitamin C in one day if kept at room temperature.

If kept in cool, well-ventilated conditions, carrots and onions will keep longer – several weeks – and potatoes will keep for several months but will tend to lose much of their Vitamin C content.

Some fresh vegetables are suitable for freezing and this causes very little loss of nutrients. Sweetcorn, spinach, seakale beet, broccoli, carrots, peas, and beans (runner and broad) are all good.

To freeze, prepare the vegetables as directed below and blanch them by plunging into boiling water for a minute; do about 450g (1lb) at a time, so that the water does not cool down too much. (Blanching destroys the enzyme that causes deterioration.) Drain the vegetables and plunge immediately into cold water to prevent further cooking. Drain again, using a salad spinner or dryer. Freeze on a tray in a single layer, covered with a plastic bag. Pack in boxes or bags. They will keep for up to a year. Use straight from frozen and do not thaw first, or the vitamin content will be significantly reduced.

Preparation
Many vegetables are best eaten raw, for both flavour and nutrition. If you have any suspicion that your vegetables may have been contaminated by chemicals, it is advisable to wash or scrub them.

Be sure not to soak when washing. Water leaches out sugars, vitamins, and minerals, so foods should be exposed to as little as possible, whether by soaking or cooking. Apart from destroying vitamins, a mere 4 minutes' boiling of whole vegetables will cause 20 to 45 per cent of the mineral content and 75 per cent of the sugars to go the same way. With cut and peeled food it is even worse. Unless the water is used in soups and sauces all those nutrients go down the drain.

Oil-soluble vitamins such as A are less likely to be lost in cooking but they, too, are sensitive to heat and oxygen. Left at room temperature, green and yellow vegetables slowly lose their A, B_2, and C vitamins.

You may not realize how delicious uncooked vegetables can be until you try, say, a bit of raw turnip or cauliflower. Raw plants are such important sources of fibre, minerals, and vitamins (especially C) that salad should be on the menu every day. Green ones are best because deep green leaves have higher concentrations of nutrients than most fruits and other vegetables. Cooked greens are good but they do lose nutrients so how, without salads, would we manage? Salad foods must be kept dry, chilled, and uncut until soon before serving. Toss them in a dressing to keep oxygen from the surfaces once cut.

Root vegetables and tubers should be scrubbed and cooked in their skins. In general, do not peel first: scrubbing removes most pesticides, and much of the goodness of root vegetables is contained in or near the skin. Potatoes can lose up to 25 per cent of their protein if peeled too coarsely. Celeriac is the exception that does need peeling before cooking. Peel others (except potatoes) after cooking and chop, slice, or dice them. Jerusalem artichokes, small turnips, especially the young white French ones, and small kohlrabi can also be left whole, and all can be mashed or puréed.

Some vegetables (Jerusalem artichokes, celeriac, potatoes) go brown when cut: to prevent this, drop them in water, preferably lightly acidulated by adding 3–4 teaspoons of lemon juice or vinegar to each litre (2 pints) of water, or rub with lemon juice. Aubergines also go brown, but this does not matter as when cooked it will not show. It is really not necessary to salt them to draw out their bitter liquid, as many books recommend.

With okra, cut off the conical cap at the stalk end, salt and leave them for an hour, then rinse carefully and dry. Cut fennel in thin slices across, discarding the stems and, if particularly tough, the bottom.

Spinach and other leaf vegetables should be well washed and drained before cooking. Do not discard the outer leaves: they are often the most nutritious, but must of course be well washed to remove any pesticides.

Cooking

When choosing vegetables for a meal, calculate about 225g (8oz) per person for a main dish, but a bit less for a side dish.

The most nutritious way to eat vegetables is raw because the more a food is processed the greater the loss of nutrients. Of course some vegetables, such as potatoes, are unpalatable unless cooked, but there are ways of cooking that minimize nutrient losses.

Of the many different ways of cooking vegetables, boiling is one of the most popular. It is also one of the least desirable, as up to 45 per cent of the minerals and 50 per cent of the Vitamin C may be lost. If you must boil vegetables, use the minimum amount of water and make sure it is boiling when you add the vegetables. Never add bicarbonate of soda: it may keep the colour in, but it destroys Vitamin C. Instead, use a drop of vinegar to acidify the water. Salt draws out nutrients and is not good for you, so avoid that, too. For green vegetables, 1cm (½in) water should be enough. If spinach has been thoroughly rinsed and not too well drained, it will need no further liquid. Root vegetables should be barely covered. Keep the pan tightly covered – this will help prevent vitamin loss – and cook as shown on p.75.

Steaming is a good way to hold on to nutrients because if little water is used, if there is a tight-fitting lid, and if heat is kept so low that no steam gets out, nutrients that escape into the steam are reabsorbed into the food by the time it is cooked. Put the vegetables in a basket over a pan of boiling water. If you use a pressure cooker, time it carefully.

Coating with oil is another way to avoid contact with oxygen. Frying is not good for the health but stir-frying and sautéeing are different because so little oil is used – 10ml (2 tsp) oil is enough to coat the vegetables and keep juices in while cooking. Make sure the food is dry or the oil will not cling, and stir it into hot oil. Cover the pan, lower the heat once food is heated through, and it will cook in its own moisture.

You can also coat with milk. Milk covers the surfaces as oil does and food cooks in its own juices, keeping its colour beautifully. The taste is sweeter and milder than cooking with water, and the milk is lovely in soup.

Vegetables can be baked or grilled but oil them first to stop oxygenation and loss of Vitamin C, aggravated by long, slow heating. Baking or roasting is particularly suited to root vegetables and potatoes. Prick the skins first to prevent them from bursting. Green vegetables can also be baked successfully, particularly Brussels sprouts, but first brush both the sprouts and the cooking dish with a little oil. This produces a crisp cooked vegetable, the leaves on the outside well cooked and the inside tender.

To braise vegetables, brown them lightly in a little oil and bake in the oven, adding a little hot liquid, in a covered dish. When using a casserole, get both it and the oven hot before adding vegetables with hot liquid. Unless the liquid covers the food, keep the lid on.

Asparagus is best cooked with the stems in boiling water but the tops out of it, so that the tender tips cook in the steam.

Cooking vegetables in the microwave is similar to steaming: vegetables cook quickly, they keep their bright colour and crunchy textures, and vitamin loss of water-soluble vitamins like Vitamin C is minimal. Cooking times vary, but leaf vegetables normally need 30ml (2 tbsp) water for 450g (1lb), and take about 6–8 minutes on High in a 700W oven. Beans and peas need the same amount of water for 450g (1lb) and take 5–10 minutes on High in the same oven. Consult a microwave vegetable cooking chart for full details.

Most B vitamins disappear when the temperature is above boiling, as in frying or pressure cooking, but E and K seem to survive. Aromatic oils that give foods flavour are lost in proportion to how long the cooking takes, so serve vegetables firm, not mushy.

VITAMIN LOSSES IN COOKING

Overcooking is one of our commonest sins. Peeling is another because so many nutrients lie just under the skin. The water-soluble vitamins, such as Vitamin C, are destroyed most readily by cooking and other processing. See what happens to the Vitamin C in a 100g (3oz) serving of peas:
- fresh or frozen, uncooked: 25mg
- fresh or frozen, boiled: 15mg
- canned garden: 9mg
- canned processed: trace only
- freeze dried: trace only

Even if left untouched at room temperature, leafy vegetables can lose half their C in a day, and light destroys half their B_2. Cutting exposes more surface to destructive contact with light and air, and cooking can have a devastating effect. This is what happens to the most important vitamins in spinach when prepared:

	B_1	C	folic acid
raw, shredded	no loss	30% loss	25% loss
steamed	30% loss	50% loss	75% loss
boiled	total loss	total loss	total loss

PREPARING AND COOKING VEGETABLES

Washing vegetables
- Clean quickly in cold water. Never soak.
- Brush root vegetables. Do not scrape.
- Dry thoroughly.
- Store in bags in the vegetable compartment of the refrigerator.

Preparing vegetables
- Cut food while still chilled.
- Peel only when you absolutely have to.
- Save peelings for soup.
- Save tops (for example, radish and carrot tops) for soups or salads, or to cook as a vegetable.
- Toss cut foods in a little lemon juice or vinegar to prevent discoloration and preserve nutrients.

Cooking vegetables
- Do not cook in copper or iron pans.
- Never add soda.
- Add a drop of vinegar to hard water.
- Steam if possible. Otherwise, boil very little water, add food, return to boil. Cover pan tightly, then simmer.
- Cook on High in the microwave with 2 tbsp water or as recommended.
- Cook until barely tender.
- Save vegetable water for soups, sauces, or the next lot of cooking.

COOKING TIMES AND METHODS FOR DIFFERENT VEGETABLES

Aubergines are usually sautéed and/or baked, often with a stuffing: see detailed recipes for specific cooking instructions.
Tomatoes can be grilled for 3–4 minutes. No times have been giving for frying or sautéing as these will be found in specific recipes.

Spinach* is not strictly speaking boiled, but cooked in the water adhering to it after rinsing.
All the times listed below give *very lightly cooked* vegetables, many with a crisp, crunchy texture. If you prefer softer vegetables, you will need to increase the cooking time.

Vegetable	Steam	Boil	Bake (whole)	Braise	Stir-fry
Potatoes	25–30 minutes	20 minutes	1–1½ hours	15–20 minutes	–
Carrots	20 minutes	10–15 minutes	45–60 minutes	15–20 minutes	yes
Turnips	25–30 minutes	10–15 minutes	–	15–20 minutes	yes
Swedes	25–30 minutes	20 minutes	–	15–20 minutes	yes
Parsnips	–	15–20 minutes	45–60 minutes	15–20 minutes	–
Celeriac & kohlrabi	20 minutes	10–15 minutes	–	15–20 minutes	yes
Salsify & scorzonera	30–40 minutes	20–30 minutes	–	–	–
Sweet potato	25–30 minutes	20 minutes	1–1½ hours	–	–
Jerasulem artichokes	–	15–20 minutes	–	–	–
Radish/daikon	–	–	–	–	yes
Beetroot	–	40–60 minutes	–	–	–
Asparagus	–	10–15 minutes	–	–	–
Fennel	12–15 minutes	10–12 minutes	–	15–20 minutes	yes
Onions	–	–	45–60 minutes	–	–
Leeks	15–20 minutes	10–15 minutes	–	8–10 minutes	–
Celery	12–15 minutes	8–10 minutes	–	10–12 minutes	yes
Globe artichokes	–	30–40 minutes	–	–	–
French beans	4–8 minutes	–	–	–	yes
Broad beans	–	10–15 minutes	–	–	–
Peas	–	8–12 minutes	–	–	yes
Mangetout peas	6–8 minutes	–	–	–	yes
Okra	–	15–20 minutes	–	–	–
Mushrooms	–	–	–	–	yes
Sweetcorn	–	8–15 minutes	–	–	yes
Cabbage	4–6 minutes	–	–	–	yes
Red cabbage	–	–	–	45–60 minutes	–
Brussels sprouts	6–10 minutes	–	25–30 minutes	–	yes
Cauliflower	4–8 minutes	–	–	–	–
Broccoli	4–8 minutes	–	–	–	yes

Continued overleaf

COOKING TIMES AND METHODS FOR DIFFERENT VEGETABLES

Vegetable	Steam	Boil	Bake (whole)	Braise	Stir-fry
Spinach*	–	*6–8 minutes	–	–	–
Pak choi	4–8 minutes	–	–	–	yes
Spinach beet	10–12 minutes	–	–	–	–
Chard (seakale beet)	10–12 minutes	–	–	–	–
Endive	–	–	–	10–12 minutes	–
Chicory	–	–	–	–	yes
Chinese leaves	4 minutes	–	–	–	yes
Courgettes	4–8 minutes	–	–	–	yes
Marrow	10–20 minutes	–	45–60 minutes	–	yes
Peppers	–	–	–	–	yes
Cucumbers	5–10 minutes	–	–	–	–

Salad Vegetables

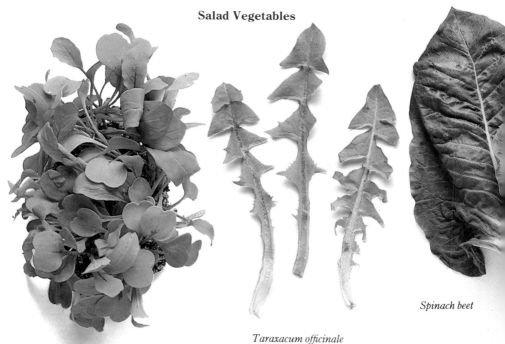

Spinach beet

Eruca sativa
Rocket
*Rocket is deservedly popular in
Italy and parts of France. The
young, tender leaves become toothed
and taste quite peppery.*

Taraxacum officinale
Dandelion
*Dandelion leaves offered for sale
have been blanched (like celery and
chicory) to reduce their bitterness.
If you want to use wild dandelions,
pick only the young leaves.*

Valerianella olitoria
Lamb's lettuce
Also known as corn salad and (in France) as mâche, *this is a very useful winter salad.*

Chicory

Chard

Cichorium intybus
Chicory
Endive and chicory have a similar slightly bitter taste. Both are usually blanched by the grower to reduce this bitterness. Chicory can be eaten raw, or stir-fried.

Beta vulgaris
Chard; Spinach beet
Chard (Swiss chard or seakale beet) and spinach beet are the same species; they resemble spinach, but lack its distinctive flavour. The central spines of chard are often cut out and cooked separately.

Radicchio rosso

Batavian endive

Cichorium endivia
Endive
*Endive is valuable as a salad plant;
the most popular kinds are curly
endive (the French* frisée*), the
more wavy Batavian endive, or
escarole, and the crisp radicchio
rosso from Treviso in north Italy.*

Curly endive

Levisticum officinale
Lovage
*The young, reddish leaves (above)
are good in salads; the older leaves
(bottom) and the stems help to make
powerful flavourings.*

Brassica chinensis
Pak choi
*Less well known than some other
leaf vegetables, pak choi, or
Chinese cabbage, is crisp and
delicate-tasting and needs little or
no cooking at all.*

Rumex acetosa
Sorrel
*Sorrel is high in oxalic acid. This
gives it a fresh, sharp taste but also
impedes assimilation of minerals,
notably calcium and iron. Garden
sorrel is less acid.*

Sprouts

Easy and quick to grow at home, sprouts
provide fresh, uncontaminated green
vegetables of outstanding nutritional value:
they contain valuable amounts of protein as
well as Vitamins A, B complex, C, and E,
minerals, and enzymes.

The changes that take place as the seed
grows are incredible. The total vitamin content
can increase by 800 per cent in a few days.

Buying
Buy untreated seeds from a healthfood shop or
a firm specializing in organically grown
produce, as almost all seeds sold for planting
will have been treated with fungicides and
pesticides. Split beans or seeds will not sprout.

Growing
If you do not have proper tiered sprouting
trays, fine sieves, or mesh trays, or a wide-
necked jar with a cover of muslin or other
porous substance, will do very well. Pick over
the seeds, removing tiny stems and stones.

Put two tablespoons of seeds in a jar and soak
them in plenty of lukewarm water overnight, to
encourage them to germinate more quickly.
Next day, drain off the water. Put the seeds on
a suitable tray or leave them in the jar. Put in a
warm place but not in direct sun (the airing
cupboard is ideal). They need good ventilation

and a constant temperature of 13–21°C
(55–70°F). Remember to allow enough space
in the container for the growth of the sprouts.

Every night and morning pour warm water
over the seeds. Turn the jar, if you are using
one, upside down so the water can drain away
completely. If not properly drained the sprouts
can go mouldy, but be careful not to rinse them
so vigorously that you damage the delicate
shoots. Grain sprouts take 2–3 days, beans and
lentils 5–7 days, to be at their best. When
ready, give them a final rinse.

Storing
Sprouts keep in the refrigerator for up to 4
days. Use an airtight container with a double
layer of kitchen paper or muslin at the bottom,
to absorb excess moisture.

Using
All sprouts can be eaten raw in salads. The
delicate green leaves of mustard, cress, and
alfalfa look particularly pretty and can also be
used to garnish. Aduki bean sprouts have a
distinct flavour of peanuts; mung beans taste a
little like delicate peapods, but if grown for too
long will lose some of their nutritive value.
Fenugreek sprouts taste spicy.

The best known and easiest to sprout are
mustard and cress, mung beans, and alfalfa.
Sprouts are good used on bread: use wheat
sprouts, or alfalfa sprouts, which have been
grown to only 0.5cm (¼in) in height.

Sprouts

Mung beans
(Phaseolus aureus)

Alfalfa *(Medicago sativa)*

Wheat *(Triticum vulgare)*

Growing sprouts
Sprouts from wheat (and other grains such as rye) and from lentils are best when grown to about the length of the seeds. Aduki bean sprouts should be about 1cm (½in) long, mung beans can be grown to 2.5cm (1in). Mustard and cress are eaten at the two-leaf stage, when 3–4cm (1–1½in) long, so are alfalfa sprouts, which take 5–6 days. Fenugreek sprouts are best when not more than 2–3 times the length of the seed, which normally takes 3–6 days.

Cress *(Lepidum sativum)*

Mustard *(Sinapis alba)*

Aduki beans
(Phaseolus angularis)

Fenugreek *(Trigonella foenum-graecum)*

Lentils
(Lens esculenta)

Pod and Root Vegetables

Hibiscus esculentus
Okra
This is also known as lady's fingers and gumbo. The edible part is the pod, picked and eaten while still unripe, as when fully ripe it becomes fibrous and indigestible. It is very mucilaginous and when added to soups and casseroles gives them a rich, thick consistency.

Winter radish

Raphanus sativus
Winter radish
A useful vegetable for winter salads, much grown in China and Japan. The large roots are crisp, but not quite so tender as spring radishes. It is excellent when used in stir-fries.

Okra

Brassica oleracea
Kohlrabi
*A variety of cabbage, also called
turnip-rooted cabbage, although the
apparent root is actually the swollen
stem. Both green and purple
varieties are good when young,
crisp and tender: they can then be
eaten raw and have a delicate,
slightly turnip-like flavour. Weight
for weight they have more Vitamin
C than oranges.*

Kohlrabi

Foeniculum vulgare var. *dulce*
Fennel
*Often known as Florence fennel,
the "bulb" is the swollen leaf-base
and has a pronounced anise
flavour. It is usually served raw
in salad dishes.*

Fennel

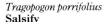

*Jerusalem
artichoke*

Helianthus tuberosus
Jerusalem artichoke
*No relation to globe artichokes, but
a cousin of the sunflower, this has a
sweet, nutty flavour.*

Raphanus sativus
Daikon
*A large winter radish, also known
as Japanese white radish or mooli.
It has a crisp texture and a milder
flavour than ordinary winter
radishes. It is used like them, in
salads and stir-fries. All winter
radishes have slightly more
nutritional value than
spring ones.*

Daikon

Salsify

Tragopogon porrifolius
Salsify
*Also called oyster plant or vegetable
plant, as its subtle taste is supposed
to resemble that of oysters. "Black
salsify" is the related scorzonera,
which is similar in appearance but
black-skinned.*

Ipomoea batatas
Sweet potato
*This name is also sometimes given
to the brown-skinned yam, which is
similar in taste but has little
nutritive value.*

Sweet potato

Herbs and Spices

The word "herb" comes from the Latin word *"herba"*, meaning grass or herbage. Herbs are usually annual plants and are mostly grown from seed. The flowers, leaves, seeds, stems, and roots are used as flavourings in cooking, or for medicinal purposes. The amount used in cooking depends partly on individual taste, and partly on the type of herb. Strongly flavoured herbs should be used only sparingly. Many herbs, such as parsley, basil, fennel, marjoram, or thyme do not grow too vigorously and can easily be kept in small pots on the windowsill.

Buying and storing herbs

Most herbs should be bought and used fresh whenever possible, although a few (principally oregano, marjoram, sage, bay leaf, and dill) keep their aroma well when dried. Buy small amounts of dried herbs, if possible, from a wholefood shop or somewhere where there is a high turnover of stock.

To dry your own herbs, pick them when the leaves are dry, preferably just before flowering. Tie the items in bunches and hang them upside down in a cool, dark place. When dry, crumble up the leaves, leaving out the stalks, and put them into small jars.

Some herbs can also be frozen for use as a flavouring rather than as a garnish: parsley, coriander leaves, chives, tarragon, and chervil are all suitable. Blanch in boiling water for a few seconds (otherwise they will lose their colour and look unappetizing). Blanching also helps to retain flavour and aroma. Drain them, leave in sprigs and open freeze. Wrap in polythene bags and keep for not more than 3–4 months. Keep dried herbs away from light or heat, in airtight containers to prevent any deterioration in the flavour.

Using herbs

To get the best flavour from fresh herbs, tear or snip them rather than chop them, except parsley. Dried herbs are more pungent in flavour than fresh, so use only 1 teaspoon of the dried herb where you would need to use at least 2–3 teaspoons of the fresh variety.

SPICES

Even a small amount of spice, judiciously used, alters the whole character of a dish. The term generally refers to the dried roots, bark, pods, berries, or seeds of aromatic plants. Most spices come from countries in the East, but allspice, chilli peppers, and vanilla originated in the New World.

Buying and storing spices

Buy spices whole whenever possible as they keep their flavour and freshness much better. Turmeric, pepper, cayenne, and paprika are generally sold ready ground, but red dried chilli peppers can be bought whole and then ground. Keep in airtight containers, in a dark place.

Preparing spices

Some spices can be crushed in a pestle and mortar: they include allspice, cardamom, cloves, coriander, cumin, dill and fennel seed, juniper, black peppercorns, and saffron. Poppy seeds are tough and need a proper nut mill, which can of course also be used for other spices. Aniseeds, capers, caraway, celery, dill, and fennel seeds are generally used whole. Green peppercorns are not strictly speaking a spice, as they are not dried. They are easily crushed or mashed. Nutmeg needs grating: a cheese grater does perfectly well. Ginger can also be grated, especially when fresh, or it can be sliced thinly or chopped. Always prepare spices just before they are to be cooked.

Fresh chilli peppers can be chopped (remove the seeds unless you are sure you like the chilli hot), or kept in a jar of oil to impart their flavour. Keep topping up with oil as you use it – you will need only a few drops at a time.

Saffron threads are often mixed with a little warm water, when they will expand and give out their colour and flavouring more easily. They may also be lightly crushed and put in a warm oven for a few minutes.

Using spices

Many spices benefit from being lightly fried in a little oil before being added to the dish they are to flavour. This seems to bring out and

COOKING WITH HERBS CHART						
Herb	Soups	Stews	Sauces	Salads	Garnish	Other remarks
Basil	yes		yes	yes	yes	Goes particularly well with tomatoes; an essential ingredient of pesto.
Bay leaf	yes	yes	yes			A bay leaf, a sprig of thyme, and some parsley make a *bouquet garni*.
Chervil	yes	yes	yes	yes	yes	The mixture known as *fines herbes* is made of finely chopped chervil, parsley, tarragon, and chives.
Chives			yes	yes	yes	Particularly good with potato salad.
Coriander leaves	yes	yes	yes	yes	yes	Use like parsley.
Dill leaves			yes	yes	yes	Good with potatoes and green vegetables.
Garlic	yes	yes	yes			Extremely versatile and enhances other flavours.
Lemon balm	yes	yes				Use to flavour summer drinks and tisanes.
Sweet marjoram	yes	yes				Goes well with nuts, eggs, and tomatoes.
Mint			yes	yes	yes	Use to flavour young vegetables, especially peas and new potatoes, or add to yogurt or bean dishes. Also good with fruit and summer drinks.
Oregano	yes	yes	yes			Indispensable to many Greek and Italian dishes.
Parsley	yes	yes	yes	yes	yes	Use generously both as flavouring and as garnish.
Rosemary	yes	yes				Good with oily foods. Strong camphor-like flavour.
Sage		yes				Use sparingly: very pungent.
Savory	yes	yes		yes	yes	Use like thyme or marjoram; good with beans.
Tarragon	yes	yes	yes		yes	Particularly good with cheese, cream, eggs, sauces, and some vegetables.
Thyme	yes	yes				Good with most vegetables, such as tomatoes, courgettes, aubergines, and peppers.

reinforce their aroma, removing any suspicion of rankness or coarseness, and applies particularly to coriander, cumin, cardamom, ginger, and fenugreek.

Cinnamon and mace, being difficult to grind, are often used whole to flavour liquids – sauces or drinks – from which they can be easily extracted once they have yielded their aromatic flavour. In the same way, a vanilla pod can be used to flavour drinks, syrups, custards, and other sweet desserts.

Coriander, cumin, cardamom, peppercorns, turmeric, cloves, ginger, and chilli peppers are the most important spices for curry. Some recipes call for "garam masala", a combination of spices. This can be bought, or you can make your own: there is no standard recipe (the name means "hot mixture"). It is a starting mixture rather than a complete curry powder. A mixture could be 4 parts coriander, 1 part cumin, 1 part chilli, all lightly roasted or fried and added to 1 part ground black peppercorns.

Herbs

Salvia officinalis
Sage
There are many varieties. It dries well, but can become musty if it is kept for too long.

Allium sativum
Garlic
Sold all the year round, a garlic bulb is separated into cloves which are used one or two at a time. An essential ingredient in many casseroles, curries, and soups.

Origanum vulgare
Oregano
This is wild marjoram, which for the best flavour must be grown in strong sun. Luckily it keeps all its aroma when it is dried.

Petroselinum crispum
Parsley
Available curled (left) or flat (above), parsley is a good source of both Vitamin C and iron. Flat parsley is thought to have a finer taste than curled parsley.

Coriandrum sativum
Coriander
Also known as Chinese or Japanese parsley, it is lavishly used in the East as with parsley.

Laurus nobilis
Bay leaf
Good in milk puddings as well as savoury stews and sauces. A bay leaf (left) kept in a packet of grains will give them a delicate taste.

Anthriscus cerefolium
Chervil
Very popular in France, chervil can be used in the same way as parsley but has a more delicate taste with a hint of anise.

Satureja montana
Winter savory
Its German name means "bean-herb", which indicates its traditional use. Summer savory (S. hortensis) is similar and even more aromatic.

Artemisia dracunculus
Tarragon
If possible, make sure that you are getting French tarragon (left), not Russian which is far less aromatic.

Rosmarinus officinalis
Rosemary
A wonderfully aromatic herb with a strong camphor-like flavour. The spiky needles, however, can be a menace when dried.

Thymus vulgaris
Thyme
This popular herb contains an essential oil, thymol, which helps to digest fatty foods.

Melissa officinalis
Lemon balm
The crushed leaves give off a wonderful lemony scent. They can be used generously in salads.

Ocimum basilicum
Basil
If you cannot find fresh, do not use dried; substitute another herb. A pot of basil in the kitchen will help keep any flies away.

Mentha spp.
Mint
There are many species of this popular herb, from spearmint to the fresh-tasting peppermint used for making soothing tisanes.

Anethum graveolens
Dill
The leaves are known as dill weed, one of the most popular herbs used in Scandinavia.

Allium schoenoprasum
Chives
Mostly eaten raw, but also good in omelettes, chives are widely used from China and Japan to Europe and America.

Origanum majorana
Marjoram
Sweet marjoram, native to the Mediterranean, is very fragrant and can be dried successfully.

Apium graveolens
Celery
The slightly bitter taste of
celery seeds goes well in bread, egg
dishes, and salads.

Pimenta officinalis
Allspice
Also called Jamaica pepper; the
taste combines cloves, cinnamon,
and nutmeg.

Capsicum frutescens
Chilli
Ripe chilli peppers dry and keep
well. "Chilli powder" often
includes other spices.

Pimpinella asinum
Aniseed
This is popular in Mexico and all
over the Mediterranean for its
liquorice flavour.

Coriandrum sativum
Coriander
Mild but aromatic, coriander seed
is an important ingredient in Arab
and Eastern food.

Carum carvi
Caraway
Looks like cumin seed and often
confused with it, but the taste is
quite different.

Cuminum cyminum
Cumin
The pungent seed is often
combined with coriander seeds to
make a basic curry mixture.

Capsicum frutescens
Cayenne
A very hot, pungent red chilli sold
ready ground. Use sparingly.

Vanilla planifolia
Vanilla
Fruit of an orchid plant from
Mexico, traditionally used to
flavour chocolate. Expensive, but
good in many sweet dishes.

Anethum graveolens
Dill
Popular in eastern and northern Europe, dill seed is much used in pickle making.

Capsicum annuum
Paprika
Made from very mild, sweet peppers, popular in Hungary and Spain. Use generously.

Foeniculum vulgare
Fennel
Like the bulb, fennel seeds have a slight aniseed flavour. Good with fruit and salads.

Piper nigrum
Pepper
Unripe whole peppercorns are green. When dried they turn a brown-black colour.

Trigonella foenum-graecum
Fenugreek
Produces spicy sprouts. Use the ground seed sparingly.

Papaver rhoeas; P. somniferum
Poppy seed
White poppy seed is much used in curries, blue is popular in pastries and bread.

Brassica alba; B. nigra
Mustard
The white (or yellow) seed is milder in flavour than the black (or brown) seed.

Curcuma longa
Turmeric
Always sold ground. Do not confuse with the more expensive saffron. The taste is mustier.

Myristica fragrans
Nutmeg
Always buy whole and grate as required: ready-ground nutmeg quickly loses its aroma. Sometimes coated with lime to repel insects.

Crocus sativus
Saffron
Always buy the stigmas or "threads" of this extremely expensive spice, as the powder is very easy to adulterate.

Juniperus communis
Juniper
The berries have a pungent, slightly resinous flavour. They go well with cabbage and add a light touch to oily or heavy dishes.

Myristica fragrans
Mace
Mace, in "blade" form, resembles the outer net-like covering of nutmeg. It is sold both in blades and ready-ground, as it is difficult to grind at home.

Eugenia caryophyllata
Cloves
These are buds of an evergreen tree, widely used in curries, marinades, mincemeat, fruit dishes, and mulled wine. Use sparingly, as the taste is very strong.

Capparis spinosa
Capers
The buds of a small Mediterranean bush, these are usually sold pickled in vinegar and should not be allowed to dry out. Capers are used mostly in sauces and salads.

Elettaria cardamomum
Cardamom
The flavourless pod encloses black aromatic seeds used in curries and pastries and to flavour drinks, including coffee.

Zingiber officinale
Ginger
Fresh root ginger is firm and juicy. It needs peeling before being grated or chopped for use in curries, stir-fries, or puddings.

Cinnamomum zeylanicum
Cinnamon
The "quills" of dried bark can flavour drinks and syrups; the powder is widely used in breads and different sweet dishes.

Seasonings and Flavourings

Any well-stocked vegetarian store cupboard should contain a wide range of flavourings and seasonings, from spices and vinegars, seaweeds and syrups, to flavourings made from nuts and vegetables and the indispensable soya products.

Soya bean products

The soya bean, difficult to digest when whole, is easily assimilated when fermented and provides nutrients as well as flavourings. The best known fermented products are shoyu, tamari, and miso. The soya sauce familiar to many non-vegetarians, is too often a rather synthetic reproduction.

Miso is a living food rather in the same way that yogurt is, and contains bacteria and enzymes which are destroyed by boiling. It is therefore usually added as a flavouring at the end of cooking, often mixed with a little warm water so it dissolves easily. The most commonly available is mugi miso, a combination of soya and barley with a warm, mellow flavour. Hatcho miso, made from soya beans alone, is denser and more strongly flavoured, while genmai miso, made with rice, is lighter and sweeter.

Tamari, shoyu, and miso all keep well but should not undergo sudden changes of temperature. Miso may develop a white mould: this is a natural yeast by-product and can simply be mixed straight back in.

Rock salt, held by some to have the finest taste, and sea salt are preferable to refined table salt, which may have additives. Both can be used for cooking and at the table. Salt substitutes often consist of potassium salts. One of the most successful combinations of salt with other flavourings is gomashio, or sesame salt, whose nutty flavour complements many dishes. It will keep for up to two weeks.

Both the strong English mustard powder and the gentler, more aromatic, made-up French mustard have their place in the kitchen. With mustard powder, make up only as much as you are going to need at any one time.

Horseradish sauce can be bought, but does not compare with sauces made from the freshly grated root, as the aroma is very volatile. The best substitute is dried horseradish.

Nuts and seeds provide useful flavourings, from peanut butter to tahini, a beige paste of similar consistency made from sesame seeds.

Dried mushrooms add rich natural flavouring and are popular in Japan and China. They keep well in an airtight container and are reconstituted by soaking in warm water for at least half an hour.

Vegetable concentrates, stock cubes, and yeast extracts are all quick ways of adding flavour. Yeast extracts in particular are rich in nutrients, but high in salt so should not be used too generously. They are sold in screwtop jars and will keep for at least six months.

Shoyu
Naturally fermented soya sauce, made from soya beans with barley or wheat, is known as shoyu or tamari, and should not be confused with the manufactured soya sauce, which is not the same and usually contains sugar and other additives.

Tamari
True tamari, a liquid made from the manufacture of miso, contains no wheat and is therefore suitable for people on gluten-free diets, but is very difficult to find.

Dried mushrooms
These are available in several varieties, from the strongly flavoured cep (Boletus edulis) to the ordinary cultivated mushroom (Agaricus bisporus) shown here. Even this kind makes a valuable contribution of flavour.

Brewer's yeast
This is exceptionally high in protein as well as in calcium, iron, and B vitamins. It can be sprinkled over cereals or used as part of a topping, and adds an interesting flavour as well as nourishment.

Japanese gomashio
Also called sesame salt, this is available from healthfood shops, but it is easy to make by grinding four–five parts roasted sesame seeds with one part salt. Keep in an airtight container and use instead of salt.

Grated horseradish
When fresh, grated horseradish is very pungent, and much liked in Germany and Scandinavia as well as Britain. It can be used rather in the same way as mustard.

Mugi miso

Hatcho miso

Vegetable concentrates
Like stock cubes, vegetable concentrates are a quick way of adding flavour to stocks, soups, and casseroles, and for making hot drinks. They can also be used as a spread on toast.

Yeast extracts
Yeast extracts are made from a mixture of brewer's yeast and salt, which produces a highly flavoured brown residue, full of protein, iron, potassium, and B vitamins, some with added B_{12}.

Genmai miso

Miso
Like shoyu and tamari, miso is a product of the fermented soya bean, a little like peanut butter in texture. All misos have quite a high salt content, although lighter coloured miso has slightly less.

Vegetable stock cubes
These are quite widely available, but make sure they contain no artificial additives. They should be a concentration of vegetables, yeast, and vitamins.

Tahini
Tahini is sesame seed paste, widely used in the Middle East. Strong, with a nutty flavour, it can be used as a dip, on its own, or to flavour other dips and sauces.

Peanut butter
This is not only a nutritious spread but can be adapted to other uses, particularly as a flavouring for sauces and dressings.

Wholegrain mustard
Usually from France, this contains the whole mustard seed and is often flavoured with herbs such as tarragon. It is used as a relish.

English mustard powder
Made mainly from black mustard seed, its clean, sharp taste makes it ideal for flavouring sauces, dressings, and dips.

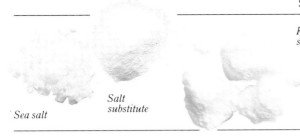

Sea salt

Salt substitute

Rock salt

Sodium chloride
Salt
Salt comes from the sea, either as sea salt or as bay salt, which is directly evaporated from sea water, or as rock salt deposits left by vanished prehistoric seas. Salt substitutes are also available.

Sea Vegetables

Most seaweeds are like salty rubber but there are, surprisingly, around 70 edible species. We would do well to know about them because they provide an excellent, cheap, seemingly inexhaustible supply of protein, vitamins, and minerals. As a source of B vitamins they are unusual in having B_{12}, not often found in vegetables. They are hard to beat for their mineral content, supplying all we need, and are particularly rich in calcium, potassium, sodium, iodine, and iron.

We eat some seaweed without knowing it – it is used in manufactured vegetable gelatines, ice cream, salad dressing, soups, sauces, and sausage skins. Those who eat it knowingly are the Celts, Chinese, and Japanese. A variety eaten in Wales is red seaweed called laver, which smells like cabbage and looks like spinach. In the Far East kelp, or brown seaweed, is particularly popular, used as a garnish for rice or as a seasoning.

Buying and storing
It is usually best to buy from a healthfood shop, where sea vegetables are sold already cleaned, dried, and packaged. Unopened, they will keep indefinitely; once opened, they will last up to four months in an airtight container.

Preparation
Dried nori, dulse, kombu, wakame, and arame need a preliminary brief soaking for 5 minutes or so to soften them, although this is not necessary if they are to be added straightaway to a soup or stew. The exception is dulse, which needs to be rinsed and then soaked again for 10 minutes. Nori need not be softened if it is to be crumbled over a salad. Carrageen may need rinsing before use.

Nori, intensively farmed in Japan, is similar to laver and normally sold in sheets. It is traditionally toasted and wrapped around small rice balls which are then dipped in shoyu. After its preliminary soaking, it can be used to flavour soups or as a salad ingredient, when it should be rinsed and boiled for 15 minutes.

Dulse can be eaten raw, or, if dried, simmered for 30 minutes after being soaked. Widely available, it is a dark, leafy vegetable with a sweet, tangy taste and is particularly good with cooked cabbage.

Kombu, valued and cultivated in Japan, is eaten both raw and cooked. The flavour is sweet and it is used to enhance stocks and soups (see page 121).

Wakame should have the central vein cut out after soaking. It can then be either simmered for 10 minutes, or cut into small pieces and served as a salad.

Arame has a broad leaf and is usually shredded into hair-like threads. It is similar to hijiki, which is shredded more coarsely. Both can be steamed, sautéed, or eaten as salad. Arame is a good introduction to seaweeds because of its mild taste.

Agar is a vegetable gelatine, available in powder or flake form. The powder is easier to use and ensures better results. Make sure it is thoroughly dissolved in boiling water or liquid before use, otherwise it will not set. Use 10ml (2tsp) of agar powder to 600ml (1 pint) of boiling liquid for a delicate jelly.

Carrageen, or Irish moss, is still enjoyed in Ireland, where it is most often used to make carrageen mould or blancmange. Soak 10–15g (½oz) dried carrageen in water for 15 minutes. Drain, rinse and cover with 570ml (1 pint) milk; bring to the boil and simmer, covered, for 20–30 minutes. Strain, cool slightly, sweeten to taste, pour into a wet mould and leave to set.

Sea Vegetables

Agar flakes   *Agar powder*

Agar
Agar (or agar-agar, from a Malay word meaning jelly) is obtained from several different species of sea vegetables. Also called Japanese or Ceylon moss, it is used as a substitute for animal gelatine.

Chondrus crispus
Carrageen
Also called Irish moss, carrageen is still eaten in Ireland, and used to be valued as a cure for bronchial diseases and tuberculosis.

Rhodymenia palmata
Dulse
Dulse grows in the North Atlantic and is eaten in Ireland and New England, as well as Iceland and parts of Canada.

Porphyra spp.
Nori
Nori is intensively grown in Japan, where it is usually sold in sheets which can be wrapped round rice. Laver, still used in Wales, is a similar sea vegetable.

Eisenia bicyclis
Arame
This has a mild taste that blends well with other flavours, and is a good introduction to sea vegetables. It is rich in iron.

Laminaria spp.
Kombu
This is much cultivated in Japan and considered suitable for offering to people as a gift.

Undaria pinnatifida
Wakame
This is another Japanese favourite. Softer than kombu, it can be used in many of the same ways, particularly in soup.

Sweetenings

Rather than substituting one kind of sugar for another, it is important to monitor your intake of sugar and cut down on the total. There is little difference nutritionally between white and brown sugar, but brown sugar does contain a little fibre.

A product of cane sugar, molasses, especially blackstrap molasses, contains small amounts of minerals, including calcium and iron, and some B vitamins. Its strong flavour makes it suitable for fruit breads. It will keep for up to six months in an airtight jar.

Honey is twice as sweet as sugar, so you need to use only half the amount of sugar given in a recipe (reduce the liquid elsewhere to allow for the water content of honey). Look for the word "pure" on the label: blended honey may contain sugars, syrups, and possibly additives. A jar of clear honey may crystallize if stored at a low temperature. Simply warm gently and the honey will become clear again.

Maple syrup is not so sweet as honey, but it does contain some minerals, especially calcium. Other syrups available include corn syrup, rice syrup, sorghum syrup, and barley syrup, also known as malt extract.

Fruit juice concentrates are very useful flavourings and can be combined with other sweetenings, such as honey, to reduce the total amount of sweetening needed in cakes and pastries – on their own the taste is too strong. Add them to fruit salads, sauces, and cereals. Once opened, store the bottle in the refrigerator for up to three weeks.

Carob powder, or carob flour, made from the seeds of the Mediterranean carob tree, tastes very similar to chocolate. Naturally sweeter than cocoa, it has no caffeine, a lower fat content and also contains some vitamins. When substituting carob for cocoa, use about half the quantity suggested.

Corn syrup
Corn syrup, or glucose syrup, is made by heating cornstarch and water with a little sulphuric or hydrochloric acid.

Muscovado sugar
This is a dark, moist, partly refined sugar with a strong distinctive flavour. It is sometimes called Barbados sugar.

Molasses
Sometimes called black treacle, molasses is the residue left when cane sugar is refined. It has some vitamins and minerals.

Demerara sugar
Demerara can be white sugar dyed with caramel. If the country of origin is stated on the packet, it is less likely to be dyed.

Maple syrup
This comes from the sugar maple and black maple. It takes 50 gallons of sap to make one gallon of syrup, so it is a very concentrated form of sweetening.

Light brown sugar
As with demerara, check the packet for the country of origin.

Apple juice concentrate
This and other concentrated fruit juices are useful flavourings for fruit salads, sauces, and cereals.

Malt extract
Sometimes also called barley syrup, this is not so sweet as sugar; it is used to flavour drinks and malted breads and cakes.

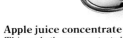

Carob powder
Carob pods, the size of a banana, but flat and dark brown, contain small black seeds, so uniform in size that the word "carat" as a weight measure derives from them.

Oils, Fats, Dairy Products, and Alternatives

Oils are used mainly as a cooking medium for frying and sautéing, as a condiment for salads, and as shortening in baking. Fats are solids, a good source of energy, and unrefined contain many vitamins and minerals.

Dairy products like milk provide protein, vitamins, and minerals such as calcium and phosphorous. Nutritious soya bean produce has evolved from the Chinese and provides excellent low-fat alternatives.

Oils

There are three main types of oil that are obtained from seeds, beans, and nuts.

Cold pressed oil is still extracted using the ancient method of hydraulic pressing. Much of the oil remains in the pulp, but that which is extracted is high quality and full of flavour. Unfortunately true cold pressed oil is very expensive to buy.

Semi-refined oil requires greater pressure and higher temperatures. The extraction rate is higher, but the vitamin content suffers.

Refined oil, confusingly labelled "pure", is produced by a method called solvent extraction, which removes most of the goodness as well as bleaching and deodorizing the oil. Many of the vitamins are then added back artificially along with preservatives to prevent the oil from going rancid. This is generally the cheapest type available.

Buying
This depends on what you want your oil for: dressing salads, frying vegetables and grains, or baking. For eating raw, as a salad dressing, use cold-pressed or unrefined oil: it tastes much the best to most palates and nutritionally is the most valuable.

Olive oil has a rich flavour, but one that varies widely depending on the country of origin. "Virgin oil" means oil from the first pressing. It is the best quality of oil and is highly recommended for use in different salad dressings.

Safflower oil is pale in colour, with a delicate flavour, high in linoleic acid and low in cholesterol, which justifies its high price.

Sunflower oil is perhaps the best all-purpose oil. It is high in linoleic acid, second only to safflower oil, and slightly cheaper.

Sesame oil does not go rancid quickly, and food containing it will not go stale, which makes it a good oil for baking.

Corn oil is cheap to produce, almost tasteless and popular as a cooking oil. It is also widely used as an ingredient in margarine.

Peanut oil is another very popular oil. It is particularly good for frying as it can be heated to very high temperatures without burning. *Soya oil* is also cheap and popular.

Walnut oil has a strong, nutty taste and is very expensive to buy, so it is used chiefly for dressing salads.

Storing
Cold pressed oils, apart from sesame oil, do not keep well. They are not heat-treated or otherwise stabilized and may go rancid, so buy comparatively small quantities (enough for a month or two) and keep in a cool, dark place. If it is too cold and the oil congeals, do not worry – the oil will liquefy very quickly when brought to room temperature. Semi-refined oils will keep for up to three months.

Fats

Butter is high in saturated animal fats and as such should not be overindulged in, but current medical thinking is that animal fats do not have an adverse effect on cholesterol levels if eaten in conjunction with twice the amount of polyunsaturated fats. Since most of us could do with reducing our total fat intake, this leaves a comparatively small amount of butter available, but still an appreciable one, and for its addicts there is no real substitute, either for taste or quality. So unless you need to keep to a low-cholesterol diet use butter (preferably unsalted) for cooking where taste matters.

Margarine is often presented as the healthy alternative to butter. In fact many margarines are highly refined and contain additives. Soft margarines contain about 30 per cent polyunsaturated fat. In hard margarines the original polyunsaturated fats have been hydrogenated, so they are not much better for you than butter, from the point of view of fat content. If you do not eat any animal product, then you will want a vegetable-based margarine; if you do eat butter but want to cut down on cholesterol, an excellent compromise is to mix equal parts of butter and good quality oil (safflower or sunflower). This will keep for several days in the refrigerator.

Ghee is clarified butter, popular in cooking because any impurities have been removed and it can be heated to a much higher temperature than ordinary butter without burning. To make your own, simply melt butter and filter it through muslin. Vegetable ghee is also available. This is vegetable oil that has been hydrogenated to make it solid at room temperature. So has *solid vegetable fat*, which is hard enough to grate. Neither should contain any unwelcome additives.

Milk products

Milk is a very useful product that contains the essential Vitamin B_{12}, which is lacking in a strictly non-animal diet. Milk is a very good source of protein, vitamins, and minerals, particularly calcium and phosphorous. However, it also contains saturated fat. Skimmed milk has had most of the fat content removed and in the process has also lost Vitamins A, D, and E (but not B). Goat's milk is often a good substitute for people who find it difficult to tolerate drinking cow's milk.

Buttermilk has a similar protein and mineral content to whole milk, but contains less Vitamin A and the fat content is much lower.

Yogurt is a living food, in which bacteria act on the milk sugars to produce lactic acid, a job normally done by our digestive juices. It is easy to assimilate, being in a sense pre-digested, and eating it regularly helps the digestion. Many commercial yogurts contain additives, preservatives, and colouring agents, so it is worth making your own. There are yogurt-makers available that can maintain the milk at exactly the right temperature while it ferments. (See *Making Yogurt*, pp. 105–106.)

Soya bean products

Soya bean foods have become very popular recently because of their varied uses for vegetarians. *Soya milk* is an easily digested substitute for dairy milk and recommended to sufferers of milk allergies. To make it, soak soya beans in water overnight (one cup of beans will produce about 8 cups soya milk). In the morning, strain them and grind them to a meal with the same volume of water (each cup will have roughly doubled in size, so add two cups of water for each original cup of beans). Put this in a large pan and add the same quantity of water (another four cups for each original cup). Bring to the boil and boil for 20 minutes, uncovered. It should be at a fairly fast boil to ensure that all toxins are destroyed. You will find that the water froths up considerably – sprinkling cold water on top will help to settle it. Strain before use. Soya milk makes an excellent substitute for milk in custards, puddings, and milk shakes.

Tofu is soya bean curd. This is another way of utilizing the soya bean. Its high protein content (it is also rich in iron, calcium, and B vitamins, while containing few calories or saturated fats, and no cholesterol) makes it a nutritious substitute not only for meat and fish, but also for dairy products – the Chinese hardly use milk. In Chinese and Japanese cooking it is a most versatile ingredient, whether marinated, stir-fried, or deep-fried, beaten into dressings and sauces, or added to soups, burger mixes, and even some puddings.

It is available in various forms. Silken tofu is the softest, a mixture of some curds and whey, with a consistency like firm junket. It is best for mashing, or blending for dips, dressings, and sauces. It is usually sold in a carton or tetrapak, which will keep unopened and unrefrigerated for 6 months. Once opened, it should be used within 2 days.

Firm tofu is a heavily pressed version, with a dense texture like firm cheese; it can be cubed, sliced, and marinated. When sold loose, you will usually find it refrigerated, submerged in deep buckets of water. It will keep fresh for a week immersed in water in the refrigerator, with the water changed daily. It is also sold in vacuum packs, which keep, if not opened, for 3–4 weeks. Once opened, keep the tofu under water and treat it just like loose tofu, otherwise it will develop a fresh skin. Soft tofu, with a texture between firm and silken, can be treated like firm tofu.

Tofu can be frozen, which drastically changes its look and texture. Squeeze out thawed tofu to get rid of excess water.

Fats

Solid vegetable fat
This is the only vegetarian alternative to lard or suet. Vegetable oils are hydrogenated to make them solid at room temperature.

Ghee
Ghee generally denotes clarified butter but a vegetable version (above) made from hydrogenated vegetable oils is also available.

Milk products

Buttermilk
This is the liquid remaining after fresh cream has been churned to make butter. Much of the buttermilk sold today is cultured and soured by adding bacteria to form lactic acid.

Yogurt & Strained Yogurt
One of the most popular fermented milk products, yogurt is a natural antibiotic, the acid in it killing almost all harmful organisms. It is easily digested, especially goat's milk yogurt (below).
Strained yogurt (below right), popular in Greece, is much smoother, creamier and sweeter than ordinary yogurt, not unlike crème fraîche. It is an excellent substitute for cream.

Yogurt

Strained yogurt

Firm tofu

Soya bean products

Soya milk
Soya milk can be used as a substitute for dairy milk. Commercial soya milk sometimes contains sugar.

Silken tofu

Tofu
This product of the soya bean is generally available as silken tofu, made from lightly pressed soya bean curd, and firm tofu, which is more heavily pressed. Soft or regular tofu has a texture in between the two.

Soft tofu

Cheese and Eggs

Strict vegetarians eat only cheese made with non-animal rennet. These can be found in healthfood shops and include Cheddar and other hard cheeses, as well as the soft cheeses such as cottage cheese, Ricotta, and Feta, some varieties of which do not use rennet anyway. Although a good source of protein, cheese made from whole milk is high in fat and cholesterol, so use it sparingly and substitute low fat cheese wherever possible.

Eggs
It is hard to ignore the horrors of battery farming. Vegetarians will prefer to buy humanely produced free-range eggs, which are generally considered to have a superior taste, although nutritionally there is little difference.

Eggs, particularly the yolks, are an excellent source of protein and contain all the essential amino acids. They are also high in fat and cholesterol, which is why many people are advised to limit their consumption of eggs. Store eggs in a cool place. There is no need to keep them in the refrigerator. If the shell is soiled, wipe it with a dry cloth; washing removes the protective film. Avoid shiny shells as this is an indication of age.

Substitutes for eggs
Eggs in cooking can be replaced in a number of ways. All the following variations will alter the texture and flavour to a certain extent, but it is worth experimenting to cut down on cholesterol.

Where eggs are used to enrich a dish such as pastry or bread dough, use soya flour instead. One to two tablespoons mixed with 225g (8oz) flour gives a richer pastry; 50g (2oz) soya flour in 450g (1lb) flour gives a rich bread dough. Soya flour mixed to a cream with water can be used instead of an egg-wash, or glaze. One to two tablespoons of soya flour can be added to savoury bakes as a substitute for an egg, but will not bind the mixture in the same way. Tahini (see page 90) can be used instead of an egg as a binding agent.

Cheeses

Hard cheeses

All the cheeses on these two pages are made without animal rennet: Double Gloucester; Botton (an English farmhouse cheese from Yorkshire) made with chives; farmhouse cheese made with celery seeds; hard goat's cheese, and Cheddar. Other hard cheeses available include Gouda and Munster.

Farmhouse

Cheddar

Botton

Double Gloucester

Hard goat's cheese

Cream cheese
Made, as the name indicates, from cream, this cheese therefore has a very high fat content. It is valued for its smooth, rich taste and creamy texture.

Curd cheese
Soft cheese made from whole cow's milk, this is usually set without using rennet. It is sometimes known as lactic curd cheese.

Cottage cheese
Cottage cheese is a type of low fat curd cheese made from cooked skimmed cow's milk. It is drained, washed, and coated with thin cream, and has a granular appearance.

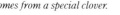

Geska
A Swiss whey cheese, this is also known as Sapsago, Schabzieger, or Glärnerkäse. It can be used instead of Parmesan. The greenish colour comes from a special clover.

Coulommiers
Coulommiers is a mild French cheese, similar to Brie (it is also called Brie de Coulommiers). Usually eaten unripened, it is often sprinkled with paprika or herbs.

Chèvre
Chèvre, or French goat's cheese, is a traditional soft cheese with a distinctive taste. It is usually found in the shape shown here, or as a small cylinder.

Ricotta
This is a very low fat cheese made from whey, not from pressed curds. It is sometimes available in mature hard form for grating.

Feta
This is the best known Greek cheese: with tomato and cucumber, it becomes "Greek salad". Traditionally made from sheep or goat's milk, it is curdled naturally without the addition of rennet.

CHAPTER FOUR

BASIC VEGETARIAN COOKERY TECHNIQUES

If you are switching to a healthier diet, you may wish to make your own basic foods – bread, for example, is easy to make and better than anything bought from a shop, even a healthfood shop, as you will know exactly what ingredients have been used in your loaf. Nothing can beat the delicious smell of a newly baked loaf of bread, fresh from the oven!

No special equipment is needed in order to make yogurt; a thermos flask will do very well. In fact, basic kitchen equipment and some muslin is all that you will need for making smetana, curd cheese, hung yogurt, and tofu.

Most pastry is made out of refined flour and is not very nutritious, but there are healthier ways of making it. Hot water crust pastry, shortcrust pastry, yeasted pastry, and strudel pastry can all be made using wholewheat flour and less fat.

Vegetarian cookery involves the frequent use of dried pulses and dried fruit, and you will need to know how to reconstitute these. Grains, too, are easy to cook once you know how.

Home produce

Foods cooked, or made at home always taste that much better. Top left: Using a yogurt maker (see p. 106); Top right: Making strudel pastry (see p. 113); Bottom left: Making tomato sauce (see p. 119); Bottom right: How to stir-fry (see p. 121).

Making bread

It is worth making your own bread, as many of the so-called wholesome and healthy brown loaves available in the shops are neither. Often the flour used is wheatmeal, which contains only 85 per cent of the whole grain, so many of the nutrients and much of the fibre are lost. Even the distinctive brown colouring may come from caramel. Such loaves often have as many additives as white bread, and are manufactured in much the same way, having no real fermentation time to enhance the flavour.

When making your own bread, choose a strong, stoneground, 100 per cent wholewheat or wholemeal flour. Strong or hard flours, usually made from American or Canadian wheat, have a high gluten content, thus ensuring a strong, elastic dough which is needed for good results. I add a soft, low-gluten flour like soya for extra flavour and protein which the dough might otherwise lack. You can also add oil to improve the texture.

Once you have got used to making the basic loaf, try a variety of flours, also adding nuts, seeds, or wheatgerm, cooked grains or even beansprouts for different flavours, and textures. Richer bread doughs can be made using milk, yogurt, or eggs as part of the mixing liquid. For naturally sweet loaves, use honey, molasses, or dried fruits. If you are on a strictly salt-free diet, you can leave out the salt from the basic recipe but the taste and texture of the loaf will be quite different.

Wholewheat bread

Along with grains and pulses, wholewheat bread is one of the staples of a vegetarian diet – it is high in protein, fibre, vitamins, and minerals. It is also very easy to make at home. Bake in a preheated oven at gas mark 7, 220°C (425°F), for 35–40 minutes. Once cooked, the bread should sound hollow when tapped a couple of times on its base.

Ingredients
25g (1oz) fresh yeast
25g (1oz) soya flour
425ml (³/₄ pint) warm water
700g (1½lb) wholewheat flour
up to 5ml (1 tsp) salt
Makes two 450g (1lb) loaves

Making wholewheat bread

1 *Whisk the yeast and soya flour with 150ml (¹/₄ pint) of the warm water. Leave in a warm place for 5 minutes or until the mixture becomes frothy.*

2 *Mix most of the flour and salt in a large bowl. Pour in the yeast mixture and add the remaining flour. Mix all the liquids in with a wooden spoon.*

3 *Draw up the flour with your hands to form a dough, turn out on to a floured surface and knead thoroughly until the dough has a smooth, velvety surface.*

4 *Put into a clean bowl and leave covered in a warm place for 1 hour to rise. This process is called "proving". It also enhances the flavour of the bread.*

5 *After an hour, turn the dough out on to a floured surface, punch your fist into the dough, and knead it again thoroughly for a few minutes.*

6 *Divide the dough and shape it into two loaves. Put these into two greased tins and leave them to prove for another 10 minutes before baking.*

Sourdough

This is a delicious sharp-tasting continental bread whose flavour is enhanced if it is kept for one day. Mix together the rye flour, milk, and salt, and leave at room temperature for 48 hours.

Blend the yeast with half the water and the sourdough starter. Mix in half the rye flour, and leave overnight at room temperature. Mix the remaining rye flour with the salt. Add to the dough with the remaining water, then add the wholewheat flour and knead well. The dough should be moist, but not sticky. Form into a loaf and prick all over. Place on a floured baking sheet. Leave to rise for 45 minutes. Bake at gas 6, 200°C (400°F), for 1¼–1½ hours.

Ingredients
For the sourdough starter
100g (4oz) rye flour
100ml (4fl oz) milk
2.5ml (½ tsp) salt
For the dough
50g (2oz) yeast
500ml (17fl oz) warm water
450g (1lb) rye flour
10–15ml (2–3 tsp) salt
225–300g (8–10oz) wholewheat flour
Makes one 1kg (2.2lb) loaf

Rye bread

A characteristic of rye bread is its close, moist texture. In this recipe, moistness is achieved by adding buckwheat flour and some yogurt or buttermilk to the ingredients. In the batter method of making bread used here, the wholewheat flour is mixed with the yeast first to start the dough rising properly. The low-gluten rye flour (which does not rise as easily) is then beaten into the risen mixture. Bake in a preheated oven at gas mark 7, 220°C (425°F), for 35 minutes. The bread is cooked if it sounds hollow when tapped lightly on the base.

Ingredients
25g (1oz) fresh yeast
10ml (2 tsp) molasses
300ml (½ pint) lukewarm water
450g (1lb) wholewheat flour
pinch of salt
175g (6oz) rye flour
50g (2oz) buckwheat flour
10ml (2 tsp) anise seeds
up to 150ml (¼ pint) yogurt or buttermilk
Makes two 575g (1¼lb) loaves

Making rye bread

1 *Mix together the yeast, molasses, and water. Leave in a warm place for 10 minutes until frothy. Add half the wholewheat flour and beat in thoroughly.*

2 *Cover and leave to rise for 45 minutes. Beat in the remaining ingredients, adding enough yogurt or buttermilk to make a soft dough.*

3 *Turn out on to a floured surface and knead thoroughly until the dough feels smooth, adding more flour or liquid as necessary.*

4 *Shape into two cobs and place on lightly oiled baking sheets or in 450g (1lb) tins. Leave to prove for 30 minutes before putting in the oven.*

Dairy products

Yogurt can be made from any milk – cow, goat, sheep, or soya, skimmed or whole, long-life or fresh – in either a wide-necked thermos flask or a special yogurt maker. I prefer yogurt made from skimmed, long-life (UHT) milk. It has a thicker consistency than yogurt made from whole milk, and because it has already been heat-treated there is no need to scald it before adding the culture.

Both yogurt and smetana are made using commercial starters for the first batch. These can be bought from most healthfood shops.

Home-made yogurt

To start your first batch of home-made yogurt, you will have to use either a commercially made natural yogurt, or a culture powder (advisable for anyone with an allergy to milk). For successive batches, just keep back 30ml (2 tbsp) of the yogurt each time. Yogurt can be made thicker by adding 15ml (1 tbsp), or more, of skimmed milk powder to the milk.

Ingredients
600ml (1 pint) long-life skimmed milk, or fresh skimmed milk
30ml (2 tbsp) natural yogurt
15–30ml (1–2 tbsp) skimmed milk powder (optional)
Makes 600ml (1 pint) yogurt

Using a thermos flask

1 *Bring the long-life milk to a temperature of 43–44°C (110–115°F), or scald the skimmed milk and cool to this temperature.*

2 *Stir in the yogurt starter and add the required amount of skimmed milk powder, if you are using it, to thicken your yogurt.*

3 *Pour into a clean, warmed thermos flask (the neck should be wide enough for you to get the finished yogurt out). Leave overnight, or until set.*

4 *Transfer the yogurt to a clean container and put in the refrigerator. The mixture will thicken slightly as it begins to cool.*

Using a yogurt maker

1 *Bring the long-life milk to a temperature of 43–44°C (110–115°F), or scald the skimmed milk and cool down to this temperature.*

2 *Pour into clean yogurt pots, screw on the lids, and switch on the machine. Leave to set according to the manufacturer's instructions.*

Hung yogurt

Ingredients
600ml (1 pint) fresh yogurt
Makes 175g (6oz) hung yogurt

By hanging fresh yogurt in muslin it is possible to drain off excess whey, leaving a thick, creamy textured yogurt similar to curd cheese. The longer the yogurt is left, the thicker it will be.

Making hung yogurt

1 *Suspend a muslin cloth or jelly bag over a clean bowl. Pour the fresh yogurt into it.*

2 *Leave for at least 4 hours. Turn it out into a clean container and keep in the refrigerator.*

Smetana

Smetana is a low-fat soured cream made from skimmed milk and cream. Two types are available commercially – smetana and creamed smetana – and these can be bought from larger supermarkets and delicatessens. When making smetana yourself, you will need to use a commercial brand as a starter for your first batch, using half single cream and half long-life skimmed milk. Make sure that you bring the milk to the correct temperature and incubate it for slightly longer than for yogurt.

Ingredients

300ml (½ pint) long-life skimmed milk
300ml (½ pint) single cream
30–45ml (2–3 tbsp) smetana
Makes 600ml (1 pint)

Making smetana

1 *Put the milk into a saucepan and stir in the single cream. Heat gently to 43–44°C (110–115°F).*

2 *Using a spoon, add the smetana to the contents of the saucepan, and mix in thoroughly.*

3 *Transfer to a clean, warm, wide-necked thermos flask and leave for 12 hours, or until set.*

4 *Transfer the smetana to a clean container and keep refrigerated for up to a week.*

Curd cheese

Ingredients
600ml (1 pint) whole milk
150ml (¼ pint) cultured buttermilk
15ml (1 tbsp) lemon juice
Makes 150g (5oz) curd cheese

Like yogurt, curd cheese is a versatile ingredient in healthy eating – it can be used as a thickener, a garnish, or a main ingredient. One of the best things about this low-fat, soft cheese is its freshness and creaminess – it makes commercially produced soft cheese seem cloying in comparison. Although the taste is mild, it gives plenty of scope for flavouring: add chopped chives, sage, paprika, coriander, or garlic for a savoury cheese, and dried or fresh fruit for a sweet one.

Once made, keep refrigerated in a sealed container for up to a week. This cheese also freezes successfully, but once thawed beat well in a liquidizer or blender to ensure a smooth texture.

Making curd cheese

1 *Put the milk (either cow's milk or goat's milk) into a saucepan and then scald it. Place a thermometer in the pan and allow the mixture to cool to 21°C (70°F).*

2 *Mix in the buttermilk and gently heat the mixture to a temperature of not more than 77°C (170°F). Stir the mixture every 5 minutes, being careful not to break up the curds.*

3 *Curds form at 49–60°C (120–140°F). Keep the mixture at this heat until the curds have separated. Add fruit juice if curds do not separate with heat alone.*

4 *Put a colander inside a large bowl and line it with two or three thicknesses of muslin. Use a slotted spoon to scoop out all the curds into the muslin.*

5 *When most have been removed, gently pour the remaining curds and whey down the side of the muslin, taking care not to break up the curds as you pour.*

6 *Allow the curds to drain for 2 hours or until they are quite firm. Turn them out into a clean bowl and keep refrigerated. They will keep for up to a week.*

Making pastry

Pastry in general is not very nutritious – it is high in calories due to the fat content and, when made with white flour, is low in fibre, vitamins, and minerals. However, there are healthier ways of making pastry, using fewer fats. By switching to wholewheat flour, you can improve the nutritional content of your pastry. This is because wholewheat flour is higher in protein, fibre, vitamins, and minerals than refined flour, and at the same time is also free from any additives.

Until you have had some practice with wholewheat pastry, you may find it slightly difficult to handle. Due to its fibre content, you will need to add more liquid (whether water, skimmed milk, oil, or eggs) than you would for refined flour, and you should allow a resting period of 30 minutes. This will give the fibre a chance to absorb the liquid and to swell. Another important point to bear in mind is that wholewheat pastry has a much denser texture than refined pastry.

To guarantee a lighter effect to the finished pastry, I encourage beginners to add baking powder to the flour until they get used to handling the dough. Also, remember always to roll out wholewheat pastry more thinly than normal, as a little tends to go a long way.

Low-fat pastry

This alternative to shortcrust pastry (see p.110) uses oil, not fat, to provide the richness. It is therefore low in saturated fats and high in polyunsaturates.

Always let pastry rest before rolling it out. This allows the gluten in the flour to lose its elasticity. If this is not allowed for, the pastry will shrink once it is rolled out. It will also shrink badly during the baking process, leaving an unsightly gap around the edge of your flan or pie.

Ingredients
175g (6oz) wholewheat flour
15ml (1 tbsp) soya flour
pinch of salt
6.5ml (1½ tsp) baking powder
15ml (1 tbsp) sunflower oil
skimmed milk to mix
Makes enough for a 23–25cm
(9–10in) flan case

Making low-fat pastry

1 *Sift the flours, salt, and baking powder together into a mixing bowl. Use a wooden spoon to push all the flour through the sieve.*

2 *Add the oil and milk and mix to a soft dough. Let the dough rest for at least 10 minutes in a cool place before starting to roll it out.*

Shortcrust pastry

This pastry has a nuttier taste and more ingredients than white-flour pastry. It also contains more vitamins and other nutrients, as it is made with wholewheat flour. If you prefer a healthier pastry, try using vegetable fat.

Pastry always tastes better and has a lighter texture if it is made in cool surroundings. If your hands tend to be warm, use a pastry blender to mix the fat into the flour. Always use lightly chilled fats in pastry-making. They rub into breadcrumbs without becoming soft and greasy. A marble slab makes an ideal board for rolling out the pastry, as it is cool to the touch.

Ingredients
100g (4oz) wholewheat flour
pinch of salt
up to 5ml (1 tsp) baking powder
50g (2oz) fat (butter, solid vegetable fat, margarine, or a mixture)
10ml (2 tsp) oil
30–45ml (2–3 tbsp) water
squeeze of lemon juice
Makes enough for a 23–25cm
(9–10in) flan case

Making shortcrust pastry

1 *Mix the flour and salt in a bowl and add the baking powder. Using just the tips of your fingers, rub the fat well into the flour.*

2 *Mix together the oil, water, and lemon juice in a separate bowl. Sprinkle two-thirds of this over the rubbed-in mixture.*

3 *Draw the dough together. If it is not wet enough to hold together, add the rest of the liquid.*

4 *Wrap the pastry in plastic film or foil and leave for 30 minutes or so before rolling out.*

Hot water crust pastry

Despite being the pastry traditionally used for raised meat pies, hot water crust is ideal for vegetarian dishes, both sweet and savoury. The fat and water are boiled together then mixed with the flour, to produce a soft dough which is extremely pliable when hot. It therefore has to be moulded into the spring mould or baking tin when warm, so you should always have the filling for the pie made in advance. Once a pie is made, however, it does not matter if it stands for a few hours before being cooked. Put the pie into a hot oven, then reduce the oven temperature so that it finishes cooking properly.

Ingredients
350g (12oz) wholewheat flour
pinch of salt
150g (5oz) solid vegetable fat
100ml (4fl oz) water
Makes enough for a 18cm (7in) spring mould

Making hot water crust pastry

1 *Put the flour and salt into a bowl. Chop the cooled fat into small pieces.*

2 *Put the water in a saucepan, add the fat and bring the mixture to a steady boil.*

3 *Immediately pour the liquid on to the flour and stir it in thoroughly with a wooden spoon. Leave it for a few minutes to cool slightly.*

4 *As soon as the mixture is cool enough to handle, draw it into a dough. If it seems dry and crumbly, add as much boiling water as needed to keep it supple.*

Yeasted pastry

This cross between a bread and a pastry has a good, light texture so long as it is rolled out thinly. For an egg-free variation, use 100ml (4fl oz) milk and add 15ml (1 tbsp) soya flour to the fermenting yeast mixture. Then proceed as for the main recipe. Remember to leave the pastry for 10 minutes before starting to roll it out.

To prevent the base of pastries from becoming soggy, bake the pastry blind. To do this, roll out the pastry thinly and line a flan tin with it. Press down the base and sides firmly and prick the base all over with a fork. Bake for 5 minutes at gas mark 6, 200°C (400°F), then put in the filling and bake as instructed.

Ingredients
75ml (3fl oz) skimmed milk, warmed
5ml (1 tsp) honey
5ml (1 tsp) fresh yeast
175g (6oz) wholewheat flour
pinch of salt
25g (1oz) butter, melted
1 egg, beaten
Makes enough for a 23–25cm (9–10in) flan case

Making yeasted pastry

1 *Mix the milk and honey. Crumble yeast into a bowl.*

2 *Pour the milk mixture on to the yeast and whisk together to blend.*

3 *Add half the flour to the bowl and stir in thoroughly.*

4 *Cover with a cloth and set aside for 30 minutes.*

5 *Add the remaining flour, salt, melted butter, and egg.*

6 *Mix to a dough and knead on a floured surface for 5–7 minutes.*

Strudel pastry

This is a versatile wholewheat alternative to the traditional Greek *filo* pastry, and it can be served with both sweet and savoury fillings. With practice, strudel pastry is not hard to make. The secret is to knead the dough thoroughly so that it becomes very elastic. If this is done properly, you will be able to pull and stretch it out very thinly. When stretching the dough, work on a well-floured cloth as this helps to grip the dough, and prevents it from shrinking back once stretched out. Once the dough is stretched out, leave it to dry slightly before covering with the chosen filling and carefully rolling up.

Ingredients
150g (5oz) wholewheat flour
pinch of salt
10ml (2 tsp) sunflower oil
100ml (4fl oz) water
oil for brushing
Makes enough for one strudel
pastry for 4–6 people

Making strudel pastry

1 *Mix the flour and salt together in a bowl. Add the oil and water and mix to a soft dough. Put the dough on a board for kneading.*

2 *Knead thoroughly by picking up the dough and slapping it down on the surface. Do this until the dough becomes elastic in texture.*

3 *Brush the dough with oil to retain this elasticity. The oil will also prevent a skin from forming on the dough while it is resting.*

4 *Cover the dough with a warm dish and leave it on one side to rest for about 10–15 minutes.*

5 *Brush with oil again and place on a clean, floured cloth. Use your knuckles to flatten the dough.*

6 *Using the back of your hands, stretch the dough out gently until it is thin and almost transparent.*

Fruit, pulses, and grains

Pulses, one of the main staples of a wholefood vegetarian diet, are sold dried. Of these, the larger beans and peas need to be soaked in water before cooking. The same is true of many dried fruits.

Although the food has usually been cleaned, it is often a good idea to rinse grains, dried fruit, and pulses before reconstituting them, to remove any remaining dust or, in the case of dried fruit, traces of preservative.

Fruit

Dried fruit is a useful standby for the store cupboard. All dried fruits are high in vitamins, fibre, and minerals, and are delicious raw as snacks, in salads, or cooked for fruit salads and compôtes. Try spicing the soaking water with nutmeg, cinnamon, or vanilla essence for extra flavour, but do not add any extra sugar to the water, as the sugar content of dried fruit is already highly concentrated.

Reconstituting dried fruit

1 *Put the fruit in a large bowl and cover with plenty of water. Leave to soak overnight.*

2 *The fruit will double or treble in size. Cook it in its original soaking liquid.*

Pulses

Soaking pulses (which include peas, beans, and lentils) before cooking speeds up cooking times. Before soaking, pick over the pulses carefully to remove any sticks or stones, and then soak in plenty of water. Pulses do cause flatulence, but by changing the soaking water two or three times this problem can be reduced. When you boil dried beans (step 3), flavour the water with vegetables (onions, carrots), and seasonings (caraway, fennel, aniseed, or kombu sticks) to make a good bean stock. Pulses usually take 30–50 minutes to cook (they will be soft all the way through when ready); in a pressure cooker they cook in roughly a third of the normal cooking time.

Reconstituting pulses

1 *Put the pulses in a large bowl and cover by at least 5–7.5cm (2–3in) cold water. Leave overnight.*

2 *Drain away the soaking water. Rinse the pulses thoroughly in cold water.*

3 *Put in a saucepan, cover with water and bring to the boil. Add any flavourings except for salt as this toughens the skins. Boil for 10 minutes, removing any white scum from the surface.*

4 *Lower the heat and cook until the pulses are tender. Drain the pulses, keeping the liquid for stock (see p. 120). Use the pulses immediately, or store, covered, in a refrigerator for up to 4 days.*

Tofu

Also known as bean curd, tofu is made from a ground soya bean and water mixture which is then strained and pressed to form firm, off-white cakes. It is richer in protein than any other food of equivalent weight and is therefore a useful addition to a vegetarian diet. It is, however, more notable for its texture than its taste, which is rather bland, so dishes using it should always be well flavoured. Tofu can be bought from most Chinese supermarkets, and will keep for three days in the refrigerator.

Ingredients
200g (7oz) soya beans
juice of 2 lemons
Makes 275g (10oz) okara, 275g (10oz) tofu

Making okara and tofu

1 *Put the beans in a bowl, cover them with water and leave them overnight in a cool place. Do not leave the beans anywhere warm, or they may start to ferment.*

2 *Drain and rinse thoroughly. Liquidize the beans to a creamy consistency, using one cup of water for each cup of beans. This mixture is called Go.*

3 *Bring 6 cups of water to the boil in a large saucepan or preserving pan. When boiling, add the liquidized soya beans. Bring the mixture back to the boil.*

4 *When the mixture boils up to the top of the pan, sprinkle cold water over it; this will stop the boiling and the liquid will sink back.*

5 *Repeat this 3 times, stirring occasionally. This stage is very important as it destroys any toxins present in the bean skins.*

6 *Put a colander into a clean bowl and line it with a layer of muslin. Strain the mixture through the muslin into the bowl.*

7 *The crumbly residue in the muslin is called okara or soya bran. The liquid is soya milk.*

8 *Return the soya milk to a clean pan and bring it to the boil. Pour it into a clean bowl.*

9 *Add the lemon juice, stir, then leave the mixture to curdle. If it does not, repeat steps 8 and 9.*

10 *Using a fine sieve, press lightly against the curds in the bowl and then scoop out all the available liquid with a ladle.*

11 *Very gently tip the curds into a colander lined with muslin. Allow the moisture to drain off. This is soft or silken tofu.*

12 *For a firmer tofu, wrap curds in muslin and weigh down. The heavier the weight and the longer it is left, the more solid the tofu.*

Grains

Once you have weighed out the amount of grain required, pour it into a measuring cup or jug to establish how many cups it makes. Follow the chart on page 47 to gauge the amount of cooking water needed, and the length of time you will need to cook each type of grain. Put the grain in a sieve and rinse thoroughly before cooking; it will not need soaking. Buckwheat and millet are best lightly roasted before boiling. Do not stir rice more than twice during cooking, or it will break up.

Roasting grains and seeds
Brush a thick-based pan lightly with oil. Heat, add the dry grains or seeds and cook until they are pale brown (about 4 minutes). Stir with a wooden spoon to prevent them sticking. Cook as normal.

Cooking grains

1 *Weigh out the required amount of grain. Pour into a measuring cup to establish the number of cups, and the required amount of water.*

2 *Bring the correct amount of water to the boil (see the chart on p.47) and add the grain. Stir the contents of the pan once.*

3 *Bring the pan back to the boil, cover and simmer until all the water has been absorbed. Add more boiling water if necessary.*

Making sauces

There are three basic sauces used in wholefood cookery which can be adapted to serve with a variety of grain, pulse, and vegetable dishes. They are white sauce, tomato sauce, and brown sauce, and the recipes are given here. When cooking all sauces, it is important to stir them continuously when this is indicated, to prevent them from becoming lumpy. You may wish to adjust the seasoning slightly according to your taste.

White sauce

When made with wholewheat flour, white sauce always has a nuttier flavour than with refined flour, and a fuller texture. Not surprisingly, it also tends to be slightly browner in colour.

It is best to infuse the milk to improve the flavour, especially if you are cutting down on seasoning. Use half an onion, peppercorns, a bay leaf, mace or nutmeg, or a small sprig of thyme or parsley. When using oil for the base of a roux, you must not overheat it before adding the flour, otherwise the flour fries, and cannot absorb the oil properly.

For a nutritious variation on this sauce, try adding 50–100g (3–4oz) grated cheddar cheese, or 15–30ml (1–2tbsp) chopped fresh herbs, such as dill, tarragon, or parsley.

If you are really concerned about your fat intake, try a low-fat white sauce instead. This recipe has the added advantage of being low on calories because no fat is mixed with the flour to make the normal roux paste. Instead, rice flour is used as the thickening agent, mixed with skimmed milk.

Ingredients
300ml (1/2 pint) skimmed milk
30ml (2 tbsp) sunflower oil
20g (3/4oz) wholewheat flour
white pepper
For the infusion
1/2 onion
6 peppercorns
1 bay leaf
1 blade mace
Makes 300ml (1/2 pint) sauce

Ingredients for a low-fat white sauce
15ml (1 tbsp) rice flour
300ml (1/2 pint) skimmed milk, infused as above
white pepper
Makes 300ml (1/2 pint) sauce

Making white sauce

1 *Heat the milk with the infusion ingredients. Bring to the boil, remove from the heat, cover and stand for 10 minutes. Strain the milk into a jug or into a bowl.*

2 *Gently heat the oil. When it is just hot add the flour and mix it in thoroughly, stirring all the time. Cook the oil and flour together for a few minutes.*

3 *Add the milk gradually, stirring well until completely smooth. Bring to the boil, and simmer for 3–5 minutes. Season with white pepper.*

Making low-fat white sauce

1 *Heat skimmed milk with infusion ingredients, see opposite. Leave to cool. Put the rice flour in a saucepan and mix to a paste with a little of the milk.*

2 *Stir in the remainder of the milk, bring to the boil and simmer for 5–7 minutes. Season to taste with the white pepper.*

Tomato sauce

This is a good example of a sauce made with vegetables and their own juices. To vary the flavour of the sauce, try adding two finely chopped sticks of celery to the recipe, or a couple of large, chopped broccoli florets (defrosted, if frozen). The herb marjoram can also be substituted instead of the oregano or fresh basil detailed, if preferred.

Ingredients
10ml (2 tsp) olive oil
1 small onion, finely chopped
1–2 cloves garlic, crushed
450g (1lb) tomatoes, skinned and roughly chopped
15–30ml (1–2 tbsp) tomato purée
5ml (1 tsp) miso, dissolved in a little water
5ml (1 tsp) oregano or 10ml (2 tsp) fresh basil
black pepper
Makes 300ml (½ pint) sauce

Making tomato sauce

1 *Heat the oil and cook the onion and garlic over a very low heat for 10–15 minutes – they should not colour. Add the remaining ingredients.*

2 *Cover and simmer for 45 minutes. If you want a smooth sauce, purée the mixture in a food processor or liquidizer. Season with black pepper.*

Brown sauce

It is much healthier to avoid all highly salted gravy mixes –
vegetarian and otherwise. The points about oil and the thorough
cooking of the flour (see p.118) also apply to this recipe. I find
stock from aduki beans or continental lentils provides a
particularly good flavour, although you could use any dark
vegetable or bean stock. Miso, which should be dissolved in a
little water, and shoyu add colour as well as seasoning to the
sauce. Wholewheat flour adds its own delicious taste, but must
be thoroughly cooked to avoid a rather gluey result.

Ingredients
1 onion, chopped
50g (2oz) mushrooms, chopped
30ml (2 tbsp) sunflower oil
20g (³/₄oz) wholewheat flour
300ml (¹/₂ pint) dark stock
1 bay leaf
1 sprig fresh thyme
2.5ml (¹/₂ tsp) mustard powder
up to 5ml (1 tsp) miso
up to 5ml (1 tsp) shoyu
black pepper
Makes 300ml (¹/₂ pint) sauce

Making brown sauce

1 *Heat the oil and fry the
vegetables gently for 5 minutes. Add
flour, stir and cook for 3 minutes.*

2 *Pour on the stock and bring to
the boil, stirring constantly to mix
the ingredients thoroughly.*

3 *Add the herbs and mustard.
Simmer for 7–10 minutes. Add
miso, shoyu, and pepper to taste.*

Stock

Any liquid left over from cooking beans, pulses, or grains can be
used as the basis for a stock. Dark stocks are best made from
red or black beans; for pale stocks use chickpeas or white bean
cooking liquid.

To make the stock, first heat the oil and gently fry the
vegetables. Add the water and simmer for 1–1¹/₂ hours. Take
the pan off the heat and tip the vegetables and water into a sieve
held over a clean bowl or other container. All the vitamins and
minerals from the vegetables will have leached out into the
water and the vegetables can be thrown away. Season the
resulting stock to taste with some miso or shoyu.

Ingredients
15ml (1 tbsp) olive or sunflower oil
2 carrots, roughly chopped
1 large onion, roughly chopped
1 stick kombu
1 bay leaf
1 sprig thyme
1.5 litres (2¹/₂ pints) water
miso or shoyu
Makes 1.1 litres (2 pints)

Steaming and stir-frying

Steaming is an excellent way of preserving most of the minerals and vitamins in vegetables. There are two basic types of steamer; specially designed metal ones that act as container for both the food and the boiling water, and expandable steel baskets which hold the food but have to be placed inside a saucepan containing boiling water, as shown in the picture. Whichever method you use, the layer of vegetables should not be deeper than 1–5cm (½–2in).

Sprouting seeds
Sprouts have a very high vitamin and mineral content, and are useful if you want cheap, fresh salads and stir-fries all year round. I have found mung beans, aduki beans, alfalfa, mustard cress, and whole lentils easy to grow.

Steaming
Boil up a small amount of water in a pan and fit a steaming basket inside. Then add the chopped vegetables and steam until just tender.

Stir-frying

In this cooking technique the vegetables are cooked rapidly in the minimum amount of very hot oil so that they retain all their flavour and crisp texture. The traditional piece of equipment is a wok: a thin, round-bottomed metal pan that conducts the heat well, allowing the food to cook quickly and evenly. Peanut oil is good to use as it can be heated to high temperatures with no flavour loss.

Stir-frying vegetables

1 *Chop the vegetables into evenly sized pieces. Heat a wok over a high heat until smoke rises. Add 22.5ml (1½ tbsp) oil and swirl it around gently to coat the wok.*

2 *Add the chopped vegetables one at a time, putting in the ones requiring the longest cooking first, and the others at short intervals so that they will be ready together.*

3 *Just before the vegetables are cooked, add the seasoning, and then add some liquid – water or stock, to taste – to finish off cooking with a burst of steam.*

· CHAPTER FIVE ·

HEALTHY VEGETARIAN RECIPES

This chapter contains recipe suggestions to help you towards good health. Based on the high-fibre, high-protein, low-fat principle, each recipe is accompanied by a nutritional profile (*see below*). This shows you which nutrients are contained in each dish.
A frequent criticism of vegetarian food is that it takes a long time to prepare. The secret of success is making sure that time is allowed for preparation. Many dishes freeze well, so make extra quantities for later meals.

HOW TO USE A NUTRITIONAL PROFILE

NUTRIENTS PER PORTION
110
Calories
Protein 25g ● ● ●   *Fibre 16g* ● ● ●
Polyunsaturated fats 17g ● ● ●   *Saturated fats 4g* ● ●
Vitamins A, B1, B2, B6, B12, C, D, E, FA, N
Minerals Ca, Cu, Fe, Mg, Zn

Each recipe has its own nutritional profile, so that you can see at a glance, in grams, exactly how much protein, fibre, polyunsaturated fat, saturated fat, and calories each portion, or meal, contains. The profile also shows which vitamins and minerals are found in significant quantities. The bullet system indicates how good the source is: three bullets shows an excellent source, two bullets a very good source, and one bullet a good source.

Tempting foods
Delicious and attractive-looking dishes can be made using a wide variety of vegetarian ingredients. Top left: Vegetable terrine (see p.135); Bottom: Hot stuffed mushrooms (see p.137); Right: Aubergine dip (see p.134).

SOUPS

A pot of lentils or beans, pasta or rice, onions, celery or tomatoes, all simmered in a savoury broth made from fresh vegetables, and seasoned with shoyu, herbs, and spices – this is more than a welcome hot soup: it is a meal in itself, rich in protein, full of flavour, and with a nutritious balance of beans, grains, and vegetables. For summer evenings, light purées of green vegetables such as fresh peas or watercress, or chilled fruit soups, make tempting first courses.

It needs no special skill to produce a splendid home-made soup; nor, in most of these recipes, much preparation. The bulk of the work, including pre-soaking peas and beans, can often be done well in advance; indeed many of the soups detailed benefit from being made the day before and given time to rest and to develop their flavour.

Clockwise from left: Fennel soup (see p. 126); All Saint's broth (see p. 126); Pease pottage (see p. 126).

All Saints' broth

Illustrated on page 125
Ingredients
*50g (2oz) dried chestnuts, soaked
overnight in 1.1 litres (2 pints)
water, or 100g (4oz) fresh chestnuts
10ml (2 tsp) sunflower oil
1 medium onion, finely grated
100g (4oz) aduki beans, soaked
overnight
225g (8oz) celeriac, peeled and
chopped
30ml (2 tbsp) tomato purée
5ml (1 tsp) dried thyme
15ml (1 tbsp) shoyu
black pepper
Serves 4–6*

NUTRIENTS PER PORTION
120 Calories
*Protein 8g ● ● ●   Fibre 10g ● ● ●
Polyunsaturated fats 2g ● ● ●   Saturated fats 0.5g ● ● ●
Vitamins C
Minerals –*

This soup is perfect nutritionally – high in protein and fibre, low in fat. Serve with dishes high in minerals and vitamins.
1 Place the chestnuts and their soaking water in a saucepan. Bring to the boil, cover, and simmer for 40–50 minutes or until soft. Leave to cool, then liquidize.
2 Heat the oil in a large saucepan and gently fry the onion for 4–5 minutes or until just brown. Drain the beans.
3 Add the beans and celeriac to the pan and cook for 3 minutes.
4 Pour in 900ml (1½ pints) chestnut stock. Stir in the tomato purée and thyme. Bring to the boil and boil fast for 10 minutes. Reduce the heat, cover, and simmer for 40–50 minutes or until beans are cooked. Season with shoyu and pepper. Serve hot.

Pease pottage

Illustrated on page 125
Ingredients
*10ml (2 tsp) sunflower oil
1 medium onion, chopped
1 medium carrot, chopped
1 medium parsnip, chopped
100g (4oz) green split peas
900ml (1½ pints) vegetable stock
(see p. 120)
1 bay leaf
2.5ml (½ tsp) mustard powder
10ml (2 tsp) gomasio, or salt if
preferred
black pepper
Serves 4–6*

NUTRIENTS PER PORTION
140 Calories
*Protein 7g ● ● ●   Fibre 6g ● ● ●
Polyunsaturated fats 1g ● ● ●   Saturated fats 0.5g ● ● ●
Vitamins A, B₁, C, E
Minerals Fe*

Choose brightly coloured split peas for this iron-rich soup.
1 Heat the oil in a large saucepan and gently fry the onion for 4–5 minutes, or until soft.
2 Add the carrot, parsnip, and green split peas. Cook for 5 minutes, stirring frequently.
3 Stir in stock, bay leaf, and mustard. Bring to the boil, cover, and simmer for 50 minutes. Season with gomasio and pepper.

Fennel soup

Illustrated on page 124
Ingredients
*10ml (2 tsp) sunflower oil
450g (1lb) fennel, trimmed and
diced
40g (1½oz) cashew nut pieces
150ml (¼ pint) skimmed milk
300ml (½ pint) vegetable stock (see
p. 120)
1.25ml (¼ tsp) anise seeds
5–10ml (1–2 tsp) lemon juice
gomasio, or salt if preferred
black pepper
Serves 4*

NUTRIENTS PER PORTION
95 Calories
*Protein 4g ● ● ●   Fibre 3g ● ●
Polyunsaturated fats 2g ● ● ●   Saturated fats 1g ● ● ●
Vitamins –
Minerals –*

This subtle-tasting, high-protein soup is low in saturated fats.
1 Heat the oil in a large saucepan and gently fry the fennel for 10–15 minutes, or until soft.
2 Add the cashew nuts, milk, and stock. Bring to the boil, cover, and simmer for 15 minutes.
3 Cool, liquidize until smooth, adding anise seeds and lemon juice. Season with gomasio and pepper. Reheat before serving.

Minestrone alla Genovese

NUTRIENTS PER PORTION
190
Calories
Protein 11g ● ● ● *Fibre 10g* ● ● ●
Polyunsaturated fats 1g ● *Saturated fats 0.5g* ● ● ●
Vitamins A, B₁, C, E, FA
Minerals Ca, Cu, Fe, Mg

Illustrated below
Ingredients
100g (4oz) cannellini or haricot
beans, soaked overnight
10ml (2 tsp) olive oil
1 medium onion, chopped
3 cloves garlic, crushed
100g (4oz) cabbage, shredded
100g (4oz) mushrooms, sliced
225g (8oz) courgettes, diced
1 small aubergine, diced
350g (12oz) tomatoes, skinned and
chopped
30ml (2 tbsp) tomato purée
10ml (2 tsp) dried oregano
900ml (1½ pints) bean stock
(see p. 120)
50g (2oz) wholewheat pasta
45–60ml (3–4 tbsp) finely chopped
fresh parsley
15–30ml (1–2 tbsp) shoyu
black pepper
Serves 6–8

There is a fine distinction between a hearty soup and a casserole, and although this highly nutritious soup comes into the former category, it needs only wholewheat bread to make it a complete and satisfying meal.

1 Drain the beans. Cover with plenty of fresh water, bring (uncovered) to the boil, and boil fast for 10 minutes. Reduce the heat, skim, cover, and simmer for 45–50 minutes or until soft. Drain and reserve the cooking water for stock. Make up to 900ml (1½ pints) if necessary.
2 Heat the oil in a large saucepan and gently fry the onion and garlic for 4–5 minutes or until the onion is soft. Add the cabbage, mushrooms, courgettes, aubergine, and tomatoes and cook for 5 minutes.
3 Stir in the tomato purée, oregano, beans, and the reserved bean stock. Bring to the boil, cover, and simmer for 45–50 minutes. Add more stock if necessary.
4 Add the pasta and parsley and cook for a further 10 minutes.
5 Season with shoyu and pepper. Serve hot.

Minestrone alla Genovese (see above).

Clockwise from left:
Country vegetable broth
*(*see opposite*); Onion*
*soup (*see opposite*);*
*Miso julienne (*see
p. 130*).*

Onion soup

120
Calories

NUTRIENTS PER PORTION
Protein 3g ● ● *Fibre 4g* ● ● ●
Polyunsaturated fats 3g ● ● ● *Saturated fats 1g* ● ● ●
Vitamins A, C, E, N
Minerals Ca, K

Illustrated opposite
Ingredients
22.5ml (1½ tbsp) sunflower oil
450g (1lb) onions, finely chopped
1–2 cloves garlic, crushed
1 medium carrot, roughly chopped
1 small white turnip, grated
salt and pepper
1 bay leaf
1 tsp celery seeds
¼ tsp English mustard powder
570ml (1 pint) dark vegetable stock
(see p. 120)
10ml (2 tsp) shoyu
5ml (1 tsp) miso
For garnishing
2 tbsp parsley or chervil, finely chopped
1 tbsp sesame seeds
Serves 4–6

A vegetarian adaptation of the traditional French onion soup which makes a welcome start to a winter meal.
1 Heat the oil in a large, heavy-based pan and add the onions, garlic, carrot, and turnip. Cover the pan and cook the vegetables for 15–20 minutes over a very gentle heat. Sprinkle over a little salt to bring out extra juices.
2 Add the bay leaf, celery seeds, mustard powder, stock, and shoyu. Stir well, bring to the boil, cover, and simmer for 20 minutes. Remove the bay leaf and carrot (unless you prefer to leave the pieces of carrot in for extra colour).
3 Blend the miso with 15ml (1 tbsp) of the soup in a small bowl. Stir it back into the soup, mixing well, and season to taste.
4 Simmer gently for another 5 minutes and serve sprinkled with the chopped parsley or chervil and the sesame seeds.

Country vegetable broth

220
Calories

NUTRIENTS PER PORTION
Protein 6g ● ● *Fibre 5g* ● ● ●
Polyunsaturated fats 4g ● ● ● *Saturated fats 1g* ● ● ●
Vitamins C, E, N
Minerals Ca, K, Mg, Zn

Illustrated opposite
Ingredients
25g (1oz) pot barley
25g (1oz) wheat berries
25g (1oz) green split peas
25g (1oz) red lentils
1 medium onion, finely chopped
1 medium parsnip, diced
1 medium turnip, diced
1 medium potato, diced
30ml (2 tbsp) sunflower oil
700–900ml (1¼–1½ pints)
vegetable stock (see p. 120) or water
15ml (1 tbsp) shoyu
2 tsp rosemary, finely chopped
1 tsp thyme, finely chopped
salt and pepper
Serves 4–6

If you do not have the individual grains, peas, and lentils readily to hand, a "soup mix", obtainable in many healthfood shops, makes an ideal base.
1 Steep the grains, peas, and lentils in hot water for 1 hour and then drain well.
2 Gently soften the vegetables in the oil for 10 minutes, using a large, heavy-based pan with a lid. Add the grains, peas, and lentils to the mixture, and fry them gently for a further 5 minutes, stirring occasionally.
3 Add the stock and shoyu, bring to the boil, cover, and simmer for 50–60 minutes.
4 Stir in the herbs and season to taste. You can serve the soup immediately, just as it is, or blend it briefly in a liquidizer if you prefer a smoother texture, but do not liquidize it completely or it will lose its character.

Illustrated on page 128

Miso julienne

Ingredients
5g (¹/₄oz) arame
¹/₂ tsp sliced ginger root
15ml (1 tbsp) peanut oil
10ml (2 tsp) sesame oil
225g (8oz) carrots, cut into
julienne strips
225g (8oz) daikon, cut into
julienne strips
570ml (1 pint) dark vegetable stock
(see p. 120)
30ml (2 tbsp) shoyu
15ml (1 tbsp) miso, preferably mugi
Serves 4–6

100
Calories

NUTRIENTS PER PORTION
Protein 2g ● ● *Fibre 2g* ● ●
Polyunsaturated fats 1g ● ● ● *Saturated fats 0.5g* ● ● ●
Vitamins A, C
Minerals Ca, K, Mg, Zn

With its strong, salty flavour, miso makes an excellent warming basis for a clear stock. This recipe includes a julienne of carrots and daikon, the subtly flavoured Japanese white radish. The sea vegetable arame contributes a rich mineral content.
1 Soak the arame in hot water for 10 minutes and drain. Either chop it finely or, if you prefer, leave it in strips.
2 In a large, heavy-based pan, fry the ginger in the peanut oil for 2–3 minutes over medium heat.
3 Add the sesame oil, carrots, daikon, and arame, cover, and continue to cook over gentle heat for 15 minutes.
4 Add the stock and stir in the shoyu and miso. Bring to the boil, cover, and simmer for a further 10 minutes. Serve the soup immediately.

Illustrated opposite

Cream of potato soup with garlic

Ingredients
For the stock
10ml (2 tsp) sunflower oil
2 medium onions, quartered
12 cloves garlic
2 medium carrots, cut into chunks
1 bay leaf
sprig of thyme
For the soup
10ml (2 tsp) sunflower oil
1 medium onion, finely chopped
2 cloves garlic, crushed
225g (8oz) potatoes, diced
15ml (1 tbsp) shoyu
10ml (2 tsp) miso, dissolved in a
little water
Serves 4

75
Calories

NUTRIENTS PER PORTION
Protein 2g ● *Fibre 2g* ●
Polyunsaturated fats 1g ● ● ● *Saturated fats 0g* ● ● ●
Vitamins C
Minerals –

Do not be put off by the amount of garlic in this recipe – the cloves add a wonderfully subtle flavour to the stock. Serve with a high-protein, high-fibre dish for balance.
1 For the stock: heat the oil in a large saucepan and gently fry the onion, whole cloves of garlic and carrot for 15–20 minutes.
2 Add the bay leaf, thyme, and 900ml (1¹/₂ pints) water. Bring to the boil, cover, and simmer for 1–1¹/₂ hours. Strain, and reserve all the stock.
3 For the soup: gently heat the oil in a large saucepan and fry the onion and garlic for 4–5 minutes until lightly browned, stirring frequently.
4 Add the potato and fry for a further 5–8 minutes until lightly browned.
5 Pour over the garlic stock. Bring to the boil, cover, and simmer for 20 minutes.
6 Cool slightly, then liquidize until smooth, adding the shoyu and miso. Reheat gently before serving.

Cauliflower and coriander soup

NUTRIENTS PER PORTION
170 *Calories*
Protein 7g ● ● ● *Fibre 7g* ● ● ●
Polyunsaturated fats 2g ● ● *Saturated fats 2g* ● ●
Vitamins A, B1, B6, C, FA
Minerals Fe

Illustrated below

Ingredients
50g (2oz) pot barley
50g (2oz) yellow split peas
10ml (2 tsp) sunflower oil
1 medium onion, finely chopped
1 clove garlic, crushed
5ml (1 tsp) fresh root ginger, grated
2.5ml (½ tsp) turmeric
2.5ml (½ tsp) coriander seeds,
crushed
2.5ml (½ tsp) cumin seeds
1 medium cooking apple, cored,
and chopped
1 medium carrot
1 fresh green chilli, deseeded and
finely chopped
900ml (1½ pints) vegetable stock
(see p. 120)
1 cauliflower, divided into florets
30ml (2 tbsp) fresh coriander
leaves, finely chopped
gomasio, or salt if preferred
black pepper
25g (1oz) grated cream coconut
Serves 6–8

Although coconut cream is high in saturated fats, the quantity used here is small enough to be allowable, and just sufficient to add a delicate, velvety texture to the soup.

1 Place the barley and yellow split peas in a bowl. Cover with hot water and leave to soak for 1 hour. Drain.

2 Heat the oil in a large saucepan and gently fry the onion and garlic for 4–5 minutes or until soft. Add the ginger, turmeric, coriander, and cumin, and cook for 3–4 minutes.

3 Add the apple, carrot, chilli, barley, and yellow split peas, and fry for 2–3 minutes.

4 Pour over the vegetable stock, bring to the boil, cover, and simmer gently for 1 hour.

5 Add the cauliflower and chopped coriander to the soup and cook for a further 10 minutes or until the cauliflower is just tender. Season with gomasio and pepper.

6 Place the creamed coconut in a bowl. Pour over 150ml (¼ pint) boiling water, and stir to dissolve. Mix the coconut liquid into the soup, and allow to heat through before serving.

From left to right:
Cream of potato soup with
garlic (see opposite);
Cauliflower and coriander
soup (see above).

STARTERS, SAUCES, AND RELISHES

Whether you eat a formal meal with separate courses, or whether you follow the example of many vegetarians and combine several dishes at the same time, something to start with is always welcome. This can be simple, perhaps eaten with a drink before the meal – pâté spread on little biscuits, raw vegetables with various dips – or more elaborate, such as a vegetable terrine or stuffed vine leaves.

Vegetarian food lends itself admirably to the occasion and offers endless possibilities. In addition to the recipes given here, you will find many dishes in other sections of the book, which can be scaled down to make ideal first courses. Soufflés, quiches, or stuffed vegetables are always welcome. For a substantial start to a meal, try a pasta dish or a risotto, while for a lighter one, salads are perfect.

Sauces need not be thickened with flour. Vegetable and fruit purées make delicious bases, as in the broccoli and sunflower sauce, or the apricot and tomato relish. Nut-based sauces play a large part in vegetarian cuisine and supply extra protein.

Clockwise from left: Leek and tomato terrine (see p. 134); Cheese devils (see p. 135).

Leek and tomato terrine

Illustrated on pages 132–33

Ingredients
550g (1¼lb) leeks
15ml (1 tbsp) olive oil
15ml (1 tbsp) white wine vinegar
*10ml (2 tsp) concentrated apple
juice*
2.5ml (½ tsp) whole grain mustard
1 clove garlic, crushed
gomasio, or salt if preferred
black pepper
*225g (8oz) tomatoes, skinned and
sliced*
*2.5ml (½ tsp) green peppercorns,
lightly crushed*
For serving
*radicchio, lamb's lettuce, endive,
wholewheat bread (see p. 102)*
Serves 4–6

NUTRIENTS PER PORTION
85 Calories
Protein 3g ● ● *Fibre 5g* ● ●
Polyunsaturated fats 0.5g ● ● *Saturated fats 0.5g* ● ● ●
Vitamins A, B₁, B₂, B₆, C, E, FA, N
Minerals Ca, Cu, Fe, Mg, Zn

This is a colourful way to serve leek vinaigrette, with the
buttery taste and smooth texture of the leeks contrasting well
with the sharp dressing. Thin slices of wholewheat bread, rolled
up with cottage or curd cheese, could be a good accompaniment
to serve with this starter.
1 Clean the leeks and chop them in 2.5cm (1in) pieces. Steam
for 5–8 minutes until soft. Drain well.
2 Mix the olive oil, vinegar, apple juice, mustard, and garlic
together. Season with gomasio and pepper.
3 Add the dressing to the warm leeks and toss.
4 Put a layer of half the leeks in the base of a lightly oiled 450g
(1lb) loaf tin. Cover with a layer of tomatoes, sprinkle over the
peppercorns, then top with the remaining leeks. Weight the
mixture down well. Leave to cool.
5 When cold, turn out onto a bed of salad leaves. Serve in
slices accompanied by wholewheat bread.

Aubergine dip

Illustrated on page 136

Ingredients
1 large aubergine
60ml (4 tbsp) yogurt
15–30ml (1–2 tbsp) lemon juice
45ml (3 tbsp) tahini
*60ml (4 tbsp) finely chopped fresh
parsley*
2 cloves garlic, crushed
gomasio, or salt if preferred
black pepper
For serving
*vegetable crudités or warm pitta
bread*
Serves 4–6

NUTRIENTS PER PORTION
90 Calories
Protein 4g ● ● ● *Fibre 1g* ●
Polyunsaturated fats 3g ● ● ● *Saturated fats 1g* ● ● ●
Vitamins –
Minerals –

In summer months, the aubergine in this Middle Eastern dip
could be barbecued to produce a more smoky flavour. Serve
with raw vegetables or wholewheat pitta bread to improve the
overall fibre content.
1 Preheat the oven to gas mark 4, 180°C (350°F).
2 Remove the aubergine stalk and prick the flesh 2–3 times.
Place in an ovenproof dish and bake for about 20 minutes or until
the aubergines feel soft.
3 Peel off the skin and chop the flesh.
4 Put the aubergine flesh, yogurt, lemon juice, tahini, parsley,
and garlic into a liquidizer or food processor and blend until
smooth. Season with gomasio and pepper.
5 Serve with crudités of carrot, cauliflower, radishes, corn, and
mangetout, or warm pitta bread.

Cheese devils

Illustrated on page 133

NUTRIENTS PER PORTION
155 Calories
Protein 11g ● ● ● Fibre 1g ●
Polyunsaturated fats 0.5g ● Saturated fats 6g ●
Vitamins A, B12, E
Minerals –

Ingredients
175g (6oz) quark
40g (1½oz) margarine
1 (large) egg
5ml (1 tsp) prepared English mustard
pinch of cayenne
black pepper
175g (6oz) asparagus
Serves 4

These delicious savouries provide a high-protein start to a light, low-calorie meal.
1 Cream the quark with the margarine in a bowl until smooth.
2 Beat in the egg and seasonings.
3 Steam the asparagus for 6–8 minutes until just tender. Cut into small pieces.
4 Meanwhile, preheat the oven to gas mark 3, 170°C (325°F).
5 Lightly oil four ramekin dishes and divide the asparagus pieces between them. Pour over the cheese mixture.
6 Bake for 30–40 minutes or until just set. Serve hot.

Vegetable terrine

Illustrated on page 136

NUTRIENTS PER PORTION
205 Calories
Protein 14g ● ● ● Fibre 3g ● ● ●
Polyunsaturated fats 4g ● ● ● Saturated fats 3g ● ● ●
Vitamins A, B1, B12, C
Minerals Ca

Ingredients
8 large spinach leaves, washed
300ml (½ pint) skimmed milk
½ medium onion
1 bay leaf
6 peppercorns
blade of mace
30ml (2 tbsp) sunflower oil
25g (1oz) wholewheat flour
herb salt, or salt if preferred
grated nutmeg
black pepper
175g (6oz) quark
1 large egg
100g (4oz) peas
100g (4oz) carrots, diced
100g (4oz) asparagus
Serves 4–6

High in both protein and fibre, and relatively low in fat, this is an impressive dish to start a meal with. It is very important, however, to make sure that the terrine is cold and well set before slicing it with a sharp knife, or the colourful effect of the layers will be lost.
1 Pour boiling water over spinach; drain after 1 minute.
2 Place the milk in a saucepan with the onion, bay leaf, peppercorns and blade of mace. Bring almost to the boil, cover and leave to infuse for 10 minutes. Strain the milk and set aside.
3 Gently heat the oil in a saucepan. Stir in the flour to make a roux. Gradually add the flavoured milk and bring to the boil, stirring constantly. Season with herb salt, nutmeg, and pepper.
4 Cool slightly, then stir in the quark and egg.
5 Lightly steam the peas, carrots, and asparagus in separate pans or compartments of a steamer for 6–8 minutes. Preheat the oven to gas mark 3, 170°C (325°F).
6 Line a 450g (1lb) loaf tin with the special spinach leaves, reserving one for the top.
7 Put in a layer of sauce, then a layer of carrot. Repeat with layers of sauce, peas, sauce, asparagus, and finally sauce.
8 Fold over the leaves and place one on the top to cover the mixture completely. Place the tin in a *bain marie* or a roasting tin filled with about 2.5cm (1in) hot water in the oven.
9 Bake for 1 hour. Cool completely before turning out on to a serving plate. When cold, slice and serve.

Clockwise from top: Vegetable terrine (see p. 135); Aubergine dip (see p. 134); Hot stuffed mushrooms (see p. 137).

Clockwise from left: Zyleone (see p. 138); Middle Eastern stuffed vine leaves (see opposite).

Hot stuffed mushrooms

Illustrated opposite

NUTRIENTS PER PORTION
165 *Calories*
Protein 8g ● ● ● *Fibre 3g* ● ●
Polyunsaturated fats 5g ● ● ● *Saturated fats 2g* ● ●
Vitamins C
Minerals Fe, Mg, Zn

Ingredients
4 large flat field mushrooms
10ml (2 tsp) olive oil
50g (2oz) button mushrooms, diced
1 small green pepper, deseeded and diced
10ml (2 tsp) capers
2 cloves garlic, crushed
40g (1½oz) fresh wholewheat breadcrumbs
5ml (1 tsp) dried thyme
15ml (1 tbsp) lemon juice
15ml (1 tbsp) sesame seeds
gomasio, or salt if preferred
black pepper
pinch of cayenne
For the dressing
200ml (⅓ pint) yogurt
15ml (1 tbsp) lemon juice
15ml (1 tbsp) tahini
1 clove garlic, crushed
Serves 4

Choose firm field mushrooms for this high-protein starter, as they have a stronger flavour than button mushrooms and are much easier to fill. The mushrooms can be grilled or baked.
1 Cut the stalks out of the large mushrooms. Lightly steam the caps for 3–4 minutes until just softened. Place in a shallow heatproof dish, rounded sides down.
2 Preheat oven to gas mark 4, 180°C (350°F), if baking them.
3 Heat the oil in a pan and gently fry the diced mushrooms, green pepper, capers, and garlic for 3–4 minutes or until soft.
4 Remove from the heat, mix in the breadcrumbs, thyme, lemon juice, and sesame seeds. Season with some gomasio, pepper, and a little cayenne.
5 Pile the mixture into the mushroom caps. Either place under a preheated moderate grill for 4–5 minutes, or, if you prefer, bake for 10–15 minutes.
6 Mix the dressing ingredients together thoroughly. Serve with the hot stuffed mushrooms.

Middle Eastern stuffed vine leaves

Illustrated opposite

NUTRIENTS PER PORTION
160 *Calories*
Protein 5g ● ● *Fibre 3g* ● ●
Polyunsaturated fats 5g ● ● ● *Saturated fats 1g* ● ● ●
Vitamins A, C
Minerals Ca, Cu, Fe

Ingredients
50g (2oz) bulgar wheat
150ml (¼ pint) vegetable stock
20 vine leaves (about 1 packet)
10ml (2 tsp) olive oil
1 medium onion, finely chopped
1 clove garlic, crushed
25g (1oz) dried apricots, diced
50g (2oz) walnuts, chopped
10ml (2 tsp) crushed coriander seeds
5ml (1 tsp) shoyu
gomasio, or salt if preferred
black pepper
Serves 4–6

Based on a classic Middle Eastern hors d'oeuvre, this low-fat dish uses fruit and nuts for substance, and bulgar wheat.
1 Soak the bulgar wheat in the stock for 15 minutes. Drain and then squeeze out any excess moisture. Spread on a clean tea, towel to dry out slightly.
2 Rinse the vine leaves and set aside.
3 Heat the oil in a saucepan and fry the onion and garlic for 4–5 minutes or until the onion is soft.
4 Add the apricots, walnuts, soaked bulgar wheat, and coriander to the pan and mix well. Cook for 10 minutes, adding a little more stock if the mixture begins to look dry. Season with shoyu, gomasio, and pepper.
5 Preheat the oven to gas mark 4, 180°C (350°F).
6 Take a vine leaf and place with the stalk nearest you. Put about 15ml (1 tbsp) of the mixture into the centre of each vine leaf. Fold in both sides to the centre, then roll the leaf up from the bottom. Place the vine leaves in a lightly oiled ovenproof dish. Cover with foil. Bake for 10–15 minutes. Serve hot.

Illustrated on page 136

Ingredients
50g (2oz) ground almonds
15ml (1 tbsp) white wine vinegar
75g (3oz) cucumber, peeled and
roughly chopped
15ml (1 tbsp) sunflower oil
225–275g (8–10oz) pear, 1 large or
2 small ones
225g (8oz) fennel, diced
For garnishing
15g (¹/₂oz) toasted flaked almonds
fennel fronds
Serves 4

Zyleone

NUTRIENTS PER PORTION
150 Calories
Protein 4g ● Fibre 6g ● ● ●
Polyunsaturated fats 4g ● ● ● Saturated fats 1g ● ● ●
Vitamins C, E
Minerals –

Meaning "green" in Russian, this is a refreshing and unusual high-fibre, low-fat starter.
1 Put the almonds, vinegar, and cucumber in a grinder, liquidizer, or food processor and blend thoroughly.
2 Add the oil drop by drop as if making mayonnaise. The mixture will thicken slightly.
3 Chop the pear into bite-sized pieces. Mix with the fennel.
4 Stir the pear and fennel into the dressing until well coated.
5 Pile into individual dishes and garnish with toasted almonds and fennel fronds. Serve chilled.

Illustrated opposite

Ingredients
6 finger avocados, peeled and
chopped
100g (4oz) cucumber, peeled and
cut into half-moons
¹/₂ pink melon, or section of
canteloupe, scooped into balls
100g (4oz) grapes
4 kumquats, halved
For the dressing
30ml (2 tbsp) orange juice
10ml (2 tsp) lemon juice
15ml (1 tbsp) sunflower oil
fresh mint
Serves 4

Cocktail kebabs

NUTRIENTS PER PORTION
150 Calories
Protein 2g ● Fibre 1.5g ●
Polyunsaturated fats 3g ● ● ● Saturated fats 1g ● ● ●
Vitamins A, C, FA
Minerals Ca, Mg

This refreshing, low-fat starter should be served with a high-protein, high-fibre main course.
1 Place prepared fruit in a bowl. Put the dressing ingredients together in a screw-top jar and mix by shaking well. Pour over fruit and marinate for 2 hours.
2 Thread the cucumber, melon, and kumquats alternately on to kebab skewers, ending with the avocado.

Illustrated opposite

Ingredients
100g (4oz) sunflower seeds
275g (10oz) silken tofu
15ml (1 tbsp) olive oil
45ml (3 tbsp) wheatgerm
100g (4oz) carrot, finely grated
2.5ml (¹/₂ tsp) dill weed
2.5ml (¹/₂ tsp) paprika
gomasio, or salt if preferred
black pepper
For serving
4–6 large tomatoes or vegetable
crudités
Serves 4–6

Golden tofu pâté

NUTRIENTS PER PORTION
330 Calories
Protein 12g ● ● Fibre 4g ● ●
Polyunsaturated fats 9g ● ● Saturated fats 6g ●
Vitamins A, E
Minerals Ca

Use this high-protein pâté as a stuffing or served as a dip.
1 Grind 50g (2oz) sunflower seeds into a fine powder in a grinder, liquidizer, or food processor.
2 Add the tofu, olive oil, and wheatgerm, and liquidize until smooth. Transfer to a serving dish if using crudités.
3 Stir in the grated carrot, remaining whole sunflower seeds, dill, paprika, and season with gomasio and pepper.
4 Cut the tops off the tomatoes, scoop out the flesh and seeds, and stuff with the tofu mixture or serve with crudités.

From left to right: Golden tofu pâté (see opposite*); Cocktail kebabs (see* opposite).

Peanut and sesame sauce

125
Calories

NUTRIENTS PER PORTION
Protein 3g ● ● Fibre 1g ●
Polyunsaturated fats 5g ● ● ● Saturated fats 2g ● ●
Vitamins –
Minerals –

Illustrated on page 140

Ingredients
30ml (2 tbsp) tahini
15ml (1 tbsp) peanut butter
15ml (1 tbsp) sesame oil
15ml (1 tbsp) red wine vinegar
10ml (2 tsp) concentrated apple juice
10ml (2 tsp) shoyu, or salt if preferred
2.5cm (1in) fresh root ginger, grated
pinch of cayenne
black pepper
Makes about 300ml (½ pint)

Relatively low in fats, this simple sauce is like a nut mayonnaise.
1 Liquidize ingredients, except the peppers.
2 Gradually add 200ml (7 fl.oz.) water, liquidizing until the sauce is smooth.
3 Season with cayenne and black pepper.

Sharp mushroom sauce

65
Calories

NUTRIENTS PER PORTION
Protein 2g ● ● Fibre 1g ●
Polyunsaturated fats 0.5g ● ● Saturated fats 0.5g ● ● ●
Vitamins C
Minerals –

Illustrated on page 140

Ingredients
10ml (2 tsp) olive oil
225g (8oz) pickling onions
225g (8oz) button mushrooms
150ml (¼ pint) tomato juice
150ml (¼ pint) apple juice
15ml (1 tbsp) red wine vinegar
5ml (1 tsp) shoyu
pinch of dried thyme
shoyu, or salt if preferred
black pepper
Makes about 450ml (¾ pint)

Low in saturated fats, this is a versatile sauce which can be served with both grain and pastry dishes.
1 Heat the oil in a saucepan and gently fry the onions for about 5–6 minutes until just brown.
2 Stir the remaining ingredients into the pan, mixing well. Bring to the boil, cover and simmer for 20 minutes, stirring occasionally. Season with extra shoyu if necessary, and pepper.

Clockwise from left: Peanut and sesame sauce (see p. 139); Carob sauce (see below); Sharp mushroom sauces (see p. 139); Ankake sauce (see opposite); Broccoli and sunflower sauce (see opposite); Apricot and tomato relish (see opposite).

Illustrated above

Ingredients

50g (2oz) dried stoned dates
15ml (1 tbsp) rice flour
300ml (½ pint) milk
5–10ml (1–2 tsp) carob powder
4–6 drops vanilla essence
Makes about 300ml (½ pint)

Carob sauce

95 Calories

NUTRIENTS PER PORTION
Protein 3g ● ● *Fibre 1g* ●
Polyunsaturated fats 0g ● ● ● *Saturated fats 2g* ● ● ●
Vitamins –
Minerals –

As you lose your taste for sugar you may find that custards need no flavouring other than vanilla. To start with, however, try this sauce sweetened with dates and carob.

1 Gently stew the dates in a little water for about 10–15 minutes until soft. Beat to a stiff purée.

2 Combine the rice flour with a little of the milk to dissolve. Then stir in the remaining milk.

3 Bring to the boil and cook gently for 5 minutes, stirring. (The rice flour will thicken the milk on standing.)

4 Liquidize the milk with the dates, carob, and vanilla until the sauce is quite smooth.

5 Reheat gently before serving.

Ankake sauce

NUTRIENTS PER PORTION
Protein 3g ● Fibre 0g
Polyunsaturated fats 0.5g ● Saturated fats 0.5g ● ● ●
Vitamins C
Minerals –

65 Calories

Illustrated opposite

Ingredients
200ml (⅓ pint) pineapple juice
5ml (1 tsp) honey
5ml (1 tsp) red wine vinegar
15ml (1 tbsp) miso
5ml (1 tsp) arrowroot
Makes about 300ml (½ pint)

This sweet and sour fruit sauce gives out a strong but pleasant flavour of miso.
1 Mix all the ingredients together in a saucepan.
2 Bring to the boil and simmer for 2–3 minutes until the sauce thickens, stirring all the time.

Broccoli and sunflower sauce

NUTRIENTS PER PORTION
Protein 4g ● ● Fibre 3g ●
Polyunsaturated fats 4g ● ● ● Saturated fats 1g ● ●
Vitamins C, E
Minerals –

60 Calories

Illustrated on page 140

Ingredients
225g (8oz) broccoli florets
25g (1oz) sunflower seeds
60ml (4 tbsp) smetana or silken tofu
10ml (2 tsp) lemon juice
gomasio, or salt if preferred
black pepper
Makes about 450ml (¾ pint)

A light, creamy sauce with a slightly nutty flavour. Serve with baked savouries or with pastry dishes.
1 Steam the broccoli florets for 8–10 minutes until tender.
2 Grind all of the sunflower seeds in a grinder, liquidizer or food processor.
3 Liquidize the broccoli with 300ml (½ pint) of the steaming water. Add the smetana, lemon juice, and sunflower seeds and liquidize again. Season to taste with gomasio and pepper.
4 Reheat very gently before serving.

Apricot and tomato relish

NUTRIENTS PER PORTION
Protein 9g ● ● Fibre 7g ● ● ●
Polyunsaturated fats 0g ● ● ● Saturated fats 0g ● ● ●
Vitamins A, C
Minerals –

250 Calories

Illustrated on page 140

Ingredients
75g (3oz) dried apricots, sliced thinly
5ml (1 tsp) coriander seeds
225g (8oz) tomatoes, skinned and chopped
1 small onion, diced
1 medium green pepper, deseeded and chopped
60ml (4 tbsp) orange juice
juice of ½ lemon
15ml (1 tbsp) tomato purée
15ml (1 tbsp) white wine vinegar
15ml (1 tbsp) concentrated apple juice
5ml (1 tsp) shoyu, or salt if preferred
1.25cm (½in) fresh root ginger, grated
Makes about 300ml (½ pint)

A tasty high-fibre fruit and vegetable relish to serve as an accompaniment to stir-fries and steamed vegetables, or baked savoury dishes.
1 Place apricots in a saucepan with 300ml (½ pint) water. Cook until soft. Drain, reserving juice.
2 Dry roast seeds (see p. 117). Cool and crush. Mix with remaining ingredients and 60ml (4 tbsp) of juice. Cover and simmer for 1–1½ hours.

SALADS

Salads of fresh, raw vegetables are a rich source of vitamins and minerals and as such play an important part in any healthy diet. Ideally, they should form part of at least one meal a day and can even form the main basis of the meal itself.

A growing number of greengrocers and specialist market gardeners are supplying a wider and wider range of vegetables and saladings, and it is worth searching these out, or growing your own fresh produce if you can. For extra nutrients add fresh or dried fruit, nuts, or sprouts. For a substantial main dish try a salad with cooked dried beans or peas, pasta, or grains. The range of dressings can be varied beyond mayonnaise and vinaigrette. Whatever kind you use, have it ready and toss the salad in it straight away to preserve nutrients. Leaf salads should be prepared and dressed at the last possible moment.

Clockwise from top: Fiesta salad (see p. 145); Tomato salad (see p. 144); Horiatiki (see p. 144); Fattoush (see p. 144).

Tomato salad

Illustrated on page 143

Ingredients
12 cherry tomatoes
1 avocado, halved, stoned, and peeled
100g (4oz) quark
juice of 1 lemon
1 clove garlic, crushed
15ml (1 tbsp) finely chopped fresh basil
gomasio, or salt if preferred
black pepper
1 bunch watercress, divided into sprigs
lamb's lettuce
6 spring onions, sliced lengthways
juice of ½ lemon
Serves 4

NUTRIENTS PER PORTION
155 *Calories*
Protein 7g ● ● ● Fibre 4g ● ●
Polyunsaturated fats 1g ● ● Saturated fats 2g ● ● ●
Vitamins – A, B6, C, E. FA
Minerals Ca, Fe

This salad is high in protein and iron, and low in saturated fat.
1 Cut a lid off the base of each tomato. Spoon out the seeds and take out the flesh.
2 Liquidize the avocado, quark, lemon juice, garlic, and basil. Season, then fill the tomatoes.
3 Toss salad ingredients in the lemon juice, and arrange the tomatoes on top.

Horiatiki

Illustrated on page 143

Ingredients
225g (8oz) tomatoes
7.5cm (3in) piece of cucumber
100–225g (4–8oz) feta cheese
12 green or black olives
For the dressing
15ml (1 tbsp) olive oil
15ml (1 tbsp) lemon juice
30ml (2 tbsp) chopped fresh parsley
1 clove garlic, crushed
15ml (1 tbsp) chopped fresh basil
black pepper
Serves 4

NUTRIENTS PER PORTION
145 *Calories*
Protein 7g ● ● ● Fibre 1g ●
Polyunsaturated fats 1g ● ● Saturated fats 4g ● ● ●
Vitamins A, B12, C
Minerals Ca

This classic Greek salad gets its protein from the feta cheese.
1 Chop the tomatoes, cucumber and feta cheese into even, bite-sized pieces.
2 Mix together with the olives in a bowl.
3 Put the dressing ingredients together in a screw-top jar and mix by shaking well.
4 Pour the dressing over the salad and toss.

Fattoush

Illustrated on page 143

Ingredients
1 cos or iceberg lettuce
1 red pepper, deseeded and diced
4 hard-boiled eggs
4 tomatoes, sliced
10ml (2 tsp) capers
16 black olives
4 thinly cut slices wholewheat bread
2 cloves garlic
15ml (1 tbsp) walnut or olive oil
For the dressing
15ml (1 tbsp) walnut or olive oil
10ml (2 tsp) white wine vinegar
15ml (1 tbsp) chopped fresh parsley
5ml (1 tsp) dried tarragon
gomasio and black pepper
Serves 4

NUTRIENTS PER PORTION
235 *Calories*
Protein 11g ● ● ● Fibre 6g ● ● ●
Polyunsaturated fats 2g ● ● ● Saturated fats 3g ● ●
Vitamins A, B1, B2, B12, C, D, E, FA
Minerals Fe, Mg, Zn

This substantial peasant dish from Syria is a rich source of protein and fibre.
1 Prepare all the salad ingredients and place in a bowl.
2 Toast the wholewheat bread and rub with the cut cloves of garlic. Lightly sprinkle with oil. Break into small pieces.
3 Put the dressing ingredients together in a screw-top jar and mix by shaking well.
4 Toss the garlic toast and dressing into the salad.

Fiesta salad

Illustrated on page 142

NUTRIENTS PER PORTION
115
Calories
Protein 4g ● ● *Fibre 4g* ● ●
Polyunsaturated fats 0.5g ● ● *Saturated fats 0g* ● ● ●
Vitamins A, C
Minerals –

Ingredients
175g (6oz) long-grain brown rice
1 papaya
1 mango
¼ cucumber, sliced
100g (4oz) peas, lightly steamed
gomasio
black pepper
For the dressing
10ml (2 tsp) sesame oil
juice of ½ lime
juice of ½ orange or 30ml (2 tbsp)
mango juice
2.5ml (½ tsp) ground cinnamon
15ml (1 tbsp) finely chopped fresh
mint
For garnishing
sprigs of mint or sweet cicely
Serves 4

The saturated fat level of the dressing is kept low by using only 10ml (2 tsp) sesame oil.

1 Measure the rice and bring twice the volume of water, about 475ml (16fl oz), to the boil. Add the rice, cover and simmer for about 25 minutes or until tender.

2 Put the dressing ingredients together in a screw-top jar and mix by shaking well.

3 Pour over the rice while it is still warm, and combine together. Allow to cool completely.

4 To prepare the papaya: cut in half lengthways. Remove the seeds and skin. Slice the flesh. To prepare the mango, cut the flesh away from the stone, then peel.

5 Mix the fruit and vegetables into the rice.

6 Season with gomasio and pepper. Garnish with mint or use some sweet cicely.

Spiced rice salad (see p.146).

Illustrated on page 145

Ingredients

1 onion, finely chopped
15ml (1 tbsp) sunflower oil
1 tsp turmeric
¼ tsp cayenne
150g (5oz) long-grain brown rice
400ml (14fl oz) boiling water
100g (4oz) green beans, chopped
100g (4oz) pineapple, diced
3 tbsp creamed coconut, grated
10–12 radishes, quartered
For the dressing
30ml (2 tbsp) sunflower oil
15ml (1 tbsp) white wine vinegar
45ml (3 tbsp) pineapple juice
½ tsp grated root ginger
salt and pepper
Serves 4

Spiced rice salad

NUTRIENTS PER PORTION
Protein 5g ● Fibre 3g ● ●
Polyunsaturated fats 7g ● ● ● Saturated fats 4g ● ●
Vitamins B1, B6, C, E, N
Minerals K

305 Calories

This is an ideal dish for a summer buffet. The high fibre in the rice and vegetables balances the fat content of the coconut.
1 Gently fry the onion in the oil for 3–4 minutes until soft.
2 Put in the spices and rice and fry for another 2–3 minutes.
3 Pour over the boiling water, bring back to the boil and simmer until all the water is absorbed and the rice is tender – about 25–30 minutes.
4 Meanwhile, steam the green beans for 3–4 minutes until barely tender.
5 Mix all the dressing ingredients together and pour over the warm rice. Season well and leave to cool.
6 When the rice is cool, mix with the remaining ingredients.

Illustrated opposite

Ingredients

225g (8oz) cooked red kidney beans
225g (8oz) cooked chick peas
225g (8oz) fresh peas, lightly steamed
6 spring onions, diced
gomasio
black pepper
For the dressing
60ml (4 tbsp) orange juice
30ml (2 tbsp) lemon juice
15ml (1 tbsp) sunflower oil
1 clove garlic, crushed
10ml (2 tsp) shoyu
5ml (1 tsp) concentrated apple juice
5ml (1 tsp) dried thyme
5ml (1 tsp) dried oregano
100g (4oz) mushrooms, thinly sliced
Serves 6–8

Tangy bean salad

NUTRIENTS PER PORTION
Protein 13g ● ● ● Fibre 12g ● ● ●
Polyunsaturated fats 3g ● ● ● Saturated fats 1g ● ● ●
Vitamins B1, B2, C, E, FA, N
Minerals Ca, Cu, Fe, Mg, Zn

215 Calories

With pulses as the major ingredients, this salad is an ideal source of both protein and fibre. The sharp citrus dressing adds a deliciously refreshing tang to the other ingredients.
1 Mix the cooked beans, chick peas, and peas together with the spring onions.
2 Mix all the dressing ingredients together, except the mushrooms, then stir in the mushrooms. Leave to stand for 30 minutes to let the flavours blend together.
3 Pour the dressing over the bean salad and toss. Season.

*Clockwise from top: Potato salad (*see p. 148*); Tangy bean salad (*opposite*); Pasta and lentil salad (*see p. 149*).*

Potato salad

Illustrated on page 147

Ingredients
450g (1lb) potatoes
½ cucumber, diced
3 artichoke hearts, sliced
3 spring onions, diced
30ml (2 tbsp) finely chopped fresh parsley
15ml (1 tbsp) sunflower seeds
5ml (1 tsp) dill weed
For the dressing
60ml (4 tbsp) mayonnaise
60ml (4 tbsp) yogurt
5ml (1 tsp) lemon juice
5ml (1 tsp) wholegrain mustard
herb salt, or salt if preferred
Serves 4

NUTRIENTS PER PORTION
260 Calories
Protein 5g ● *Fibre 3g* ● ●
Polyunsaturated fats 6g ● ● ● *Saturated fats 2g* ● ● ●
Vitamins B6, C, E
Minerals –

Potato salads are often coated in heavy, high-fat, creamy dressings. Here mayonnaise has been mixed with yogurt, but you could also use all yogurt.
1 Scrub and cube the potatoes. Bring a large saucepan of water to the boil. Add the potatoes, cover and simmer for 15–20 minutes until tender. Drain and place in a bowl.
2 Mix the dressing ingredients together. Spoon over the potatoes while they are still warm and toss together. Leave the salad to cool completely.
3 When cold, mix in the remaining salad ingredients.

Many bean salad (see opposite).

Pasta and lentil salad

Illustrated on page 147

260
Calories

NUTRIENTS PER PORTION
Protein 11g ● ● ●   *Fibre 5g* ●
Polyunsaturated fats 1g ● ●   *Saturated fats 1g* ● ● ●
Vitamins A, C, E
Minerals Fe, Mg

Ingredients
*100g (4oz) continental lentils,
cleaned
100g (4oz) wholewheat pasta shells
450g (1lb) tomatoes, quartered
For the dressing
30ml (2 tbsp) white wine vinegar
30ml (2 tbsp) olive oil
60ml (4 tbsp) finely chopped fresh
parsley
4 spring onions, very finely chopped
15ml (1 tbsp) capers, chopped
2 gherkins, chopped
herb salt, or salt if preferred
black pepper
Serves 4–6*

Unusual for a salad, this is substantially high in protein.
1 Bring the lentils to the boil in a saucepan of water. Cover and simmer for 30–40 minutes. Drain. Cook pasta in boiling water for 8–10 minutes. Drain. Mix with lentils and tomatoes.
2 Put the dressing ingredients together in a screw-top jar and mix by shaking well. Pour over salad and toss. Serve on top of lettuce leaves in a bowl.

Many bean salad

Illustrated opposite

290
Calories

NUTRIENTS PER PORTION
Protein 8g ● ●   *Fibre 9g* ● ● ●
Polyunsaturated fats 7g ● ● ●   *Saturated fats 3g* ● ● ●
Vitamins B₁, B₆, FA, N
Minerals Fe, K, Mg

Ingredients
*50g (2oz) red kidney beans, soaked
overnight
50g (2oz) chick peas, soaked
overnight
50g (2oz) lima or cannellini beans,
soaked overnight
100g (4oz) French beans, cut into
1cm (½in) lengths
For the marinade
50ml (2fl oz) white wine vinegar
75ml (3fl oz) mixed olive and
sunflower oil
15ml (1 tbsp) lemon juice
1 tsp grated lemon rind
2 cloves garlic, crushed
15ml (1 tbsp) white wine
1 dried red chilli, very finely
chopped
1 bunch spring onions, chopped
Serves 4*

The kidney beans should be soaked and cooked separately unless you want the whole salad to be pink.
1 Drain the beans and peas. Cover with fresh water, bring to the boil and boil fiercely for 10 minutes. Reduce the heat and simmer until tender. The kidney beans will take 35–40 minutes, the chick peas and lima beans up to 1 hour, depending on how fresh they are. Drain.
2 Steam the French beans for 3–4 minutes. They should be still quite crunchy, only just beginning to be tender.
3 Mix together all the marinade ingredients.
4 Mix all the beans and peas together and pour the marinade over them. Leave for several hours in a cool place before serving. Drain off any excess dressing.

VEGETABLES

Vegetable dishes are very versatile. They can form the centrepiece of a meal or act as a side dish to complement a substantial main course. A recipe for one can usually be adapted for another: for example, the vine leaf stuffing given here also goes well with peppers or courgettes. A simple preparation can be made more elaborate by adding pastry, or a topping of cornbread or nut crumble.

A meal of vegetables alone will be low in protein, so try to have a dish based on grains or beans as well. Some of the recipes here already include high protein ingredients: for example, the nuts in the green vegetable and almond stir-fry or the tofu stir-fry.

Clockwise from left: Fennel and red pepper stir-fry (see p.152); Beansprout and sesame stir-fry (see p.153); Tofu stir-fry with Ankake sauce (see p.152); Green vegetable and almond stir-fry (see p.152).

Fennel and red pepper stir-fry

Illustrated on page 150

Ingredients
350g (12oz) fennel, about 1 large bulb
1 large red pepper, deseeded
10ml (2 tsp) sunflower oil
black pepper
Serves 3–4

NUTRIENTS PER PORTION
35 Calories
Protein 1g ● ●   Fibre 2g ●
Polyunsaturated fats 1g ● ● ●   Saturated fats 0g ● ● ●
Vitamins C, E
Minerals –

High in Vitamins C and E, these vegetables have the benefit of being low in saturated fats.
1 Trim the fennel and chop into matchstick-sized pieces.
2 Slice the pepper into thin strips.
3 Heat the oil in a wok or large frying pan. When hot, stir-fry the pepper and fennel for 4–5 minutes over a high heat, stirring constantly. Season with pepper. Serve immediately.

Tofu stir-fry with Ankake sauce

Illustrated on page 151

Ingredients
1 quantity of Ankake sauce (see p.141)
225g (8oz) carrots
225g (8oz) mouli
6 sticks celery
6 spring onions
350–450g (12oz–1lb) firm tofu
10ml (2 tsp) sunflower oil
Serves 3–4

NUTRIENTS PER PORTION
205 Calories
Protein 10g ● ● ●   Fibre 3g ● ●
Polyunsaturated fats 2g ● ● ●   Saturated fats 1g ● ● ●
Vitamins A, C
Minerals Ca, Cu, Fe, Mg

This high-protein stir-fry dish is served with a tangy, sweet and sour sauce.
1 Cut the carrots, mouli, celery, and spring onions into matchstick-sized pieces. Slice the tofu.
2 Heat the oil in a wok or large frying pan. When hot, stir-fry the vegetables for 3–4 minutes over a high heat, stirring constantly, until they are just soft. Add the tofu and cook for another 2 minutes.
3 Heat the Ankake sauce and serve immediately with the stir-fried tofu and vegetables.

Green vegetable and almond stir-fry

Illustrated on page 151

Ingredients
10ml (2 tsp) sesame oil
50g (2oz) blanched almonds, halved
1 dried red chilli
225g (8oz) green beans, sliced
350g (12oz) broccoli florets
350g (12oz) Chinese leaves, shredded
15ml (1 tbsp) dry sherry
juice of 1 lemon
15ml (1 tbsp) water
gomasio, or salt if preferred
Serves 3–4

NUTRIENTS PER PORTION
145 Calories
Protein 9g ● ● ●   Fibre 7g ● ● ●
Polyunsaturated fats 2g ● ● ●   Saturated fats 1g ● ● ●
Vitamins A, C, E, FA
Minerals Ca, Fe, Mg

The liquid added at the end of the recipe provides a burst of steam to finish off the cooking.
1 Heat the oil in a wok or large frying pan. When hot, toast the almonds and chilli for 2 minutes. Remove and discard the chilli.
2 Add the vegetables and stir-fry for 3–4 minutes.
3 Mix the sherry, lemon juice, and 15ml (1 tbsp) water together. Pour over the vegetables, then stir in the toasted almonds. Cook for 1 minute.
4 Serve immediately, sprinkled with gomasio.

Stuffed tomatoes (see p. 154).

Beansprout and sesame stir-fry

Illustrated on page 151

155
Calories

NUTRIENTS PER PORTION
Protein 9g ● ● ● *Fibre 3g* ● ●
Polyunsaturated fats 5g ● ● ● *Saturated fats 1g* ● ● ●
Vitamins C, FA, N
Minerals Fe, Mg, Zn

If you cannot find fresh oyster mushrooms, use tinned ones instead for this dish.

1 Mix the sauce ingredients together. Leave to stand for 1 hour before making the stir-fry.

2 Meanwhile, prepare the beansprouts, mushrooms, cauliflower, pepper, and garlic.

3 Heat the oil in a wok or large frying pan. When hot, stir-fry the vegetables for 3–4 minutes over a high heat, stirring constantly, until just soft.

4 Serve immediately, accompanied by the sauce.

Ingredients
For the sauce
45ml (3 tbsp) tahini
30ml (2 tbsp) water
15ml (1 tbsp) shoyu
30ml (2 tbsp) dry sherry
5ml (1 tsp) concentrated apple juice
5ml (1 tsp) red wine vinegar
30ml (2 tbsp) chopped fresh coriander
For the stir-fry
225g (8oz) beansprouts, rinsed
225g (8oz) oyster mushrooms, sliced
1 cauliflower, divided into florets
1 medium red pepper, deseeded and diced
1 clove garlic, crushed
10ml (2 tsp) sesame oil
Serves 4

Illustrated on page 153

Ingredients

*100g (4oz) flageolet or cannellini
beans, soaked overnight
10ml (2 tsp) olive oil
3 spring onions, very finely chopped
2 cloves garlic, crushed
225g (8oz) tomatoes, skinned and
chopped
30ml (2 tbsp) tomato purée
12 stuffed green olives, sliced
10ml (2 tsp) dried oregano
30ml (2 tbsp) dried chervil
5ml (1 tsp) miso, dissolved in a
little water
½ avocado, peeled, stoned, and
cubed
black pepper
4 large tomatoes
50g (2oz) mozzarella cheese
(optional)
Serves 4*

Stuffed tomatoes

NUTRIENTS PER PORTION
225 Calories
*Protein 11g ● ● ● Fibre 10g ● ● ●
Polyunsaturated fats 1g ● ● Saturated fats 3g ● ●
Vitamins A, B₁, B₆, C, E, FA
Minerals Ca, Fe, Mg, Zn*

The bean filling provides the major source of protein and fibre in this dish, which is complemented by a tomato and avocado sauce. For a lower fat content, omit the mozzarella topping.

1 Drain the beans. Cover with plenty of fresh water, bring, uncovered, to the boil, and boil fast for 10 minutes. Reduce the heat, skim, cover, and simmer for another 20–25 minutes or until the beans are soft. Drain.

2 Heat the oil in a large saucepan and gently fry the spring onions and garlic for 2–3 minutes.

3 Add the tomatoes, purée, olives, oregano, chervil, and miso. Cover and cook for 25 minutes.

4 Stir in the cooked beans and avocado. Season with pepper.

5 Preheat the oven to gas mark 4, 180°C (350°F).

6 To prepare the tomatoes, slice off the base and scoop out the seeds and flesh. Season the tomato shells with pepper.

7 Fill the tomato shells with the mixture. Cover with slices of mozzarella, or simply replace the tomato "lids".

8 Place in an ovenproof dish with 30–45ml (2–3 tbsp) bean stock or water. Cover and bake for 30–35 minutes.

Illustrated opposite

Ingredients

*1 marrow, weighing about 1kg (2lb)
10ml (2 tsp) sunflower oil
350g (12oz) leeks, cleaned and
finely sliced
3 sticks celery, chopped
350g (12oz) carrots, chopped
50g (2oz) porridge oats
25g (1oz) sunflower seeds
25g (1oz) pumpkin seeds
15ml (1 tbsp) tahini
5ml (1 tsp) miso, dissolved in a
little water
gomasio, or salt if preferred
black pepper
For serving
Tomato sauce (see p. 119)
Serves 6*

Stuffed marrow

NUTRIENTS PER PORTION
260 Calories
*Protein 9g ● ● Fibre 8g ● ● ●
Polyunsaturated fats 6g ● ● ● Saturated fats 2g ● ● ●
Vitamins A, B₆, C, E, FA
Minerals Ca, Fe*

In this dish, which is an excellent source of fibre, iron, calcium, and vitamins, it is important to cook the vegetables slowly so that they have a chance to blend together well. The seeds add a contrast in taste and texture.

1 Cut the marrow in half lengthways. Scoop out and discard the seeds. Take out approximately 450g (1lb) flesh and chop finely.

2 Heat the oil in a frying pan and fry the leeks very gently for 10 minutes.

3 Add the celery, carrot, and marrow flesh. Cover and cook for 20 minutes or until the vegetables are soft, stirring frequently.

4 Preheat the oven to gas mark 4, 180°C (350°F).

5 Remove the pan from the heat and add the remaining ingredients. Mix well and season with gomasio and pepper.

6 Fill the marrow halves with the mixture, cover and bake for 45–55 minutes or until cooked.

7 Serve hot, accompanied by tomato sauce.

Spiced courgette and apple (see below).

Spiced courgette and apple

75

Calories

NUTRIENTS PER PORTION
Protein 2g ● Fibre 1g ●
Polyunsaturated fats 2g ● ● ● Saturated fats 0.5g ● ● ●
Vitamins C, E
Minerals –

Illustrated above

Ingredients
225g (8oz) courgettes
1 medium dessert apple
10ml (2 tsp) sunflower oil
10ml (2tsp) lemon juice
15ml (1 tbsp) concentrated apple
juice
2.5ml (½ tsp) ground cinnamon
2.5ml (½ tsp) grated nutmeg
25g (1oz) hazelnuts, finely chopped
gomasio, or salt if preferred
black pepper
Serves 3–4

Despite being fried, this dish remains low in saturated fat.
1 Chop the courgettes and apple into finger-sized pieces
(chunky matchsticks).
2 Heat the oil in a large saucepan and fry the courgette and
apple pieces for 3 minutes.
3 Mix in the other ingredients. Cover and cook for 10–15
minutes until the courgette and apple are just soft. Season with
gomasio and black pepper.

Stuffed marrow
(see opposite)

RICE AND PASTA DISHES

Rice and pasta can be used to form the base for many vegetarian dishes. Risottos and pilaus are filling and nutritious rice dishes. Mushrooms, fresh or dried, go well with rice; so do fresh young peas, broccoli, and courgettes. Different chopped nuts can be used to make a good contrast of textures.

Bought pasta, fresh or dried, is a great standby. It can be made from wholewheat or refined flour, with or without eggs, plain or coloured green with spinach. If you prefer it home made, there are machines to help you to turn it out in various shapes and sizes. Wholewheat pasta has a denser texture than refined pasta. Some kind of sauce or filling is always used with pasta. It may be as simple as an oil and garlic sauce for spaghetti, or it may be as robust as a mushroom lasagne.

From top to bottom: Mushroom lasagne (see p. 158); Walnut ravioli (see p. 159).

Mushroom lasagne

Illustrated on pages 156–57

Ingredients

10ml (2 tsp) olive oil
1 medium onion, finely chopped
2 cloves garlic, crushed
1 bay leaf
2.5ml (½ tsp) dried thyme
225g (8oz) mushrooms, sliced
30ml (2 tbsp) cornflour
300ml (½ pint) skimmed milk
300ml (½ pint) yogurt
gomasio, or salt if preferred
350g (12oz) broccoli florets
100g (4oz) carrots, diced
25g (1oz) pine kernels
black pepper
9 pieces wholewheat lasagne
10ml (2 tsp) cornflour
30ml (2 tbsp) freshly grated
Parmesan
Serves 4

NUTRIENTS PER PORTION
385 *Calories*
Protein 20g ● ● ● *Fibre 6g* ● ● ●
Polyunsaturated fats 3g ● ● *Saturated fats 3g* ● ● ●
Vitamins A, B1, B2, C, FA
Minerals Ca, Cu, Fe, Mg, Zn

In this lasagne, which is high in protein and fibre but low in saturated fats, a tangy yogurt sauce is used to flavour the layers of pasta. For a less sharp version, use more milk and less of the yogurt.

1 Heat the oil in a saucepan and gently fry the onion and garlic for 4–5 minutes or until the onion is soft.

2 Add the bay leaf, thyme, and mushrooms and cook the sauce over a gentle heat for 10 minutes. Dissolve the cornflour in a little of the milk.

3 Pour the remaining milk over the mushrooms. When heated through, stir in the cornflour. Cook for 5 minutes until thickened, stirring all the time. Remove the bay leaf. Remove pan from the heat and stir in 150ml (¼ pint) of the yogurt. Season with the gomasio and pepper.

4 Steam the broccoli and carrot until fairly soft. Place in a bowl, then mix in the pine kernels and season well with the gomasio and black pepper.

5 Preheat the oven to gas mark 4, 180°C (350°F).

6 Meanwhile, separate the lasagne pieces and cook in a large saucepan of boiling salted water for 8–10 minutes or until they are just *al dente*.

7 Put a layer of mushroom sauce in the bottom of a lightly oiled oblong ovenproof dish. Cover with a layer of lasagne, then the broccoli mixture, then the sauce. Repeat the layers, ending, finally, with lasagne.

8 Mix the 10ml (2 tsp) cornflour with the remaining 150ml (¼ pint) yogurt. Pour this over the lasagne. Sprinkle the top with Parmesan cheese.

9 Bake for 25–30 minutes. Serve hot.

Walnut ravioli

Illustrated on page 156

NUTRIENTS PER PORTION
Protein 25g ● ● ● *Fibre 16g* ● ● ●
Polyunsaturated fats 17g ● ● ● *Saturated fats 4g* ● ● ●
Vitamins A, B₁, B₂, B₆, B₁₂, C, D, E, FA, N
Minerals Ca, Cu, Fe, Mg, Zn

595
Calories

Ingredients
For the dough
350g (12oz) wholewheat flour
pinch of salt
2 eggs
225g (8oz) spinach, cooked and
puréed
For the filling
1 medium onion, finely chopped
or minced
4 sticks celery, finely chopped
or minced
175g (6oz) walnuts, very finely
chopped
30ml (2 tbsp) finely chopped
fresh basil
45ml (3 tbsp) finely chopped
fresh parsley
3 cloves garlic, crushed
30ml (2 tbsp) tomato purée
shoyu, or salt if preferred
black pepper
beaten egg for sealing
Serves 4 as a main course or 6 as a
starter

The dish manages to reach a nutritious ideal – it is high in protein and fibre, low in saturated fats, and is an excellent source of all the essential vitamins and minerals. Buy good-quality walnuts for this dish and store in an airtight container, otherwise the taste will be bitter.

1 For the pasta dough: mix the flour and salt together in a large bowl or on a work surface. Make a well in the centre and add the eggs and spinach. Using your fingers, or a fork, gradually draw the flour into the centre to make a dough. Knead thoroughly until the dough mixture no longer feels sticky. Cover and leave to rest for half an hour.

2 Mix the filling ingredients together in a large bowl. Season with shoyu and pepper.

3 Roll out the pasta dough very thinly to a rectangle. Mark half into 2.5–5cm (1–2in) squares. Dot a teaspoon of filling on each square. Brush the edges and in between the rows of filling with beaten egg. Cover with the remaining dough. Press firmly along the edges and between the rows to seal. Use a pastry wheel to cut out the ravioli squares. Leave to dry for 30 minutes.

4 Cook the ravioli in a large saucepan of boiling salted water for 8–10 minutes or until *al dente*. Drain. Serve hot with tomato sauce (see p. 119) or mushroom sauce (see p. 139).

Three grain pilau (see p. 160).

Paella de la Huerta

Illustrated opposite

Ingredients
10ml (2 tsp) olive oil
1 medium onion, finely chopped
2 cloves garlic, crushed
100g (4oz) peas
100g (4oz) green beans, sliced
4 artichoke hearts, halved
225g (8oz) short-grain brown rice
6 strands saffron
225g (8oz) tomatoes, skinned and chopped
5ml (1 tsp) dried oregano
5ml (1 tsp) dried thyme
30ml (2 tbsp) finely chopped fresh parsley
shoyu
black pepper
juice of ½ lemon
For garnishing
12 black or green olives
lemon slices
coriander sprigs
Serves 4

NUTRIENTS PER PORTION
280 Calories
Protein 6g ● *Fibre 5g* ● ●
Polyunsaturated fats 0.5g ● *Saturated fats 1g* ● ● ●
Vitamins B₁, C
Minerals Mg

Short-grain rice is used for this Valencian peasant dish as it provides the creamiest texture. Although low in saturated fats, paella needs to be served with a high-protein dish for full nutritional balance.
1 Heat the oil in a large saucepan and gently fry the onion and garlic for 4–5 minutes or until soft.
2 Add the peas, beans, and artichoke hearts, stirring in well, and cook over a very low heat for 5 minutes.
3 Measure the rice and have ready twice the volume of boiling water, about 500ml (16fl oz).
4 Add the rice to the pan of vegetables and cook gently for 3–4 minutes, without browning.
5 Dissolve the saffron in the boiling water, then add to the pan with the tomatoes and herbs. Bring to the boil and cook uncovered for 35–45 minutes. Stir occasionally and adjust the liquid if necessary. Season with shoyu and pepper and add the lemon juice. Garnish with olives, lemon slices, and coriander.

Three grain pilau

Illustrated on page 159

Ingredients
50g (2oz) wholewheat berries
50g (2oz) long-grain brown rice
50g (2oz) roasted buckwheat
For the sauce
10ml (2 tsp) olive oil
1 onion, finely chopped
1 clove garlic, crushed
450g (1lb) mushrooms, quartered
1 green pepper, deseeded and cut in rings
450g (1lb) tomatoes, skinned and chopped
30ml (2 tbsp) tomato purée
10ml (2 tsp) dried oregano
1 bay leaf
miso, or salt if preferred
black pepper
Serves 4

NUTRIENTS PER PORTION
175 Calories
Protein 7g ● ● ● *Fibre 6g* ● ● ●
Polyunsaturated fats 1g ● ● *Saturated fats 0.5g* ● ● ●
Vitamins B₁, B₂, C, FA, N
Minerals Cu, Fe

Cooked together, the grains used in this nutritious dish – rice, wheat, and buckwheat – allow you to taste their different flavours without one becoming dominant.
1 Rinse the grains. Bring the wheat to the boil in 425 ml (¾ pint) water, cover, and simmer for 30 minutes.
2 Add the rice and buckwheat with another 425 ml (¾ pint) boiling water. Continue to simmer for a further 25–30 minutes, or until the water is absorbed, and the grains are soft.
3 For the sauce: heat the oil in a saucepan and gently fry the onion and garlic for 4–5 minutes, or until soft. Add the mushrooms and green pepper, and cook for 3 minutes.
4 Stir in the remaining sauce ingredients, cover, and simmer for 35–40 minutes. Season with miso and pepper.
5 Put the grains into a serving dish, and pour over the sauce.

Paella de la Huerta (see opposite).

Peanut pilau with stir-fried vegetables

Illustrated below

Ingredients

225g (8oz) long-grain brown rice
For the sauce
15ml (1 tbsp) peanut oil
1 medium onion, finely chopped
1 clove garlic, crushed
1 green chilli, deseeded and diced
1.5cm (½in) fresh root ginger, grated
275g (10oz) silken tofu plus 150ml (¼ pint) water or 300ml (½ pint) skimmed milk
100g (4oz) ground roasted peanuts
5ml (1 tsp) shoyu
For the stir-fry
15ml (1 tbsp) peanut oil
175g (6oz) white cabbage, shredded
175g (6oz) fresh green beans, sliced
175g (6oz) mung bean sprouts
½ cucumber, diced
50g (2oz) peanuts
5ml (1 tsp) shoyu
Serves 4

590
Calories

NUTRIENTS PER PORTION
Protein 23g ● ● ●   Fibre 9g ● ● ●
Polyunsaturated fats 8g ● ● ●   Saturated fats 5g ● ● ●
Vitamins B1, B6, C, E, FA, N
Minerals Ca, Cu, Fe, Mg, Zn

This dish, with its crispy stir-fried vegetables coated in a creamy peanut sauce, is a perfect combination of tastes and textures. It is also an excellent source of protein and fibre.

1 Measure the rice and bring twice the volume of water, about 500ml (18fl oz), to the boil. Add the rice and stir once. Cover and simmer for about 25 minutes or until cooked. Add a little extra water at the end if necessary.

2 For the sauce, heat the oil in a saucepan and gently fry the onion and garlic for 4–5 minutes or until soft. Add the chilli and ginger and cook for 3 minutes.

3 Liquidize the onion mixture with the remaining sauce ingredients. Heat through gently.

4 For the stir-fry: heat the oil in a wok or large frying pan. When hot, stir-fry the cabbage, beans, bean sprouts, and cucumber over high heat for 3 minutes, stirring constantly. Stir in the peanuts and shoyu.

5 To serve, pile the long-grain rice on to a warm serving dish. Top with all the stir-fry vegetables and carefully pour over the hot, spicy sauce.

Peanut pilau with stir-fried vegetables
(see above)

*Beetroot Kasha (*see below*).*

Beetroot kasha

355
Calories

NUTRIENTS PER PORTION
Protein 12g ● ● *Fibre 4g* ● ●
Polyunsaturated fats 6g ● ● ● *Saturated fats 2g* ● ● ●
Vitamins B1, E, N
Minerals Ca, Fe, Mg, Zn

Illustrated above

Ingredients
10ml (2 tsp) sunflower oil
1 medium onion, finely chopped
4 sticks celery, chopped
225g (8oz) buckwheat
900ml (1½ pints) hot water
15ml (1 tbsp) shoyu
*10–15ml (2–3 tsp) grated
horseradish*
black pepper
450g (1lb) baby beetroots
For the sauce
200ml (⅓ pint) skimmed milk
1 onion
1 bay leaf
4 peppercorns
30ml (2 tbsp) sunflower oil
*20ml (1 heaped tbsp) wholewheat
flour*
*60–75ml (4–5 tbsp) yogurt or
smetana*
*5–10ml (1–2 tsp) grated
horseradish*
black pepper
Serves 4

This dish is low in saturated fats, and is a good source of all minerals except calcium.

1 Heat the oil in a large saucepan and gently fry the onion for 4–5 minutes or until soft.

2 Add the celery and cook for 2–3 minutes. Stir in the buckwheat and stir-fry for 3 minutes until lightly roasted.

3 Pour on the water, stir once, bring to the boil, cover, and cook for 20–25 minutes. Add a little boiling water if the mixture looks rather dry.

4 Stir in the shoyu and horseradish. Season with pepper.

5 Either bake the baby beetroots in a preheated oven, gas mark 4, 180°C (350°F) for about 45 minutes or steam for 20 minutes or until tender. Skin when cool enough to handle and set the beetroots to one side.

6 For the sauce, place the milk, onion, bay leaf, and peppercorns in a saucepan. Bring almost to the boil, remove from the heat and leave to infuse for 10 minutes. Strain.

7 Heat the oil in a saucepan and stir in the flour. Cook for 3 minutes, stirring.

8 Pour on the milk, stirring constantly. Bring the sauce to boiling point and simmer for 5 minutes, stirring. Cool slightly, then blend in the yogurt or smetana. Season with some horseradish and pepper.

9 To serve, pile the kasha on to a warm serving plate. Slice or arrange the baby beetroots on top. Serve the sauce separately.

*From top to bottom: Spaghetti with lentil bolognaise (*see opposite*); Tagliatelle (*see opposite*).*

Spaghetti with lentil Bolognaise

NUTRIENTS PER PORTION
Protein 26g ● ● ● *Fibre 9g* ● ● ●
Polyunsaturated fats 1g ● *Saturated fats 2g* ● ● ●
Vitamins A, B₁, B₂, B₆, C, E, FA, N
Minerals Ca, Cu, Fe, Mg, Zn

530 Calories

Illustrated opposite
Ingredients
175g (6oz) brown or continental lentils
15ml (1 tbsp) olive oil
1 medium onion, finely chopped
2 cloves garlic, crushed
350g (12oz) mushrooms, diced
5ml (1 tsp) dried marjoram
1 bay leaf
450g (1lb) tomatoes, skinned and chopped
30ml (2 tbsp) tomato purée
shoyu, or salt if preferred
black pepper
For serving
350g (12oz) wholewheat spaghetti
15–30ml (1–2 tbsp) grated Parmesan
Serves 4

Either continental or brown lentils can be used for this recipe's sauce. Lentils make an excellent introduction for a non-vegetarian to the pulse family as they are high in protein, very adaptable, easy to digest and, because of their small size, do not overpower the dish.

1 Place the lentils in a saucepan of water. Bring, uncovered, to the boil, skim, cover, and simmer for about 40 minutes or until soft. Drain.
2 Heat the oil in a large saucepan and fry the onion and garlic for 4–5 minutes or until the onion is soft.
3 Add the mushrooms, cooked lentils, marjoram, and bay leaf and cook for 10 minutes.
4 Stir in the tomatoes and purée. Cover and cook for 20–25 minutes. Remove the bay leaf. Season with shoyu and pepper.
5 Cook the spaghetti in a large saucepan of boiling salted water for about 8–10 minutes until just tender. Drain. Pile the Bolognaise sauce over the cooked spaghetti. Add Parmesan.

Tagliatelle

NUTRIENTS PER PORTION
Protein 11g ● ● ● *Fibre 3g* ● ●
Polyunsaturated fats 0.5g ● *Saturated fats 0.5g* ● ● ●
Vitamins B₁, B₁₂
Minerals –

125 Calories

Illustrated opposite
Ingredients
10ml (2 tsp) olive oil
3 spring onions, chopped
1 small red pepper, deseeded and chopped
4 canned or cooked artichoke hearts, quartered
175g (6oz) peas
175g (6oz) quark
150ml (¼ pint) skimmed milk
gomasio, or salt if preferred
black pepper
225g (8oz) fresh wholewheat tagliatelle
Serves 4

Blending quark with skimmed milk, as here, produces a light cream, lower in fat than single cream.

1 Heat the oil in a saucepan and gently fry the chopped spring onions for 4–5 minutes.
2 Add the red pepper, artichoke hearts, and peas, cover, and cook for 10 minutes, adding a little water if the mixture begins to look a bit dry.
3 Liquidize the quark with the skimmed milk until it is a smooth cream. Pour this into the vegetables and heat through gently. Season with gomasio and pepper.
4 Cook the tagliatelle in a large saucepan of boiling salted water for 3–4 minutes or until *al dente*. Drain.
5 Toss the tagliatelle well with the sauce. Serve immediately.

CASSEROLES AND ROASTS

As with pulses, the vegetarian store cupboard comes into its own with grains. Apart from rice there are many others, such as wheat, barley, millet, buckwheat, and bulgar wheat, to give different textures and unexpected flavours. Cook grains as casseroles, with fresh vegetables or dried beans and lentils, or serve them as accompaniments to other dishes, perhaps with a nut or vegetable sauce. Most grains can be used interchangeably, although the delicate taste of wild rice is probably best appreciated when it is plainly boiled.

Grain dishes are generally simple and quick to make, often using only one pan. Many can be cooked in advance and frozen. Thaw overnight in the refrigerator and reheat gently, either in the oven covered with greased paper and foil, by steaming or using the microwave. There are more ideas for cold grain dishes in the Salad section (see pp. 142–49).

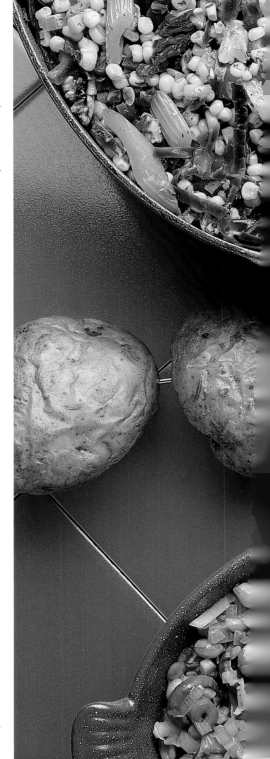

Clockwise from top: Ghiuvetch (see p. 168); Barley bourguignon (see p. 169); Peanut stroganov (see p. 168).

Illustrated on pages 166–67

Ghiuvetch

Ingredients

10ml (2 tsp) sunflower oil
1 medium onion, finely chopped
4 sticks celery, sliced diagonally
15ml (3 tsp) grated horseradish
15ml (1 tbsp) paprika
450g (1lb) frozen sweetcorn kernels
100g (4 oz) walnuts, roughly chopped
30ml (2 tbsp) finely chopped fresh parsley
5ml (1 tsp) dill weed
150ml (¼ pint) vegetable stock
225g (8oz) red cabbage, shredded
shoyu, or salt if preferred
black pepper
For garnishing
smetana or yogurt (optional)
For serving
baked potatoes
Serves 4–6

NUTRIENTS PER PORTION
315 Calories
Protein 9g ● ●   Fibre 8g ● ● ●
Polyunsaturated fats 12g ● ● ●   Saturated fats 2g ● ● ●
Vitamins B₁, B₆, C, E, FA
Minerals Fe, Mg, Zn

A quickly made, colourful vegetable stew inspired by Romanian cuisine. Extra protein and flavour are provided by the inclusion of corn and walnuts.

1 Heat the oil in a large saucepan and gently fry the onion for 4–5 minutes or until soft.

2 Add the celery, horseradish, and paprika to the pan and cook for 2–3 minutes.

3 Stir in the sweetcorn, walnuts, herbs, and stock. Cover and simmer for 10 minutes.

4 Add the red cabbage and cook for a further 10–15 minutes. Season with shoyu and pepper.

5 Serve hot, garnished with smetana or yogurt (optional), and accompanied by baked potatoes.

Illustrated on page 167

Peanut stroganov

Ingredients

10ml (2 tsp) sunflower oil
1 medium onion, finely chopped
350g (12oz) Chinese leaves, shredded
6 sticks celery, finely chopped
350g (12oz) button mushrooms
225g (8oz) roasted unsalted peanuts
2.5ml (½ tsp) caraway seeds
5ml (1 tsp) German mustard
150ml (¼ pint) red wine
shoyu, or salt if preferred
black pepper
150ml (¼ pint) smetana
For serving
wholewheat noodles
Serves 4

NUTRIENTS PER PORTION
430 Calories
Protein 21g ● ● ●   Fibre 7g ● ● ●
Polyunsaturated fats 10g ● ● ●   Saturated fats 6g ● ●
Vitamins A, B₁, B₂, B₆, C, E, FA, N
Minerals Ca, Cu, Fe, Mg, Zn

The seasonings of caraway and mustard complement the flavours of the Chinese leaves and celery well, and the smetana provides the traditional creaminess of this dish without the addition of a lot of fat.

1 Heat the oil in a saucepan and gently fry the onion for 4–5 minutes or until soft.

2 Add the Chinese leaves, celery, mushrooms, and peanuts and cook for 5 minutes, stirring frequently. Stir in the caraway seeds, mustard, and red wine.

3 Cover and cook for 10 minutes.

4 Remove from the heat and season with shoyu and pepper. Cool slightly, then stir in the smetana. Serve immediately with boiled wholewheat noodles.

Barley bourguignon

Illustrated on page 167

NUTRIENTS PER PORTION
230 Calories
Protein 9g ● ● ● *Fibre 11g* ● ● ●
Polyunsaturated fats 2g ● ● ● *Saturated fats 0.5g* ● ●
Vitamins A, B1, B2, B6, C, E, FA, N
Minerals Ca, Cu, Fe, Zn

Ingredients
100g (4oz) pot barley
10ml (2 tsp) sunflower oil
175g (6oz) leeks, finely chopped
350g (12oz) button mushrooms, quartered
225g (8oz) parsnips, chopped
5ml (1 tsp) dried thyme
5ml (1 tsp) dried sage
1 bay leaf
150ml (¼ pint) red wine
450g (1lb) tomatoes, skinned and chopped
30ml (2 tbsp) tomato purée
shoyu, or salt if preferred
black pepper
225g (8oz) broccoli florets
Serves 4

Always be careful when adding barley to a casserole or soup as a little goes a long way. It is a chewy grain which absorbs flavours well and therefore benefits from standing overnight. Serve with a cooked, dried pulse, or fresh green peas or mangetout, and a low-fat pudding for a balanced meal.

1 Dry roast the barley for 2–3 minutes in a heavy-based pan. Add enough boiling water to cover by 2.5cm (1in) and cook for 40–45 minutes. Drain, reserving the cooking liquid.

2 Heat the oil in a large saucepan and gently fry the leeks for about 5 minutes until soft.

3 Add the mushrooms, parsnips, herbs, and cooked barley. Stir in well and cook for 2–3 minutes.

4 Add the wine, tomatoes, purée, and up to 150ml (¼ pint) reserved stock. Bring to the boil, cover, and cook gently for 35 minutes. Add a little reserved stock if the mixture begins to look dry. Season with shoyu and pepper.

5 Add the broccoli florets and cook for a further 8–10 minutes or until tender. Remove the bay leaf before serving.

Georgia casserole

Illustrated on page 170

NUTRIENTS PER PORTION
210 Calories
Protein 14g ● ● ● *Fibre 18g* ● ● ●
Polyunsaturated fats 2g ● ● *Saturated fats 0.5g* ● ● ●
Vitamins A, B1, B6, C, E, FA
Minerals Ca, Fe

Ingredients
175g (6oz) black kidney beans, soaked overnight
10ml (2 tsp) sunflower oil
225g (8oz) pickling onions or shallots, peeled
2.5ml (½ tsp) ground allspice
2.5ml (½ tsp) ground cinnamon
2.5ml (½ tsp) dried thyme
100g (4oz) button mushrooms
100g (4oz) prunes
225g (8oz) tomatoes, skinned and chopped
150ml (¼ pint) tomato juice
juice and rind of 1 orange
15ml (1 tbsp) red wine vinegar
shoyu, or salt if preferred
black pepper
For serving
buckwheat or brown rice
Serves 4

High in protein because of the beans, this rich, dark casserole with its tangy sauce contains whole tiny vegetables for a contrast in texture.

1 Drain the beans. Cover with plenty of fresh water, bring to the boil and boil fast, uncovered, for 10 minutes. Reduce the heat, skim, cover, and simmer for another 35–40 minutes or until soft. Drain well.

2 Heat the oil in a large saucepan and gently fry the onions for 4–5 minutes or until just brown. Add the spices and thyme and cook for 2–3 minutes.

3 Stir in the remaining ingredients, including the beans, cover, and cook for 40 minutes. Season with shoyu and pepper. Serve with boiled buckwheat or brown rice.

From left to right: Georgia casserole (see p. 169); Spicy bean goulash (see below).

Illustrated above

Ingredients

*175g (6oz) red kidney beans,
soaked overnight
15ml (1 tbsp) olive oil
1 medium onion, finely chopped
1 clove garlic, crushed
1 small red chilli, finely chopped
3 large red peppers, chopped
225g (8oz) mushrooms, chopped
1 medium potato, diced
10–15ml (2–3 tsp) paprika
5ml (1 tsp) thyme
30ml (2 tbsp) tomato purée
5ml (1 tsp) miso, dissolved in a
little water
gomasio, or salt if preferred
black pepper
For serving
brown rice or wholewheat noodles
Serves 4*

Spicy bean goulash

205
Calories

NUTRIENTS PER PORTION
Protein 13g ● ● ●   *Fibre 14g* ● ● ●
Polyunsaturated fats 1g ● ●   *Saturated fats 0.5g* ● ● ●
Vitamins B1, B2, B6, C, FA, N
Minerals Ca, Cu, Fe, Mg, Zn

The red beans used here provide most of the high protein and fibre contained in this tasty stew.

1 Drain the beans, cover with plenty of fresh water, bring uncovered to the boil, and boil fast for 10 minutes. Reduce the heat, cover, and simmer for 40 minutes or until soft. Drain, reserving the stock.

2 Heat the oil in a large saucepan and gently fry the onion in the oil for 4–5 minutes or until soft.

3 Add the garlic, chilli, peppers, and mushrooms and cook for 5 minutes. Cover, and cook the mixture for 15–20 minutes over a very gentle heat.

4 Add the cooked beans, potato, paprika, thyme, tomato purée, and miso to the stew.

5 Simmer gently for 30 minutes, adding a little bean stock if necessary. Season with gomasio and pepper and serve hot with brown rice or wholewheat noodles.

Pine kernel roast (see below).

Pine kernel roast

Illustrated above

425
Calories

NUTRIENTS PER PORTION
Protein 10g ● ●   Fibre 7g ● ● ●
Polyunsaturated fats 7g ● ● ●   Saturated fats 3g ● ● ●
Vitamins C, E, N
Minerals Fe, Mg

Ingredients
175g (6oz) long-grain brown rice
10ml (2 tsp) olive oil
1 medium onion, finely chopped
175g (6oz) courgettes, sliced
1 small aubergine, diced
75g (3oz) pine kernels
225g (8oz) tomatoes, skinned
and chopped
75g (3oz) mixed nuts (cashews and
almonds), ground
10ml (2 tsp) ground cinnamon
6 cloves or 1.25ml (¼ tsp) ground
cloves
gomasio, or salt if preferred
black pepper
Serves 4

Only a small amount of pine nuts is needed to flavour this high-fibre, low-fat dish.
1 Weigh out the rice and cook according to the instructions given in the chart on p. 47.
2 Preheat the oven to gas mark 4, 180°C (350°F).
3 Heat the oil in a large saucepan and gently fry the onion for 4–5 minutes or until soft. Add the courgettes, aubergine, and pine kernels and cook for 10 minutes.
4 Remove from the heat and mix in the remaining ingredients and cooked rice. Season with gomasio and pepper.
5 Put the mixture in a lightly oiled 450g (1lb) loaf tin, pressing it down firmly. Bake for 50 minutes.

Buckwheat roast

Illustrated below

Ingredients

15ml (3 tsp) sunflower oil
150g (5oz) buckwheat
450ml (¾ pint) boiling water
1 medium onion, finely chopped
10ml (2 tsp) paprika
5ml (1 tsp) ground ginger
5ml (1 tsp) garam masala
pinch of cayenne
225g (8oz) red cabbage, shredded
25g (1oz) arame, soaked in warm
water for 15 minutes
45ml (3 tbsp) wheatgerm
shoyu, or salt if preferred
black pepper
For serving
sharp mushroom sauce (see p. 139)
Serves 4

NUTRIENTS PER PORTION
220 Calories
Protein 9g ● ● ●   Fibre 2g ●
Polyunsaturated fats 2g ● ● ●   Saturated fats 0.5g ● ● ●
Vitamins E
Minerals –

Buckwheat, with its strong flavour, can be an acquired taste, so try boiling and tasting the grain separately first. For balance, serve this meal with a high-fibre starter or side dish.
1 Brown the buckwheat in some oil (see p. 47). Pour over the boiling water, bring back to the boil, cover, and simmer until tender. Drain.
2 Preheat the oven to gas mark 5, 190°C (375°F).
3 Heat the remaining oil in a large saucepan and gently fry the onion for 4–5 minutes, or until just soft. Add the spices and cook for a few minutes.
4 Stir in the red cabbage, drained arame, and cooked buckwheat. Cook over a gentle heat for 10 minutes, stirring all the ingredients frequently. Add the wheatgerm and season with shoyu and pepper.
5 Pack the mixture into a lightly oiled 450g (1lb) loaf tin. Bake for 45–50 minutes.
6 Cool in the tin for 10 minutes, then turn out. Serve hot with sharp mushroom sauce (see p. 139).

Buckwheat roast (see above).

Vegetable bake (see below).

Vegetable bake

380

Calories

NUTRIENTS PER PORTION
Protein 10g ● ●   Fibre 8g ● ● ●
Polyunsaturated fats 7g ● ● ●   Saturated fats 3g ● ● ●
Vitamins A, B₁, B₆, C, E, FA, N
Minerals Ca, Cu, Mg

Illustrated above

Ingredients
For the topping
50g (2oz) porridge oats
25g (1oz) brown rice flour
50g (2oz) cashew nuts, finely chopped
30ml (2 tbsp) sunflower oil
5ml (1 tsp) dried rosemary
For the filling
1kg (2lb) root vegetables (carrots, parsnips, swede, turnip)
For the sauce
10ml (2 tsp) sunflower oil
1 medium onion, finely chopped
25g (1oz) cashew nuts
30ml (2 tbsp) brown rice flour
150ml (¼ pint) skimmed milk
300ml (½ pint) vegetable stock
5ml (1 tsp) dried rosemary
gomasio, or salt if preferred
black pepper
Serves 4

This dish is a root vegetable bake, covered with a nutty sauce and sprinkled with a crunchy topping. It is high in fibre, and low in saturated fat.

1 For the topping: put the oats, rice flour, and cashew nuts into a bowl. Mix in the oil and rosemary with the fingertips to form a light, crunchy crumble topping.

2 For the filling: scrub or peel the vegetables and cut into bite-sized pieces. Steam for 10–12 minutes until just tender. Reserve the steaming water for stock.

3 Preheat the oven to gas mark 5, 190°C (375°F).

4 Heat the oil in a large saucepan and gently fry the onion for 4–5 minutes or until soft. Add the cashew nuts and lightly brown for 3–4 minutes.

5 Mix the rice flour to a smooth paste with a little of the milk.

6 Pour the milk and reserved stock into the pan and add the rice flour paste and rosemary. Bring to the boil and simmer until thickened, stirring constantly. Season with gomasio and pepper.

7 Cool slightly, then liquidize the sauce until smooth.

8 Put the steamed vegetables into a lightly oiled, ovenproof dish. Pour over the sauce, then cover with the topping. Bake for 30 minutes and serve hot.

DESSERTS AND PUDDINGS

From a wholefood point of view, if not strictly a vegetarian one, desserts make a very positive contribution to a meal. If the main course has been light and lacking in protein, serve cheesecake made with tofu, a soufflé, mousse, or roulade using eggs, or a milk pudding. If you prefer to avoid cream, try a cashew "cream" (made with cottage cheese), yogurt, or custard made with cornmeal as an accompaniment, and use yogurt also to make delicious ice cream.

Fresh fruit salad is one of the best possible endings to a meal. Base it on a colour theme – green and white looks cool and refreshing, red soft fruit with peaches or nectarines is lovely for a party – or on a simple contrast of fruits, such as pomegranate and banana. Dried fruits really come into their own in sweets, whether individually, as mixed fruit compôtes, or puréed, and give a nutritious as well as delectable final touch to a meal.

From top to bottom: Tropical trifle (see p. 176); Baked tofu cheesecake (see p. 176).

Illustrated on page 174–75

Ingredients
For the sponge
2 eggs
*25g (1oz) concentrated pear and
apple spread*
50g (2oz) wholewheat flour
For the trifle
45ml (3 tbsp) sugar-free jam
30ml (2 tbsp) medium dry sherry
300ml (1/2 pint) fruit juice
1 papaya
2 bananas, sliced
175g (6oz) quark
90ml (6 tbsp) skimmed milk
For garnishing
toasted flaked almonds
Serves 6

Tropical trifle

NUTRIENTS PER PORTION
240 Calories
Protein 12g ● ● ●   Fibre 1g ●
Polyunsaturated fats 0.5g ●   Saturated fats 1g ● ● ●
Vitamins B12, C, D
Minerals Ca

It is quite possible to make this low-fat, seemingly rich pudding without sugar by using a well-flavoured, sugar-free jam.
1 Preheat the oven to gas mark 5, 190°C (375°F).
2 Whisk the eggs and fruit spread until very thick and creamy. Fold in half the flour, then fold in the remainder very carefully.
3 Butter and flour an 18cm (7in) sandwich tin. Spoon in the mixture evenly.
4 Bake for 20 minutes. Turn out of the tin and cool the sponge on a wire rack.
5 Cut the sponge in half, spread with jam and sandwich together again. Cut into 2.5cm (1in) cubes. Place in the bottom of a glass dish.
6 Sprinkle over the sherry. Pour over the fruit juice.
7 Cut the papaya in half lengthways. Remove the seeds and skin. Slice the flesh.
8 Arrange the banana and papaya slices in alternate layers over the sponge.
9 Liquidize the quark with the milk and spread over the fruit.
10 Decorate with some toasted flaked almonds.

Illustrated on page 175

Ingredients
For the base
*50g (2oz) butter or sunflower
margarine*
*10ml (2 tsp) concentrated pear and
apple spread*
50g (2oz) porridge oats
50g (2oz) wholewheat flour
For the filling
rind and juice of 1 orange
4 ripe bananas
594g (21oz) silken tofu
For garnishing
grapes and orange segments
Serves 6–8

Baked tofu cheesecake

NUTRIENTS PER PORTION
180 Calories
Protein 8g ● ● ●   Fibre 3g ● ●
Polyunsaturated fats 2g ● ● ●   Saturated fats 4g ●
Vitamins A, B1, C
Minerals Ca, Cu, Fe, Mg, Zn

Cheesecake is a slight misnomer as no cheese is used in this dish; protein-rich tofu is used instead. If you are trying tofu for the first time, you may wish to blend in a little cottage cheese or sweetening such as honey or maple syrup.
1 Preheat the oven to gas mark 4, 180°C (350°F).
2 For the base: cream the butter or margarine and fruit spread together until smooth. Stir in the oats and flour and mix well.
3 Spread the mixture over the base of a lightly oiled 18cm (7in) spring mould. Bake for 10 minutes.
4 For the filling: liquidize the orange rind, orange juice, bananas, and tofu until smooth. Pour over the baked base.
5 Bake for about 45 minutes until just set.
6 Leave to cool in the tin before removing. Decorate with grapes and orange segments. Chill before serving.

Cranachan

Illustrated on page 178

NUTRIENTS PER PORTION
Protein 16g ● ● *Fibre 9g* ● ● ●
Polyunsaturated fats 4g ● ● *Saturated fats 3g* ● ● ●
Vitamins B₁, B₂, B₆, C, E, FA
Minerals Ca, Fe, Mg, Zn

Ingredients
75g (3oz) hazelnuts, roughly ground
75g (3oz) medium oatmeal
300ml (½ pint) hung yogurt and 150ml (¼ pint) low-fat yogurt or 450ml (¾ pint) home-made low-fat hung yogurt
225g (8oz) black grapes, halved and deseeded
225g (8oz) strawberries, sliced
For garnishing
a few small whole strawberries
Serves 4

This high-fibre dessert can be varied according to the fruit that is in season at the time.
1 Preheat the oven to gas mark 4, 180°C (350°F).
2 Mix the hazelnuts with the oatmeal and place in a shallow ovenproof dish or on a baking sheet. Toast in the oven for 10–15 minutes until golden.
3 Using 4 wide tumbler glasses, make layers of the yogurt, fruit and oatmeal mixture. Finish with a layer of yogurt and decorate with whole strawberries. Serve chilled.

Citrus castagne

Illustrated on page 178

NUTRIENTS PER PORTION
Protein 12g ● ● ● *Fibre 2g* ●
Polyunsaturated fats 5g ● ● ● *Saturated fats 2g* ● ●
Vitamins C
Minerals Fe, Mg

Ingredients
100g (4oz) dried chestnuts, soaked overnight in 225ml (8fl oz) orange juice
30ml (2 tbsp) lemon juice
10ml (2 tsp) carob powder
60ml (4 tbsp) tahini
175g (6oz) quark
12 drops almond essence
10ml (2 tsp) maple syrup
For garnishing
grated carob chocolate and grated orange rind
Serves 4

This high-protein pudding owes its unusual taste to the inclusion of tahini and sesame.
1 Place the chestnuts and their soaking juice in a saucepan. Bring to the boil, cover, and simmer for 35–40 minutes or until they are soft. Drain.
2 Liquidize the chestnuts with the remaining ingredients.
3 Pile into 4 glasses and chill. Decorate with grated carob and the orange rind.

Clockwise from top: Cranachan (see p. 177); Citrus castagne (see p. 177).

Illustrated opposite

Ingredients

100g (4oz) dried stoned dates, chopped
5ml (1 tsp) orange rind, grated
300ml (½ pint) orange juice
40g (1½oz) butter or sunflower margarine
25g (1oz) wholewheat flour
2 eggs, separated
Serves 4

Date and orange frazzan

215
Calories

NUTRIENTS PER PORTION
Protein 5g ● Fibre 3g ● ●
Polyunsaturated fats 0.5g ● Saturated fats 0.6g ●
Vitamins B1, B12, C, D
Minerals –

Sweet, without added sugar, these fruit slices should be served to follow high-protein, low-fat dishes.

1 Place the dates in a small saucepan.

2 Add the orange rind and orange juice and cook for 10–15 minutes or until the dates are soft.

3 Meanwhile, preheat the oven to gas mark 4, 180°C (350°F).

4 Melt the butter or margarine in a large saucepan and stir in the flour until smooth. Stir in the date mixture, bring to the boil and simmer for 2–3 minutes, stirring. Cool.

5 Beat the egg yolks into the date mixture. Beat the egg whites until stiff, then fold into the mixture. Spoon the mixture into a lightly oiled ovenproof dish and bake for 30 minutes.

Wholewheat pancakes

NUTRIENTS PER PORTION
135
Calories

Protein 6g ● ● ● *Fibre 3g* ● ●
Polyunsaturated fats 1g ● ● *Saturated fats 1g* ● ● ●
Vitamins B12
Minerals Ca

Ingredients
100g (4oz) wholewheat flour
pinch of salt
1 egg
300ml (½ pint) milk
5ml (1 tsp) oil
oil or butter for frying
Makes 8–10 pancakes

This recipe can be used for sweet or savoury pancakes. Serve sweet pancakes with maple syrup, or just with a generous squeeze of lemon juice and brown sugar to taste. If you are going to eat the pancakes straightaway, stack them on top of one another on a lightly oiled plate, and keep warm in moderately hot oven or under a low grill. If you are going to keep them to use later, turn each one out on a cool surface as it is cooked. If they are stacked before cooling, their own steam will moisten them and make them soggy.

1 Mix the flour and salt in a bowl. Beat together the egg, milk, and oil. Pour this into the flour, stirring constantly and mixing in the flour until you have a smooth batter. If you use a liquidizer, first blend the milk, egg, salt, and oil for 15–30 seconds, then add the flour and blend for a further 30 seconds until a smooth, creamy batter is produced.

2 Let the batter stand for 30 minutes or more before making the pancakes. Blend or beat again just before using, as some of the flour will almost certainly have settled at the bottom.

3 Heat about 5ml (1 tsp) oil or butter in a frying pan until it smokes. Pour in 2 tablespoons of batter, quickly tipping the pan so that the batter spreads out thinly and evenly into a circle.

4 Cook for 2–3 minutes. Toss or flip over with a slice and cook the other side for a further 2–3 minutes.

Date and orange frazzan (see opposite).

Fruity oatcakes

Illustrated opposite

Ingredients
*100g (4oz) butter or sunflower
margarine
50g (2oz) date or apricot purée
100g (4oz) wholewheat flour
100g (4oz) porridge oats*
Makes 12

NUTRIENTS PER PORTION
*Protein 2g • Fibre 5g • •
Polyunsaturated fats 0.5g • • Saturated fats 4g •
Vitamins A, B₁
Minerals Fe, Mg*

These iron-rich biscuits are easy to make, and the use of a purée instead of sugar means that they have a fruity flavour.
1 Preheat the oven to gas mark 4, 180°C (350°F).
2 Cream the butter or margarine and fruit purée together in a large bowl until light. Mix in the flour and oats and beat together until a stiff dough is formed.
3 Press or roll out the dough and cut into small rounds – so that you make about 12 oatcakes.
4 Bake for 15 minutes or until just firm and lightly browned. Cool on a wire rack.

Carob digestives

Illustrated opposite

Ingredients
*50–75g (2–3oz) dates
50g (2oz) unsalted peanuts
10ml (2 tsp) aniseed
10ml (2 tsp) sesame seed
100ml (4fl oz) olive or sunflower oil
rind and juice of 1 orange
225g (8oz) flour
5ml (1 tsp) cinnamon
15ml (1 tbsp) carob powder
1 small egg*
For the topping
*1 egg white
25g (1oz) finely chopped peanuts*
Makes 18

NUTRIENTS PER PORTION
*Protein 3g • Fibre 2g •
Polyunsaturated fats 4g • • • Saturated fats 1g • • •
Vitamins B₁, E, FA, N
Minerals Fe, Mg*

These simple, low-fat biscuits have a good texture and subtle flavour, naturally sweetened by dates.
1 Preheat the oven to gas mark 4, 180°C (350°F).
2 Cook the dates gently in a little water until soft, drain and beat to a stiff purée with a fork.
3 Grind up the peanuts, aniseed, and sesame seeds, and place in a large mixing bowl.
4 Slowly mix in the olive oil, then add the orange rind and juice, and the puréed dates.
5 Add the flour, cinnamon, and carob powder. Blend in well, making sure to stir the mixture thoroughly.
6 Beat in the egg and mix to a stiff dough.
7 Turn onto a floured work surface. Roll out and cut into biscuit shapes, or divide the mixture into walnut-sized pieces and press into individual rounds.
8 Brush the biscuits with egg white and then scatter peanuts all over them.
9 Bake on a greased tray for 25–30 minutes.

Clockwise from left: Fruity oatcakes (opposite); Fruit and nut bars (below); Carob digestives (opposite).

Fruit and nut bars

315
Calories

NUTRIENTS PER PORTION
Protein 7g ● Fibre 11g ● ● ●
Polyunsaturated fats 2g ● ● Saturated fats 1g ● ●
Vitamins B₁, E
Minerals Ca, Fe, Mg

This recipe is a nutritious alternative to the standard high-fat and high-sugar snacks that are available.
1 Preheat the oven to gas mark 4, 180°C (350°F).
2 Finely chop or mince the fruit and nuts, and mix thoroughly with the other ingredients.
3 Press into a lightly greased 18cm × 18cm (7in × 7in) square tin. Bake for 15 minutes. Cut into slices while still warm.

Illustrated above
Ingredients
50g (2oz) apricots
50g (2oz) dates
50g (2oz) figs
50g (2oz) sultanas
50g (2oz) sunflower seeds
50g (2oz) hazelnuts
110g (4oz) porridge oats
15–30ml (1–2 tbsp) lemon juice
15ml (1 tbsp) concentrated apple juice
Makes 12 slices

· CHAPTER SIX ·
MENU IDEAS
FOR SPECIAL
OCCASIONS

Whether you are a full-time vegetarian or would merely
like a vegetarian meal as an occasional change from a
meat-based one, it can be difficult to structure a meal, to
decide which foods complement each other. This part of
the book is designed to help you prepare varied and
interesting meals, well balanced in taste, texture, and
nutrients. These meals are also high in fibre and protein
but low in saturated fats, and provide a good source of
vitamins and minerals.

HOW TO USE A NUTRITIONAL PROFILE

110
Calories

NUTRIENTS PER PORTION
Protein 25g ● ● ●   *Fibre 16g* ● ● ●
Polyunsaturated fats 17g ● ● ●   *Saturated fats 4g* ● ●
Vitamins A, B₁, B₂, B₆, B₁₂, C, D, E, FA, N
Minerals Ca, Cu, Fe, Mg, Zn

Each recipe has its own nutritional profile, so that you
can see at a glance, in grams, exactly how much
protein, fibre, polyunsaturated fat, saturated fat, and
calories each portion, or meal, contains. The profile
also shows which vitamins and minerals are found in
significant quantities. The bullet system indicates how
good the source is: three bullets shows an excellent
source, two bullets a very good source, and one bullet
a good source.

Appetizing meals
*Summer Dinner Party menu (see pp. 192–195). By combining
different tastes and textures, and balancing the levels of protein, fibre, and
fat, you can create interesting, special meals for all events.*

Sunday Lunch

A delicious blend of taste and texture makes this an ideal
Sunday lunch for the family. Low-protein dishes like beetroot
salad and golden fruit salad are balanced by the high-protein,
high-fibre celebration roast, and spinach soup.

1350 Calories

NUTRIENTS PER PORTION
Protein 37g ● ● ● *Fibre 39g* ● ● ●
Polyunsaturated fats 32g ● ● ● *Saturated fats 11g* ● ● ●
Vitamins A, B1, B2, C, E, FA, N
Minerals Ca, Cu, Fe, Mg

*Baked parsnips
in orange*

Hazel's potatoes

Celebration roast

Tomato sauce

Wine

Spinach soup
This nutritious, high-protein, high-fibre, low-fat soup is based on a spiced fruit stock made up from fruit juices, coriander, and ginger. The last two ingredients provide just the right amount of tang to the soup.

Celebration roast
This high-protein, high-fibre dish contrasts a creamy nut mixture with a dark, moist layer of mushrooms and walnuts.

Tomato sauce
The tomato sauce is served here to enhance the flavour of the celebration roast, not to moisten it. (See p. 119 for the recipe.)

Hazel's potatoes
Roast potatoes need not become a forbidden food once you have turned to a healthy regime of eating, as this dish proves. The potatoes here, baked lightly with a minimum amount of olive oil, are delicious, and yet low in saturated fats.

Baked parsnips in orange
After steaming, baking is the best way to preserve nutrients in cooked vegetables. The natural sweetness of the parsnips is well complemented here by the fresh orange juice.

Beetroot salad
Raw beetroot has a far better flavour than bought, pre-cooked varieties, which have often had preservatives and sugar added to them. Here the beetroot is mixed with celeriac and turnip and tossed in an oil, lemon, mustard, onion, and pepper dressing. This produces a clean-tasting salad to follow the main course.

Golden fruit salad
Using such exotic fruits as mango, passion fruit, pomegranate, and dates, this fruit salad is an ideal way to end a meal – light, naturally sweet, and fat-free.

Wine
A glass of dry, white wine will add 75 calories to the nutritional profile of this meal.

Golden fruit salad

Beetroot salad

Spinach soup

Spinach soup

Illustrated on page 185

Ingredients

10ml (2 tsp) olive oil
1 medium onion, chopped
1 clove garlic, crushed
350g (12oz) spinach, washed and shredded
450ml (³⁄₄ pint) mixed apple and orange juice
2.25cm (¹⁄₂in) fresh root ginger, grated
5ml (1 tsp) ground coriander
150ml (¹⁄₄ pint) yogurt or soured cream
gomasio, or salt if preferred
black pepper
Serves 4

NUTRIENTS PER PORTION

110 Calories

Protein 7g ● ● ●   Fibre 6g ● ● ●
Polyunsaturated fats 0.5g ● ●   Saturated fats 1g ● ● ●
Vitamins A, C, E
Minerals Ca, Cu, Fe, Mg

A good source of Vitamins A, C, and E, and high in minerals, protein, and fibre, this soup uses a spiced fruit stock to add another dimension to the spinach flavour.

1 Heat the oil in a large saucepan and gently fry the onion and garlic for 4–5 minutes, or until the onion is soft.

2 Add the spinach and stir-fry for 2–3 minutes over a high heat until it becomes limp.

3 Pour over the fruit juices, ginger, and coriander. Bring to the boil, cover, and simmer for 20 minutes.

4 Cool slightly, then liquidize until smooth. Stir in the yogurt or cream. Season with gomasio and pepper. Reheat the soup gently before serving.

Celebration roast

Illustrated on page 184

Ingredients

30ml (2 tbsp) sunflower oil
1 medium onion, finely chopped
5 sticks celery, finely chopped
15ml (1 tbsp) wholewheat flour
300ml (¹⁄₂ pint) white wine or stock
200g (7oz) almonds, ground
50g (2oz) wholewheat breadcrumbs
50g (2oz) porridge oats
1 apple, grated
2 eggs
juice of ¹⁄₂ lemon
gomasio, or salt if preferred
black pepper
For the filling
10ml (2 tsp) sunflower oil
1 medium onion, finely chopped
350g (12oz) mushrooms, diced
1 clove garlic, crushed
150g (5oz) walnuts, chopped
Serves 6–8

NUTRIENTS PER PORTION

775 Calories

Protein 41g ● ●   Fibre 15g ● ● ●
Polyunsaturated fats 7g ● ● ●   Saturated fats 2.5g ● ● ●
Vitamins B1, B2, B6, B12, C, D, E, FA, N
Minerals Ca, Cu, Fe, Mg, Zn

Successful nut roasts should be moist. They should include plenty of vegetables, otherwise the nut and breadcrumb mix becomes too reminiscent of stuffing. This attractive dish, made with a creamy nut "meat" filled with a contrasting layer of mushrooms and walnuts, provides a near perfect nutritional balance for a meal.

1 Heat the oil in a large saucepan and gently fry the onion for 4–5 minutes, or until soft. Add the celery and fry for 5 minutes.

2 Sprinkle over the flour. Cook for 1–2 minutes, stirring, then pour over the wine or stock. Cook and stir for 1–2 minutes.

3 Mix the almonds, breadcrumbs, oats, grated apple, and eggs together in a large bowl. Add the sauce and lemon juice. Season.

4 Preheat the oven to gas mark 5, 190°C (375°F).

5 For the filling: heat the oil in a saucepan and gently fry the onion until soft. Add other ingredients and cook for about 10 minutes, stirring.

6 Lightly oil and line a 1 litre (2–2¹⁄₂ pint) savarin or ring mould with greaseproof paper. Spoon in a third of the creamy nut mixture, add the dark filling, then cover the top of the dish with the remaining nut mixture.

7 Bake for 50–55 minutes. Cool in the tin for 10 minutes.

Hazel's potatoes

NUTRIENTS PER PORTION
Protein 3g • Fibre 2g •
Polyunsaturated fats 1g • • Saturated fats 1g • •
Vitamins C
Minerals –

165 Calories

Illustrated on page 184
Ingredients
450g (1lb) potatoes
30–45ml (2–3 tbsp) olive oil
juice of ½ lemon
Serves 4

These roast potatoes are low in saturated fats.
1 Preheat the oven to gas mark 6, 200°C (400°F).
2 Peel and cut the potatoes into pieces. Place in a saucepan of water, bring to the boil, and parboil for 10–15 minutes until almost cooked. Drain.
3 Heat the olive oil in an ovenproof dish in the oven for a few minutes.
4 Put the potatoes in the dish and sprinkle with lemon juice. Bake for 20–25 minutes until well cooked and lightly browned.

Baked parsnips in orange

NUTRIENTS PER PORTION
Protein 2g • • Fibre 5g • •
Polyunsaturated fats 1g • • • Saturated fats 0g • • •
Vitamins C, E, N
Minerals –

80 Calories

Illustrated on page 184
Ingredients
450g (1lb) parsnips
juice of 1 orange
30–45ml (2–3 tbsp) water
10ml (2 tsp) sunflower oil
Serves 4

After steaming, baking is the best way to preserve nutrients.
1 Preheat the oven to gas mark 6, 200°C (400°F).
2 Scrub or peel the parsnips and cut lengthways. Put in a lightly oiled ovenproof dish.
3 Mix together the orange juice, water and oil. Pour this over the parsnips.
4 Bake for 40–50 minutes, adding more water or orange juice during the cooking if the parsnips begin to look dry. Serve hot.

Golden fruit salad

NUTRIENTS PER PORTION
Protein 2g • Fibre 6g • • •
Polyunsaturated fats 0.5g • Saturated fats 0.5g • • •
Vitamins A, C
Minerals –

120 Calories

Illustrated on page 185
Ingredients
1 mango
1 ugli fruit or pink grapefruit
2 passion fruit
1 pomegranate
8 fresh dates
6 yellow plums
5ml (1 tsp) lemon juice
15ml (1 tbsp) white grape juice
Serves 4

In a healthy diet fruit salads come into their own – naturally sweet and fat-free.
1 Peel the mango and chop the flesh into bite-sized pieces.
2 Peel the ugli fruit or grapefruit and segment the flesh.
3 Halve the passion fruit and pomegranate and scrape out the seeds, taking care to remove the bitter white pith from the pomegranate.
4 Stone the dates and plums and chop into bite-sized pieces.
5 Mix fruits together with the juices. Leave for 2–3 hours.

Quick and Tasty Supper

This delicious supper menu is for when time is at a premium, just allow time for the ice cream to set. Filling and lighter dishes happily mix together. The meal also shows how the addition of wholewheat noodles and courgettes can improve the level of fibre.

NUTRIENTS PER PORTION
875 Calories
Protein 34g ● ● ● Fibre 17g ● ● ●
Polyunsaturated fats 12g ● ● ● Saturated fats 9g ● ● ●
Vitamins A, B₁, B₂, C, E, FA
Minerals Ca, Cu, Fe, Mg, Zn

Papaya and lime salad with mint
This light, easy-to-prepare starter uses papaya (a tropical fruit containing the digestive enzyme pepain) at its simplest – just peeled and sprinkled with lime juice to offset its natural sweetness.

Tofu bobotie
This spicy fruit casserole is an adaptation of the traditional South African dish. This version makes excellent use of tofu, a high-protein soya bean product. Although tofu has little taste of its own when uncooked, it absorbs the flavours of what it is cooked with very well.

Wholewheat noodles
Wholewheat noodles are a good standby item to keep in the store cupboard. They have been used here as an alternative to potatoes or rice. They are a good way of making up the fibre levels in a meal which may otherwise be rather too low.

Steamed courgettes
Steaming is one of the best ways of preserving the nutrients in vegetables. Salt should ideally not be added – gomasio could be tried instead. If you find you cannot do without a dab of butter on the vegetables, try using a margarine high in polyunsaturates, or use yogurt or chives, instead.

Papaya and lime salad with mint

Sweetcorn salad with beansprouts
This crisp salad is a good choice to make when serving a substantial dish like tofu bobotie because its lightness and range of ingredients make such a pleasing and varied contrast.

Iced cashew cream
Containing no double cream, this pudding owes its richness to the pulverized nuts and fruit. The fat level in this dish is desirably low.

Mineral water
Mineral waters, whether still or carbonated, are a refreshing, calorie-free accompaniment to meals. Read the bottle's label to check for the specific mineral content.

Iced cashew cream

*Sweetcorn salad
with beansprouts*

Steamed courgettes

Wholewheat noodles

Mineral water

Tofu bobotie

Papaya and lime salad with mint

Illustrated on page 188

Ingredients
2 papayas
1 lime
Chinese leaves and
watercress sprigs
For garnishing
sprig fresh mint
Serves 4

50
Calories

NUTRIENTS PER PORTION
Protein 0.5g ● *Fibre 0g*
Polyunsaturated fats 0g ● ● ● *Saturated fats 0g* ● ● ●
Vitamins –
Minerals –

Also known as pawpaw or papaw, this tropical fruit contains the digestive enzyme pepain.

1 Cut the papayas in half lengthways and discard the seeds.

2 Squeeze the juice of half the lime over the papaya flesh. Use the remaining half as garnish, cut into very thin slices, together with the sprig of mint.

3 Arrange the papaya halves on a bed of Chinese leaves and watercress sprigs.

Tofu bobotie

Illustrated on page 189

Ingredients
10ml (2 tsp) peanut oil
1 medium onion, finely chopped
450g (1lb) firm tofu, cut in chunks
5ml (1 tsp) ground allspice
5ml (1 tsp) ground cumin
2.5ml (½ tsp) ground ginger
2.5ml (½ tsp) turmeric
pinch of cayenne
6 curry leaves
450g (1lb) tomatoes, skinned and chopped
1 medium red pepper, deseeded and cut into strips
1 medium green pepper, deseeded and cut into strips
1 large aubergine, chopped
100g (4oz) sultanas
shoyu, or salt if preferred
black pepper
For the topping
2.5ml (½ tsp) cumin seeds
300ml (½ pint) yogurt
1 egg
juice of ½ lemon
Serves 4

265
Calories

NUTRIENTS PER PORTION
Protein 16g ● ● ● *Fibre 6g* ● ● ●
Polyunsaturated fats 3g ● ● ● *Saturated fats 2g* ● ● ●
Vitamins A, B1, B2, B6, C, E, FA
Minerals Ca, Cu, Fe, Mg, Zn

This dish is an adaptation of the South African spiced fruit casserole. It is perfect for tofu, which absorbs the flavouring and colouring of the vegetables and spices, while providing a good source of low-fat, low-calorie protein.

1 Heat the oil in a saucepan and gently fry the onion for 4–5 minutes, or until soft. Add the tofu and spices to the pan and fry for 5 minutes.

2 Stir in the remaining ingredients, cover and cook for 30 minutes. Season with shoyu and pepper.

3 Preheat the oven to gas mark 4, 180°C (350°F).

4 Spoon the mixture into a lightly oiled ovenproof dish.

5 Dry roast the cumin seeds in a heavy-based pan (see p.82) for 3–4 minutes, or until lightly browned. Mix the topping ingredients together and pour over the bobotie.

6 Bake for 30 minutes. Serve hot.

Sweetcorn salad with beansprouts

Illustrated on page 189

NUTRIENTS PER PORTION
Protein 5g ● ● ● *Fibre 4g* ● ●
Polyunsaturated fats 2g ● ● ● *Saturated fats 0.5g* ● ● ●
Vitamins C, E
Minerals Fe

110 Calories

Ingredients

225g (8oz) fresh or frozen sweetcorn kernels

225g (8oz) beansprouts (aduki or lentil)

100g (4oz) mouli, scrubbed and chopped

1 medium green pepper, deseeded and diced

12 radishes, sliced

For the dressing

15ml (1 tbsp) sunflower oil

5ml (1 tsp) white wine vinegar

5ml (1 tsp) fennel seeds

2.5ml (½ tsp) paprika

Serves 4

This crisp and colourful salad provides a good source of protein, fibre, and iron.

1 Cook the sweetcorn in a saucepan of boiling water for about 5 minutes, or until lightly cooked.

2 Combine the salad ingredients together in a bowl.

3 Put the dressing ingredients together in a screw-top jar and mix by shaking well. Pour the dressing over the salad and toss.

Iced cashew cream

Illustrated on page 189

NUTRIENTS PER PORTION
Protein 5g ● *Fibre 1g* ●
Polyunsaturated fats 4g ● ● ● *Saturated fats 3g* ● ●
Vitamins C, E
Minerals Mg

230 Calories

Ingredients

100g (4oz) cashew nuts

150ml (¼ pint) soya milk (unsweetened)

10ml (2 tsp) honey

2.5ml (½ tsp) vanilla essence

15ml (1 tbsp) rum (optional)

15ml (1 tbsp) sunflower oil

½ medium pineapple, diced

Serves 6

The richness and flavour of this unusual ice cream come from the nuts and fruit.

1 Grind the cashew nuts in a grinder, liquidizer, or food processor until they become a very fine powder.

2 Liquidize the milk, honey, vanilla essence, ground cashew nuts, rum (if using), and oil together until quite smooth.

3 Add the pineapple and liquidize briefly again so that the pineapple still provides some texture.

4 Transfer to a freezerproof container and freeze for about 2 hours until the cream is firm.

Summer Dinner Party

The wholewheat pancakes with their different, colourful fillings help to give substance to this party menu for a summer's evening. Extra protein is provided by the tofu in the mushroom salad and the avocado in the avocado and kiwi salad, which is also full of vitamins. A light, low-fat, ice cream dessert is the perfect dish to finish with after a filling main course.

NUTRIENTS PER PORTION
1200 Calories
Protein 40g ● ● ● Fibre 20g ● ● ●
Polyunsaturated fats 9g ● ● Saturated fats 28g ●
Vitamins A, B, B₁, B₂, B₆, B₁₂, C, E
Minerals Ca, Fe, K, Mg, Zn

Artichokes with lemon sauce
Globe artichoke served with an individual bowl of lemon and garlic sauce is a quick and easy first course which can be prepared well in advance.

Galette
A layered galette of wholewheat pancakes with three different vegetable fillings – spinach, fennel, and tomato and onion. The pancakes (see pp. 176–77) can be made in advance and frozen; the fillings will keep for 1–2 days in the refrigerator. Serve sprinkled with some grated Parmesan.

Mushroom salad in tofu
Button mushrooms are garnished with walnuts and spring onions in a tofu and lemon dressing.

Avocado and kiwi salad
A salad of avocado and kiwi fruit with a julienne of celery and cucumber, tossed in a herb vinaigrette.

Blackcurrant yogurt ice cream
This looks rich and creamy, but is low in fat and sugar. Its clean, sharp taste is enhanced with orange.

Mushroom salad in tofu

Galette

Blackcurrant yogurt
ice cream

Avocado and
kiwi salad

Artichokes with
lemon sauce

Illustrated on page 193

Ingredients
4 globe artichokes
75g (3oz) butter
15ml (1 tbsp) wheatmeal flour
300ml (½ pint) boiling water
10ml (2 tsp) lemon juice
grated rind of ½ lemon
3 cloves garlic, crushed
salt and pepper
1 tbsp snipped chives
Serves 4

Artichokes with lemon sauce

155
Calories

NUTRIENTS PER PORTION
Protein 2g Fibre 1g
Polyunsaturated fats Trace Saturated fats 9g
Vitamins A, N
Minerals –

A more elaborate variation is to prepare and cook the artichokes, cool them, remove the soft inner leaves, scoop out the inedible chokes with a teaspoon and fill them with sauce.
1 Wash the artichokes thoroughly. Remove the stalks and trim the bases so that the artichokes will sit flat. Trim the points off the leaves with scissors.
2 Bring a large pan of water to the boil and cook the artichokes, covered, for 30–40 minutes or until a leaf pulls out easily.
3 Meanwhile, melt half the butter in a pan. Add the flour and cook, stirring, over gentle heat for 2–3 minutes. Pour on the boiling water, stirring vigorously, and as soon as the mixture is smooth, beat in the remaining butter. Stir in the lemon juice, grated lemon rind and garlic. Season to taste. Keep warm, stirring from time to time, on a very low heat.
4 Drain the artichokes as soon as they are cooked and arrange them on a serving dish or on individual plates. Pour the sauce into a heated sauceboat and sprinkle it with chives.

Illustrated on page 192

Ingredients
8 pancakes (see pp. 176–77)
For the fennel filling
450g (1lb) fennel, finely sliced
50g (2oz) butter
50g (2oz) Parmesan, freshly grated
salt and pepper
For the spinach filling
450g (1lb) fresh spinach, washed
½ tsp grated nutmeg
black pepper
For the tomato filling
30ml (2 tbsp) olive oil
1 onion, chopped
1 clove garlic, crushed
450g (1lb) tomatoes, skinned and chopped
3 sticks celery, diced
½ tsp aniseeds
15ml (1 tbsp) tomato purée
salt and pepper
For serving
extra grated Parmesan
Serves 4

Galette

475
Calories

NUTRIENTS PER PORTION
Protein 22g ● ● ● Fibre 7g ● ● ●
Polyunsaturated fats 2g ● Saturated fats 14g
Vitamins A, B₁, B₂, B₁₂, C, E, FA, N
Minerals Ca, Fe, K, Mg, Zn

This makes a spectacular dish for a dinner party.
1 Blanch the fennel for 10 minutes in boiling water. Drain well.
2 Melt the butter in a small pan, put the fennel in, cover, and stew for 10 minutes over gentle heat. Purée the fennel with the grated Parmesan and add salt and pepper to taste.
3 Preheat the oven to gas mark 4, 180°C (350°F).
4 Cook the spinach in its own juices for 7–8 minutes in a covered pan. Chop and season with nutmeg and pepper.
5 Heat the olive oil in a saucepan and gently fry the onion and garlic for 3–4 minutes. Stir in the tomatoes, celery, aniseeds, and tomato purée and cook, uncovered, over moderate heat, for 10–15 minutes, or until you have a thick sauce. Season well.
6 Assemble the galette in a lightly greased 18cm (7in) spring mould. Put in one pancake, then sandwich in the different fillings (reserving some of the tomato sauce) between the pancakes. End with a pancake.
7 Bake in the oven for 10–15 minutes. Turn out and serve with the remaining tomato sauce and extra grated Parmesan.

Mushroom salad in tofu

Illustrated on page 192

NUTRIENTS PER PORTION
75 Calories
Protein 5g ● Fibre 3g ●
Polyunsaturated fats 2g ● ● Saturated fats 1g ● ● ●
Vitamins B2, N
Minerals Ca, Fe, K, Mg

Ingredients
350g (12oz) button mushrooms, sliced
15ml (1 tbsp) oil
1 clove garlic, crushed
50g (2oz) shelled walnuts
½ packet silken tofu – approx. 150g (5oz)
15ml (1 tbsp) lemon juice
salt and pepper
3–4 spring onions, sliced lengthways
Serves 4

The lemon dressing adds a pleasant tang to the salad.
1 Toss the mushrooms in the oil with the garlic.
2 Toast the walnuts for 2–3 minutes under a hot grill. Chop.
3 Mix together the tofu and lemon juice. Season well and stir into the mushroom slices.
4 Either mix in the spring onions and toasted walnuts or arrange them on top as a garnish.

Avocado and kiwi salad

Illustrated on page 193

NUTRIENTS PER PORTION
330 Calories
Protein 5g ● Fibre 4g ● ●
Polyunsaturated fats 4g ● ● Saturated fats 3g ●
Vitamins A, C, FA, N
Minerals Fe, K

Ingredients
2 large avocados, diced
4 kiwi fruit, peeled and sliced
1 tbsp finely chopped parsley
1 tbsp snipped chives
90ml (6 tbsp) vinaigrette (see p.219)
½ small cucumber, cut into julienne strips
2 sticks celery, cut into julienne strips
1 lettuce
1 bunch watercress, cleaned – approx. 50g (2oz)
Serves 4

To give contrast to the salad, use raddicchio rosso leaves instead of the green lettuce.
1 Toss avocados, kiwi fruit, and herbs in half the vinaigrette.
2 Toss the cucumber and celery in the remaining vinaigrette.
3 To serve, arrange the lettuce leaves and watercress in a dish. Pile on the avocado and kiwi fruit and arrange the cucumber and celery julienne on top.

Blackcurrant yogurt ice cream

Illustrated on page 193

NUTRIENTS PER PORTION
90 Calories
Protein 6g ● ● Fibre 2g ●
Polyunsaturated fats 1g ● ● ● Saturated fats 1g ● ● ●
Vitamins B2, C, N
Minerals Ca, K

Ingredients
570ml (1 pint) yogurt
5ml (1 tsp) vanilla essence
30ml (2 tbsp) honey
100–175g (4–6oz) blackcurrants, topped and tailed
30ml (2 tbsp) orange juice
25g (1oz) light raw sugar
2 egg whites
Serves 6

Redcurrants, blackberries, bilberries, or gooseberries could also be used, as could stoned black cherries.
1 Mix together the yogurt, vanilla essence, and honey, and freeze until mushy – about 1 hour.
2 Put the blackcurrants in a pan with the orange juice and sugar. Cover and simmer over low heat for 5 minutes (gooseberries would take about 10 minutes).
3 Remove from the heat and let the fruit steep for 30 minutes. Strain and allow to cool completely.
4 Stir the fruit into the yogurt. Freeze for 1 hour. Whisk the egg white until stiff, fold them in and freeze for 1–2 hours or until ice cream is firm.

Outdoor Lunch

A wholesome meal that can easily be popped in plastic boxes to take on a picnic. The major source of protein is the celery and green pepper flan, with the wild rice salad, fruit pie, and the slice of bread being the major sources of fibre.

NUTRIENTS PER PORTION
Protein 37g ● ● ●   Fibre 23g ● ● ●
Polyunsaturated fats 17g ● ● ●   Saturated fats 9g ● ● ●
Vitamins A, B₁, B₂, B₆, B₁₂, E, FA, N
Minerals Ca, Cu, Fe, Mg, Zn

1095 Calories

Summer soup

Wholewheat bread

Green bean julienne

Celery and green pepper flan

Summer soup

Served chilled, this high-protein soup, based on lettuce and Chinese leaves, is an ideal starter for a summer meal. The cardamom and yogurt add to the delicate flavour of the main ingredients.

Celery and green pepper flan

This high-protein, low-fat flan is a simple combination of vegetables in a well-flavoured, milky sauce. The horseradish and celery seeds add a special tang to the taste of the filling. The wholewheat pastry base is an excellent source of fibre and, because it has to be rolled out thinly, is light and delicate in texture.

Green bean julienne

Salads are often used to provide a contrast in texture, as well as taste, and this is certainly true of this dish, where raw green beans and fresh celery have been used to complement the soft filling of the flan.

Wild rice salad

This salad is an interesting combination of textures and tastes – the firmness of the rice is set off by the peppery taste of the watercress and the spiciness of the fresh root ginger.

Wholewheat bread

This type of bread is one of the best sources of fibre in our diet. It is important not to use refined flours, as most of their nutrients and roughage have been removed in manufacture.

Fresh fruit pie

Pies need not be unhealthy so long as you use the freshest ingredients. Use a good wholewheat pastry and do not use sugar. In this pie, the fresh peaches and pears are sweetened with sultanas, and they are enclosed in a light yeasted pastry.

Apple juice

High in Vitamin C, apple juice is available both still and carbonated. Always choose natural juices, and read the label to check that there are no preservatives or added colourings. A glass of apple juice only contains about 50 calories.

Apple juice

Wild rice salad

Fresh fruit pie

Summer soup

Illustrated on page 196

Ingredients

10ml (2 tsp) sunflower oil
3 spring onions, chopped
1 round lettuce, shredded
100g (4oz) Chinese leaves,
shredded
150ml (¼ pint) skimmed milk
300ml (½ pint) yogurt
8 cardamom seeds, crushed
a little lemon juice
gomasio, or salt if preferred
black pepper
Serves 4

NUTRIENTS PER PORTION
50 Calories
Protein 3g ● ● ●   Fibre 1g ●
Polyunsaturated fats 1g ● ● ●   Saturated fats 0g ● ● ●
Vitamins A, C, E
Minerals Ca, Mg

Large portions of soup can be daunting, so try serving just enough to whet the appetite. This chilled soup is high in protein and low in fat.

1 Heat the oil in a large saucepan and gently fry the onions for about 3 minutes.

2 Add the lettuce and Chinese leaves to the pan, cover, and cook for 5–8 minutes.

3 Transfer the lettuce mixture to a liquidizer and add the milk and yogurt. Liquidize until smooth.

4 Mix in the cardamom seeds and lemon juice. Season with gomasio and pepper.

5 Chill thoroughly before serving.

Celery and green pepper flan

Illustrated on page 196

Ingredients

1 quantity of low-fat or shortcrust
pastry (see p.109)
425ml (¾ pint) skimmed milk
½ onion
4 peppercorns
blade of mace
30ml (2 tbsp) sunflower oil
6 sticks celery, chopped
1 large green pepper, deseeded and
diced
2.5ml (½ tsp) celery seeds
25g (1oz) wholewheat flour
2 eggs
15ml (1 tbsp) grated horseradish
2.5ml (½ tsp) paprika
gomasio, or salt if preferred
black pepper
For garnishing
2.5ml (½ tsp) paprika
Serves 6

NUTRIENTS PER PORTION
360 Calories
Protein 13g ● ● ●   Fibre 2g ●
Polyunsaturated fats 7g ● ● ●   Saturated fats 3g ● ● ●
Vitamins B2, B6, B12, C, E, FA, N
Minerals Ca, Cu, Fe, Mg, Zn

Flans and quiches are often synonymous with rich cheese fillings and are therefore rather high in fat. It is best to use simple vegetable combinations which, when bound together with a well-flavoured sauce, produce delicious, tasty, light, and low-fat results.

1 Preheat the oven to gas mark 6, 200°C (400°F).

2 Roll out the pastry and line a 20cm (8in) flan ring. Prick the base well and bake blind for 4 minutes.

3 Meanwhile, place the milk in a saucepan with the onion, peppercorns, and mace. Bring almost to the boil, remove from the heat and leave to infuse for 10 minutes. Strain and reserve the flavoured milk.

4 Heat the oil in a large saucepan and cook the celery, green pepper, and celery seeds very slowly for 10–15 minutes.

5 Add the flour and cook for 3 minutes, stirring well.

6 Pour over the flavoured milk and mix well. Bring the sauce to the boil and simmer for 5 minutes, stirring. Cool slightly.

7 Beat in the eggs, then add the horseradish, paprika, gomasio, and the pepper.

8 Pour the filling into the pastry case and dust with paprika.

9 Bake for 30–35 minutes. Serve warm.

Green bean julienne

NUTRIENTS PER PORTION
Protein 2g ● *Fibre 3g* ● ●
Polyunsaturated fats 5g ● ● ● *Saturated fats 1g* ● ●
Vitamins C, E
Minerals –

80 *Calories*

Illustrated on page 196

Ingredients
225g (8oz) French beans
8 sticks celery
25g (1oz) sunflower seeds
For the dressing
juice of ½ lemon
15ml (1 tbsp) sunflower oil
5ml (1 tsp) concentrated apple juice
gomasio, or salt if preferred
black pepper
Serves 4

French beans are excellent raw, but if you prefer them cooked, steam them to preserve their nutrients.
1 Slice the French beans into matchstick-sized lengths. Cut the celery into julienne strips. Place in a bowl and mix together.
2 Put the dressing ingredients in a screw-top jar and mix thoroughly. Pour over salad, toss well, and add sunflower seeds.

Wild rice salad

NUTRIENTS PER PORTION
Protein 2g ● *Fibre 3g* ● ● ●
Polyunsaturated fats 2g ● ● ● *Saturated fats 0.5g* ● ● ●
Vitamins A, C, E
Minerals –

110 *Calories*

Illustrated on page 197

Ingredients
75g (3oz) wild rice
100g (4oz) carrot, grated
1 large bunch watercress
For the dressing
15ml (1 tbsp) sunflower oil
rind and juice of ½ orange
5ml (1 tsp) concentrated apple juice
1cm (½in) fresh root ginger, grated
shoyu, or salt if preferred
black pepper
Serves 4

This salad is delicious served with a high-protein bean dish.
1 Measure the rice. Bring twice the volume of water, about 225–300ml (8–10fl oz), to the boil. Add the rice, cover and simmer for 35–40 minutes, or until just tender. Drain.
2 Put dressing ingredients in a screw-top jar; mix well. Pour over warm rice and mix. Cool. Add carrot and watercress.

Fresh fruit pie

NUTRIENTS PER PORTION
Protein 11g ● ● *Fibre 8g* ● ● ●
Polyunsaturated fats 1g ● *Saturated fats 5g* ● ●
Vitamins A, B1, B2, B12, C, D, N
Minerals Fe, Mg, Zn

385 *Calories*

Illustrated on page 197

Ingredients
450g (1lb) dessert pears (Williams or Comice)
3 medium peaches, skinned
50g (2oz) sultanas
150ml (¼ pint) white wine or apple juice
2.5ml (½ tsp) ground coriander
12 cardamom seeds
5ml (1 tsp) arrowroot
1 quantity of yeasted pastry (see p.112)
1 egg, beaten
Serves 4–6

It takes time to adjust to eating sugar-free fruit dishes. Pick ripe fruit for the best flavour and use dried fruit for extra sweetness. This pie is high in most vitamins, iron, and zinc.
1 Coarsely chop the fruit. Place in a saucepan with the sultanas, wine or apple juice, coriander, and cardamon seeds. Cook, uncovered, over a gentle heat for 15–20 minutes. Remove seeds. Preheat oven to gas mark 6, 200°C (400°F).
2 Dissolve the arrowroot in a little water and add to the fruit. Bring to the boil, stirring, and simmer for 2–3 minutes.
3 Divide pastry dough in half. Roll out one portion and line a 20cm (8in) pie plate. Spoon in fruit. Moisten edges with water.
4 Roll out the remaining pastry for the lid. Seal and crimp the pastry edges. Brush with beaten egg.
5 Bake for 25–30 minutes, or until the pastry is cooked.

Light Lunch

This meal, with its creamy soup, moist main course, and aubergine side dish, looks filling but is light on calories, and it is, in fact, low in saturated fats. The lentil pourgouri and sweet red pepper soup are the major sources of protein, with mangetout being served to improve the overall balance of fibre.

NUTRIENTS PER PORTION
Protein 27g ● ● ● *Fibre 24g* ● ● ●
Polyunsaturated fats 5g ● ● ● *Saturated fats 3g* ● ● ●
Vitamins C, B₁, FA
Minerals Ca, Fe

620 *Calories*

Sweet red pepper soup

Red and white salad

Lentil pourgouri

Sweet red pepper soup
A rich soup, deriving its creaminess from high-protein, low-fat, tofu.

Lentil pourgouri
This simple, fragrant-tasting Middle Eastern dish is a combination of bulgar wheat, lentils, and courgettes. It is served with yogurt, which adds moisture to the dish.

Aubergine bake
This dish is low in saturated fats, largely because the aubergine is baked and not fried. The dwarf sweetcorn provides an appealing, crunchy texture. The moistness of the dish ensures that the intrinsic dryness of the bulgar wheat does not overpower the whole meal.

Steamed mangetout
These sweet-tasting pea pods should be so tender when raw that they need only the briefest steaming.

Red and white salad
A light way to end a substantial meal, this salad contrasts the smoothness of the lychees with the granular bite of the strawberries.

Wine
Healthy living need not preclude alcohol in moderation, and many white wines such as hock and Riesling have a low alcohol content – look for those around 9° to 10° proof. Remember, a glass of wine will add 75 calories to the meal.

Aubergine bake

Wine

Steamed mangetout

Sweet red pepper soup

Illustrated on page 200

Ingredients
*2 medium red peppers, halved
and deseeded
10ml (2 tsp) olive oil
1 medium onion, finely chopped
1 clove garlic, crushed
225g (8oz) tomatoes, skinned and
chopped
30ml (2 tbsp) tomato purée
300ml (½ pint) vegetable stock
(see p.120)
5ml (1 tsp) dried marjoram
275g (10oz) silken tofu
gomasio, or salt if preferred
black pepper*
Serves 4

NUTRIENTS PER PORTION
100 Calories
*Protein 7g ● ● ●   Fibre 2g ●
Polyunsaturated fats 2g ● ● ●   Saturated fats 1g ● ● ●
Vitamins A, B1, B2, C, FA, N
Minerals Ca, Cu, Fe*

This soup derives its richness from the tofu – a good way of providing a creamy texture while keeping fats low and protein content high.

1 Preheat the oven to gas mark 4, 180°C (350°F). Place the peppers in an ovenproof dish and bake for 15–20 minutes, turning them over occasionally so that the skin chars. Cool, then peel off the skin and dice the flesh finely.
2 Heat the oil in a large saucepan and gently fry the onion and garlic for 4–5 minutes, or until soft.
3 Add the red pepper, tomatoes, purée, stock, and marjoram. Bring to the boil, cover, and simmer for 30 minutes.
4 Cut the tofu into pieces and liquidize until smooth. Pour into the soup and stir well. Season with gomasio and pepper. Heat through gently and serve hot.

Lentil pourgouri

Illustrated on page 200

Ingredients
*10ml (2 tsp) olive oil
100g (4oz) green lentils, cleaned
5ml (1 tsp) ground allspice
12 cardamom pods, cracked
225g (8oz) bulgar wheat
25g (1oz) currants
450g (1lb) courgettes, sliced
gomasio, or salt if preferred
black pepper*
For garnishing
*30ml (2 tbsp) sesame seeds
5ml (1 tsp) coriander seeds*
For serving
*hung yogurt
steamed mangetout*
Serves 4

NUTRIENTS PER PORTION
340 Calories
*Protein 14g ● ● ●   Fibre 3g ● ●
Polyunsaturated fats 1g ●   Saturated fats 1g ● ● ●
Vitamins C, FA
Minerals Fe, Mg*

This simple, fragrant Middle Eastern dish is high in protein, low in saturated fats, and is a good source of iron.

1 Heat the oil in a large saucepan and gently fry the lentils and spices for 3–4 minutes.
2 Add 600ml (1 pint) cold water. Cover and simmer for about 30 minutes.
3 Add the bulgar wheat and currants and a little extra water if the mixture begins to look too dry. Cook for 10 minutes, stirring frequently.
4 Meanwhile, steam the courgettes for about 6 minutes. Mix the courgettes into the lentil mix. Season with some gomasio and pepper.
5 For the garnish: dry roast the seeds in a heavy-based pan for 3–4 minutes. Crush them to a fine powder using a pestle and mortar or a coffee grinder.
6 Spoon the pourgouri on to a warm serving dish and sprinkle over the garnish. Serve with the hung yogurt and steamed mangetout.

Aubergine bake

Illustrated on page 201

NUTRIENTS PER PORTION
Protein 2g ● ● *Fibre 3g* ● ●
Polyunsaturated fats 2g ● ● ● *Saturated fats 0.5g* ● ● ●
Vitamins C, E
Minerals –

141
Calories

Ingredients
1 medium aubergine
10ml (2 tsp) sunflower oil
1 medium onion, finely chopped
2.5ml (½ tsp) cumin seeds
2.5ml (½ tsp) turmeric
5ml (1 tsp) ground coriander
5ml (1 tsp) garam masala
1 medium green pepper, deseeded
and diced
100g (4oz) dwarf sweetcorn
15ml (1 tbsp) tomato purée
150ml (¼ pint) vegetable stock or
water
10ml (2 tsp) shoyu
black pepper
Serves 4

The aubergine in this recipe is baked and not fried, so the fat content remains desirably low. It can be served with other baked savouries, like pine kernel roast (see p. 169).
1 Preheat the oven to gas mark 6, 200°C (400°F).
2 Remove the aubergine stalk. Prick the skin 2–3 times. Bake for 15–20 minutes or until soft. Cool and chop the vegetable into bite-sized pieces.
3 Heat the oil in a large saucepan and gently fry the onion for 4–5 minutes. Stir in the spices and fry for 3 minutes.
4 Add the baked aubergine pieces, green pepper, and sweetcorn, and mix in well.
5 Dissolve the tomato purée in the stock. Pour all over the vegetables.
6 Transfer to an ovenproof dish. Reduce the oven temperature to gas mark 4, 180°C (350°F). Cover the dish and bake for 45 minutes. Season with shoyu and pepper. Serve hot.

Red and white salad

Illustrated on page 200

NUTRIENTS PER PORTION
Protein 2g ● *Fibre 4g* ● ●
Polyunsaturated fats 0g ● ● ● *Saturated fats 0g* ● ● ●
Vitamins C
Minerals –

80
Calories

Ingredients
350g (12oz) lychees
225g (8oz) red fruit (strawberries,
cherries, or raspberries)
15ml (1 tbsp) Kirsch
Serves 4

With the fruits used here, the dish is high in Vitamin C.
1 Peel the lychees. Using a small, sharp knife, cut in half and remove the stone. It is easier to try to find the top of the stone and work down towards the stem end, splitting open the fruit.
2 To prepare the red fruit: hull and slice the strawberries, stone the cherries, but leave the raspberries whole.
3 Mix the fruits together in a bowl and toss in the Kirsch. Leave to stand for 2 hours before serving.

Celebration Dinner Party

This is a filling and impressive meal, and most of the dishes can be prepared in advance for easy planning. It provides plenty of fibre and protein as well as a good level of vitamins and minerals.

The fat content is relatively high but there is a greater proportion of polyunsaturated fats than saturated fats. The thick mushroom soup is low on calories to prepare you for the spicy and substantial Byzantine mullet pilaf, which is balanced by the flavour of the lighter, tangy beansprout salad. The spinach is a wonderful source of fibre, protein, vitamins, and minerals, and the winter fruit compôte keeps its calories down with a delicious low-fat cashew cream sauce made with low-fat cottage cheese, cashew nuts, and honey.

NUTRIENTS PER PORTION
1085 Calories
Protein 25g ● ● ●   *Fibre 23g* ● ● ●
Polyunsaturated fats 23g ● ● ●   *Saturated fats 29g* ● ●
Vitamins A, B, B2, C, E, FA, N
Minerals Ca, Fe, K, Mg, Zn

Mushroom soup with herbs
This soup with mushrooms, and red wine, flavoured with parsley, bay, marjoram, and tarragon, can be made in advance and frozen.

Byzantine millet pilaf
A pilaf with coriander, apricots, and aubergines in sesame sauce, this dish can be prepared in advance and frozen.

Spinach darioles
Spinach leaves are stuffed with tomatoes and flavoured with basil (or oregano, if liked) and spring onions.

Beansprout salad
Mung beansprouts are combined with sweet peppers, button mushrooms, and celery. They are then tossed in a dressing made from oil, vinegar, shoyu, and seasoning, to make a colourful salad, which is chilled before serving.

Rhubarb with cashew cream
Rhubarb, pink grapefruit, and pears in wine can be served hot or cold. The "cream" to go with them is based on cashew nuts and cottage cheese.

Spinach darioles

Beansprout salad

Rhubarb with
cashew cream

Byzantine millet
pilaf

Mushroom soup
with herbs

Illustrated in page 205

Ingredients

45ml (3 tbsp) sunflower oil
1 medium onion, finely chopped
2 bay leaves
1 tsp chopped marjoram
1 tsp chopped tarragon
225g (8oz) mushrooms, chopped
425ml (3/4 pint) dark vegetable
stock (see p.120)
50ml (2fl oz) red wine
30ml (2 tbsp) tomato purée
2 tbsp chopped parsley
Serves 4

Mushroom soup with herbs

NUTRIENTS PER PORTION
130 Calories
Protein 2g Fibre 3g ● ●
Polyunsaturated fats 6g ● ● *Saturated fats 2g* ●
Vitamins A, C, E, FA, N
Minerals K

For extra flavour, you can include some dried mushrooms and use their soaking water in the vegetable stock.

1 Heat the oil in a large, heavy-based pan and sauté the onion and herbs gently for about 5 minutes.

2 Add the mushrooms and cook for another 5 minutes or until they are well browned.

3 Stir in the stock, wine, tomato purée, and parsley. Bring to the boil, cover, and simmer for 30–45 minutes.

4 Remove the bay leaves, season to taste and serve hot. Croûtons or crackers go well with this soup.

Illustrated on page 205

Ingredients

2 medium aubergines, thickly sliced
olive oil for frying
30ml (2 tbsp) tahini
30ml (2 tbsp) water
juice of 1/2 lemon
1 clove garlic, crushed
5ml (1 tsp) shoyu
For the millet pilaf
1 small onion, finely chopped
15ml (1 tbsp) olive oil
1 large clove garlic, crushed
1 tsp ground coriander
175g (6oz) millet grains
100g (4oz) dried apricots, washed
4 cloves
225ml (8fl oz) white wine or cider
450ml (16fl oz) boiling water
salt and pepper
fresh, chopped coriander
Serves 4

Byzantine millet pilaf

NUTRIENTS PER PORTION
470 Calories
Protein 8g ● ● *Fibre 11g* ● ● ●
Polyunsaturated fats 2g ● ● ● *Saturated fats 3g* ● ● ●
Vitamins A, B1, B2, B6, FA, N
Minerals Ca, Fe, K, Mg, Zn

The combination of apricots and grains, topped with aubergines baked in a sesame sauce, is greatly influenced by Middle Eastern cookery.

1 Preheat the oven to gas mark 4, 180°C (350°F).

2 Lightly sauté the aubergine slices in the olive oil until just browned and softened. Arrange them in layers in a shallow ovenproof dish.

3 Mix the tahini with the water in a bowl. Add the lemon juice, garlic, and shoyu and blend together thoroughly. Pour this over the aubergine slices and bake, uncovered, for 20 minutes. Keep warm.

4 Meanwhile, gently fry the onion in 15ml (1 tbsp) olive oil for 3–4 minutes until soft. Add the garlic, coriander, and millet and fry for another 2–3 minutes.

5 Cut the apricots into thin slivers. Add them to the frying pan together with the cloves, white wine or cider, and boiling water. Bring back to the boil and simmer for 20 minutes or until the millet is cooked. Season well and serve hot with the aubergines, sprinkled with fresh coriander.

Spinach darioles

Illustrated on page 204

50
Calories

NUTRIENTS PER PORTION
Protein 3g ● Fibre 2g ●
Polyunsaturated fats Trace Saturated fats Trace
Vitamins A, C, FA
Minerals Ca, Fe, K, Mg

Ingredients
225g (8oz) spinach
225g (8oz) tomatoes, skinned and
sliced
3–4 tsp chopped basil
2–3 spring onions, finely chopped
pepper
a little vegetable oil
1 tomato, sliced
Serves 4

Delicious with most egg dishes, the spinach also complements bakes, roasts, or pilafs such as buckwheat roast (see p. 172) or peanut stroganov. This dish looks particularly attractive in the individual moulds.

1 Preheat the oven to gas mark 4, 180°C (350°F), and bring a large pan of water to the boil.
2 Blanch the spinach for a minute in the boiling water so that it becomes slightly wilted. Drain, refresh under cold, running water, and remove any coarse stems.
3 Lightly grease 8 dariole moulds or an 18cm (7in) flan dish. Line with a little over half the spinach leaves, allowing them to overlap the top.
4 Fill with layers of tomato slices, sprinkling each layer with basil, spring onions, and pepper. Fold the edges of the spinach over the top and cover with the remaining spinach.
5 Put a small ovenproof plate or weight on top, brush any exposed leaves with a little vegetable oil, and bake for 35–40 minutes. Turn out and serve decorated with tomato slices.

Rhubarb with cashew cream

Illustrated on page 205

270
Calories

NUTRIENTS PER PORTION
Protein 9g ●● Fibre 5g ●●
Polyunsaturated fats 8g ●● Saturated fats 2g ●
Vitamins C, E
Minerals Ca, Fe, K, Mg, Zn

Ingredients
1 large, firm pear
1 tbsp demerara sugar
175ml (6fl oz) red wine
550g (1¼lb) rhubarb, chopped into
2.5cm (1in) lengths
1 pink grapefruit, peeled and
chopped
15–30ml (1–2 tbsp) honey
For the cashew cream
100g (4oz) cashew nuts
100g (4oz) cottage cheese
15–30ml (1–2 tbsp) honey
up to 150ml (¼ pint) water
Serves 4

Made with low fat cottage cheese, the nut "cream" makes a perfect accompaniment to cooked fruit – and a healthy alternative to cream.

1 Peel the pear and cut it into chunks. Dissolve the sugar in the wine in a small pan and stew the pear, covered, over very low heat for 15 minutes. Strain, reserving the juice.
2 In a separate pan, stew the rhubarb and grapefruit with the honey over low heat for 10 minutes or until the rhubarb is tender but not disintegrating. Strain, reserving the juice.
3 Put the pear juice and rhubarb juice in a pan together and boil down hard until reduced by at least half and beginning to thicken. Combine the pear, rhubarb, and grapefruit in a serving bowl and pour the juice over. Leave to cool.
4 To make the cashew cream, blend all the ingredients together until very smooth. Serve with the rhubarb.

Exotic Evening Meal

This light but filling meal is an excellent balance of protein, fibre,
polyunsaturated and, to a lesser extent, saturated fats. It also
provides a subtle range of spicy and delicate tastes – from the
earthy artichoke soup to the leafy green parcels and julienne of
vegetables through to the fruity and light taste of the mango
and orange sorbet.

NUTRIENTS PER PORTION
880 Calories
Protein 21g ● ● ●   Fibre 30g ● ● ●
Polyunsaturated fats 14g ● ● ●   Saturated fats 5g ● ● ●
Vitamins A, C, E, FA
Minerals Ca, Cu, Fe, Mg, Zn

*Chinese leaf and
grapefruit salad*

*Julienne of winter
vegetables*

Artichoke soup

Artichoke soup
Artichokes are high in protein, and they have been used in this dish to produce a thick, substantial soup which, although creamy in taste, is low in saturated fats.

Leafy green parcels
These spinach and cabbage leaf parcels, enclosing a tasty coriander-flavoured mixture of hazelnuts and spinach, are high in fibre and low in saturated fats. Their flavour is complemented by the fruity taste of the apricot and tomato relish.

Julienne of winter vegetables
The carrots, parsnips, and turnips used here have been baked, both to preserve as many nutrients as possible and to retain the vegetables' firm texture and shape.

Chinese leaf and grapefruit salad
This salad combines the tangy taste of grapefruit with the crispness of the Chinese leaves, and it is offset by a yogurt dressing.

Apricot and tomato relish
This tasty, high-fibre, low-fat fruit and vegetable relish (see p.141) is a versatile accompaniment to bakes, stir-fries, and steamed vegetables.

Mango and orange sorbet
Sorbets provide a refreshing, low-fat end to a meal, and when including the fruits used here, will be high in Vitamins A and C.

Grape juice
It is possible to buy non-alcoholic juices which nevertheless have a similar taste to light, white wines. These are ideal alternatives for those who choose not to drink. A glass will contain about 70 calories.

Grape juice

Mango and orange sorbet

Apricot and tomato relish (see p.141)

Leafy green parcels

Illustrated on page 208

Ingredients

10ml (2 tsp) sunflower oil
1 medium onion, finely chopped
450g (1lb) Jerusalem artichokes,
peeled and diced
1 small potato, peeled and diced
300ml (½ pint) skimmed milk
300ml (½ pint) vegetable stock (see
p.120)
gomasio, or salt if preferred
white pepper
Serves 4–6

Artichoke soup

NUTRIENTS PER PORTION

95 *Calories*

Protein 5g ● ● ● *Fibre 1g* ●
Polyunsaturated fats 1g ● ● ● *Saturated fats 0g* ● ● ●
Vitamins C
Minerals Ca

Artichokes are high in protein and are used here to produce a delicious creamy soup.

1 Heat the oil in a large saucepan and gently fry the onion for 4–5 minutes, or until soft.

2 Add the artichokes and potato and cook lightly for about 5 minutes but do not allow to colour.

3 Pour on the milk and stock. Bring to the boil, cover, and simmer for 25–30 minutes.

4 Cool slightly, then liquidize until smooth. Season with gomasio and pepper and reheat before serving.

Illustrated on page 209

Ingredients

8 large spinach leaves
8 spring cabbage leaves
For the filling
225g (8oz) spinach, washed
10ml (2 tsp) sunflower oil
1 medium onion, finely chopped
175g (6oz) hazelnuts, ground
50g (2oz) wholewheat breadcrumbs
30ml (2 tbsp) finely chopped fresh
coriander leaves
30ml (2 tbsp) finely chopped fresh
parsley
1 egg
15ml (1 tbsp) shoyu
black pepper
Serves 4

Leafy green parcels

NUTRIENTS PER PORTION

270 *Calories*

Protein 9g ● ● *Fibre 10g* ● ● ●
Polyunsaturated fats 4g ● ● ● *Saturated fats 2g* ● ● ●
Vitamins A, B6, C, E, FA
Minerals Ca, Fe, Mg, Zn

These attractive parcels are an excellent source of fibre and iron. Serve with tomato and apricot relish (see p. 141).

1 Wash then blanch the spinach and cabbage leaves for 2 minutes in a little boiling water. Drain.

2 For the filling: shred the spinach finely. Place in a saucepan, cover and cook, with only the water still adhering to the leaves, for 6 minutes.

3 Heat the oil in another saucepan and gently fry the onion for 4–5 minutes, or until soft. Add the hazelnuts and breadcrumbs and cook for 2 minutes.

4 Remove from the heat, add the herbs, cooked spinach, egg, and shoyu. Season with pepper.

5 Preheat the oven to gas mark 4, 180°C (350°F).

6 Take one cabbage and one spinach leaf. Place 30–45ml (2–3 tbsp) of the filling on each. Fold in the sides to the centre and roll up into a parcel. Continue using cabbage and spinach leaves alternately until you have used all the leaves.

7 Place in a lightly oiled ovenproof dish. Add 30–45ml (2–3 tbsp) water. Cover and bake for 30 minutes.

Julienne of winter vegetables

Illustrated on page 208

NUTRIENTS PER PORTION
Protein 2g ● *Fibre 4g* ● ●
Polyunsaturated fats 4g ● ● ● *Saturated fats 1g* ● ● ●
Vitamins A, C, E
Minerals –

180 Calories

Ingredients
30ml (2 tbsp) sunflower oil
10ml (2 tsp) maple syrup
10ml (2 tsp) whole grain mustard
550g (1¼lb) mixed root vegetables,
cut into matchstick-sized pieces
gomasio, or salt if preferred
black pepper
Serves 4

Serve with a high-protein and high-mineral dish.
1 Preheat the oven to gas mark 6, 200°C (400°F).
2 Heat oil in ovenproof dish. Mix syrup and mustard together.
3 Put vegetables in the dish, add mustard mix and toss well.
4 Cover and bake for 25–30 minutes. Add water if vegetables begin to look dry. Season with gomasio and pepper. Serve hot.

Chinese leaf and grapefruit salad

Illustrated on page 208

NUTRIENTS PER PORTION
Protein 5g ● ● *Fibre 1g* ●
Polyunsaturated fats 6g ● ● ● *Saturated fats 2g* ● ●
Vitamins A, C, E, FA
Minerals Ca, Fe, Mg

160 Calories

Ingredients
1 grapefruit
350g (12oz) Chinese leaves,
shredded
For the dressing
1 egg yolk
45ml (3 tbsp) sunflower oil
15ml (1 tbsp) grapefruit juice
30ml (2 tbsp) hung yogurt
For garnishing
salad cress
Serves 4

If you are watching your fat intake, use plain not hung yogurt.
1 Place the grapefruit on a board and cut downwards to remove the peel and pith. To separate each segment from its membrane, hold the grapefruit over a bowl to catch the juice cut on either side of the membrane to release skinless segments. Dice the segments. Reserve 15ml (1 tbsp) grapefruit juice.
2 For the dressing, beat the egg yolk. Add the oil a drop at a time to make a mayonnaise. When 30ml (2 tbsp) have been added, mix in the grapefruit juice.
3 Add remaining oil, 5ml (1 tsp) at a time, then the yogurt.
4 Combine the Chinese leaves and grapefruit in a bowl.
5 Mix dressing into salad, toss and garnish with cress.

Mango and orange sorbet

Illustrated on page 209

NUTRIENTS PER PORTION
Protein 2g ● *Fibre 2g* ●
Polyunsaturated fats 0g ● ● ● *Saturated fats 0g* ● ● ●
Vitamins A, C
Minerals –

110 Calories

Ingredients
2 mangos
juice of 1 orange
5ml (1 tsp) orange rind
15ml (1 tbsp) Cointreau (optional)
1 egg white, beaten
Serves 4

Use a liquidizer to blend the frozen purée and egg white.
1 Peel the mangos and cut the flesh away from the stone.
2 Put the mango flesh, orange juice and rind, Cointreau, if using, into a liquidizer and blend until smooth. Transfer to a freezerproof container and freeze for 1–2 hours.
3 Remove from freezer and liquidize until broken up.
4 Beat the egg white until stiff and fold into the fruit purée. Freeze again for 2–3 hours.

Weekday Supper

This substantial meal is both satisfying and simple to prepare. It provides both protein and fibre, but remains low in fat. The relatively low protein levels of the strudel and salads are balanced out by the meals as a whole, which, apart from the nutritional element, is a happy blend of colour, texture, and taste.

NUTRIENTS PER PORTION
1175 Calories
Protein 36g ● ● ●   Fibre 27g ● ● ●
Polyunsaturated fats 17g ● ● ●   Saturated fats 7g ● ● ●
Vitamins A, B1, B6, C, E, FA, N
Minerals Ca, Cu, Fe, Mg, Zn

Crunchy green salad

Fennel risotto

Spiced bean pâté and banana raita

Beans make excellent bases for vegetarian pâtés because they are high in protein and fibre but low in fat. The bean pâté shown here was well flavoured with coriander and cumin, and made slightly hot with the addition of ginger and chilli. The spiciness is complemented by a cooling raita, and the whole dish is served with crisp crudités of yellow peppers, cucumber, and celery.

Fennel risotto

High in fibre and low in fat, this tangy-tasting rice dish has all the creaminess of a classic risotto. The walnuts add a crunchiness to the overall texture of the dish.

Crunchy green salad

Despite a creamy mayonnaise dressing, this salad remains low in saturated fats. This is largely because yogurt and fruit juice have been used instead of oil. Chinese leaves were used to make up this salad, but crispy white cabbage could have been chosen.

Radicchio salad

In a meal that already has ample sources of protein and fibre, this salad is used to provide additional variety of texture and colour. Radicchio was used here, and mixed with carrot, chicory, mustard, and cress before being tossed in an olive oil, lemon juice, mustard, and black pepper dressing. Chinese leaves or lamb's lettuce can be used instead of the radicchio.

Apple strudel

This light fruit pudding, based on the classic European pastry, is high in fibre and, for pastry, low in fat, especially when served with yogurt or smetana instead of cream.

Fruit juice

Avoid artificially flavoured drinks and those with added preservatives. Choose fresh fruit juice or water instead. (A glass of orange juice contains about 65 calories.) For a long, refreshing drink, add some sparkling water to the juice.

Fruit juice

Spiced bean pâté and banana raita

Radicchio salad

Apple strudel

Illustrated on page 213

Ingredients

100g (4oz) Dutch brown beans or
ful medames, soaked overnight
5ml (1 tsp) coriander seeds
2.5ml (½ tsp) cumin seeds
5ml (1 tsp) black mustard seeds
30ml (2 tbsp) sunflower oil
1 medium onion, finely chopped
1 clove garlic, crushed
1 fresh green chilli, deseeded and
diced
1cm (½in) fresh root ginger, peeled
and grated
1.25ml (¼ tsp) garam masala
1.25ml (¼ tsp) turmeric
15ml (1 tbsp) tomato purée
juice of 1 lemon
gomasio, or salt if preferred
black pepper
For the banana raita
1 banana, sliced
150ml (¼ pint) yogurt
2.5ml (½ tsp) roasted cumin seeds
Serves 4–6

Spiced bean pâté

NUTRIENTS PER PORTION
190 *Calories*
Protein 9g ● ● ●   *Fibre 8g* ● ● ●
Polyunsaturated fats 4g ● ● ●   *Saturated fats 1g* ● ● ●
Vitamins B1, C, N
Minerals Ca, Fe, Mg

Beans make excellent bases for vegetarian pâtés because they are high in protein and fibre but low in fat. They do, however, need to be well flavoured with spices or herbs. The taste improves if the pâté is kept covered in the refrigerator for a few days before serving.

1 Drain the beans. Cover with plenty of fresh water, bring uncovered to the boil, and boil fast for 10 minutes. Reduce the heat, skim, cover, and simmer for about 40 minutes, or until soft. Drain.

2 Dry roast the coriander, cumin, and mustard seeds in a heavy-based pan for about 3–4 minutes, until they start to pop, shaking the pan from time to time.

3 Add the oil to the pan and lightly fry the onion and garlic for 4–5 minutes until soft. Stir in the chilli, ginger, garam masala, and turmeric and cook for 3–4 minutes. Add the cooked beans and stir well.

4 Liquidize the mixture until smooth, adding the tomato purée and lemon juice. Season with gomasio and pepper. Leave overnight for the flavours to blend.

5 To make the banana raita, mix the banana, yogurt, and cumin seeds together. Serve with the pâté.

Illustrated on page 212

Ingredients

10ml (2 tsp) sunflower oil
1 medium onion, finely chopped
5ml (1 tsp) grated lemon rind
450g (1lb) fennel, diced
225g (8oz) short-grain brown rice
350ml (12fl oz) boiling water
350g (12oz) tomatoes, skinned and
chopped
juice of ½ lemon
50g (2oz) walnuts, roughly chopped
gomasio, or salt if preferred
black pepper
For garnishing
a fennel fond
Serves 4

Fennel risotto

NUTRIENTS PER PORTION
320 *Calories*
Protein 7g ●   *Fibre 7g* ● ● ●
Polyunsaturated fats 6g ● ● ●   *Saturated fats 1g* ● ● ●
Vitamins B6, C, E, FA
Minerals Cu

This tangy rice dish is high in fibre and low in fat, despite having all the creaminess of a classic risotto.

1 Heat the oil in a large saucepan and gently fry the onion for 4–5 minutes, or until soft.

2 Add the lemon rind and fennel and cook for 2–3 minutes.

3 Add the rice and one cup, about 250ml (8fl oz), of the boiling water. Stir, bring to the boil and cook covered, until all the water has been absorbed, whilst stirring occasionally.

4 Add the tomatoes, lemon juice, walnuts and ½ cup, about 100ml (4fl oz), boiling water. Stir again and cook until all the liquid is absorbed. If the rice is not yet cooked, add a little more boiling water if necessary.

5 Once cooked, the risotto should be creamy. Season with gomasio and pepper. Garnish with a fennel frond. Serve hot.

Crunchy green salad

NUTRIENTS PER PORTION
100 Calories
Protein 2g ● Fibre 2g ●
Polyunsaturated fats 3g ● ● ● Saturated fats 1g ● ●
Vitamins C
Minerals –

Illustrated on page 212

Ingredients
*225g (8oz) white cabbage or
Chinese leaves, shredded
1 small green pepper, deseeded and
diced
3 sticks celery, chopped
3 spring onions, diced
For the dressing
45ml (3 tbsp) mayonnaise
30ml (2 tbsp) yogurt
15ml (1 tbsp) orange juice
5ml (1 tsp) grated orange rind
herb salt, or salt if preferred
For garnishing
½ bunch watercress*
Serves 4

This is the ideal salad to serve with a rich grain or pulse dish.
1 Prepare and mix the vegetables together in a large bowl.
2 Stir the dressing ingredients together to make a thin cream.
3 Mix the dressing, pour over the salad and toss. Garnish with watercress. Serve chilled.

Apple strudel

NUTRIENTS PER PORTION
410 Calories
Protein 8g ● Fibre 7g ● ● ●
Polyunsaturated fats 3g ● ● Saturated fats 2g ● ● ●
Vitamins B1, E
Minerals Ca, Cu, Fe, Mg

Illustrated on page 213

Ingredients
*1 quantity of strudel pastry (see
p.113)
For the filling
15g (½oz) butter
50g (2oz) wholewheat breadcrumbs
450g (1lb) crisp dessert apples
100g (4oz) raisins
50g (2oz) flaked almonds
10ml (2 tsp) ground cinnamon
5ml (1 tsp) grated lemon rind
5ml (1 tsp) maple syrup
little melted butter
For the glaze
5ml (1 tsp) malt extract
5ml (1 tsp) concentrated apple juice*
Serves 6–8

This version of the classic pastry is slightly less rich, being virtually sugar-free. As it is high in fibre it is ideal to serve after a low-fibre main course. Breadcrumbs are incorporated here to absorb some of the fruit juices, to prevent the pastry from becoming soggy.
1 Melt the butter in a pan and gently fry the breadcrumbs for about 3 minutes until very lightly toasted.
2 Preheat the oven to gas mark 6, 200°C (400°F).
3 Finely slice the apples and mix with the raisins, flaked almonds, cinnamon, lemon rind, and maple syrup.
4 Pull out the dough very thinly on a floured cloth to form a rectangular shape.
5 Sprinkle over the breadcrumbs. Cover with the apple filling to within 1.5cm (½in) of the edges.
6 Brush the edges of the dough with melted butter. Fold in the long side edges over the filling so that they meet in the centre. Roll up the strudel like a Swiss roll.
7 Put on a lightly oiled baking sheet. Brush the top with a little melted butter. Bake for 45–50 minutes.
8 Remove from the oven. Mix the malt extract and concentrated apple juice together and brush over the strudel.

Impromptu Dinner Party

Colourful meal that is quick to prepare. The main pasta dish is an excellent source of carbohydrate, protein, and fibre. The vegetable dishes add a good level of vitamins and minerals.

NUTRIENTS PER PORTION
Protein 32g ● ● ●   *Fibre 17g* ● ● ●
Polyunsaturated fats 10g ● ● ●   *Saturated fats 21g* ● ●
Vitamins A, B, B1, B2, B6, B12, C, D, E
Minerals Ca, Fe, K, Mg, Zn

1380 *Calories*

Spaghetti with oil, garlic, and chilli sauce
Spaghetti aglio, olio, e peperoncino is the Italian name for this quickly made dish of pasta with garlic and chilli, much liked in its native land. Grated cheese is an optional extra.

Broccoli roulade
A roulade always looks impressive, but in fact is easy to make once you have mastered the technique – it only needs one or two practice runs.

Tomato sauce
Tomato sauce is easy to make in quantity and keeps well, whether frozen or in the refrigerator (see p.119).

Mangetout and mushroom salad
Make an impromptu salad with whatever you have to hand: use leftover grains or beans, and nuts or raisins as well as fresh salad vegetables as shown here, dressed with a vinaigrette sauce.

Steamed potatoes
Potatoes, lightly steamed and sprinkled with toasted almonds, are a good accompaniment to the roulade, but steamed carrots or celery would be good too (see Cooking *times for vegetables,* pp.74–75).

Marinated oranges
Fresh oranges can be sliced and marinated in orange and lemon juice with honey and Grand Marnier to taste, and then decorated with some orange zest.

Tomato sauce

Steamed potatoes

Mangetout and
mushroom salad

Broccoli roulade

Marinated oranges

Spaghetti with oil,
garlic and chilli sauce

Illustrated on page 217

Ingredients

*500g (1lb 2oz) fresh wholewheat
spaghetti*
30ml (2 tbsp) olive oil
2–3 cloves garlic, crushed
1 dried chilli, very finely diced
2–3 tbsp finely chopped parsley
salt and pepper
Serves 4–6

Spaghetti with oil, garlic, and chilli sauce

NUTRIENTS PER PORTION

460 Calories

Protein 18g ● ● ●   Fibre 9g ● ● ●
Polyunsaturated fats 3g ● ● ●   Saturated fats 5g ● ● ●
Vitamins A, B1, B2, B12, C, E, FA, N
Minerals Fe, K, Mg, Zn

Pasta must always be freshly cooked. Bring a large pan of water to the boil and put in plenty of salt. If the pan is big enough, there is no need to add a little oil as some cooks do to prevent the pasta from sticking together. It should be cooked *al dente* – until just tender but offering a very slight resistance to the bite. The only way to be sure of this is to test a piece by biting. Wholewheat spaghetti will take from 8–10 minutes to cook. This is one of the quickest of all pasta sauces. It can be made while the spaghetti is cooking.

1 Using a large, heavy-based pan, heat the oil and sauté the garlic and chilli over moderate heat for 2–3 minutes. The garlic should turn golden, but must on no account burn.

2 As soon as the pasta is cooked, drain it, turn it into the pan and mix quickly to coat it with the oil. Mix in the parsley and season with salt (and pepper if necessary). Serve immediately.

Illustrated on page 217

Ingredients

225g (8oz) broccoli florets
40g (1½oz) butter
25g (1oz) wholewheat flour
150ml (¼ pint) milk
3 eggs, separated
salt and pepper
Filling
tomato sauce (see p.119)
For garnishing
2–3 tbsp freshly grated Parmesan
tomato slices (optional)
Serves 4–6

Broccoli roulade

NUTRIENTS PER PORTION

250 Calories

Protein 12g ● ●   Fibre 2g ●
Polyunsaturated fats 1g ● ●   Saturated fats 8g ● ●
Vitamins A, B2, B12, C, D, FA, N
Minerals Ca, K

To vary the dish, substitute 100g (4oz) green or brown lentils for the broccoli. Simmer them in plenty of water for 35–40 minutes and drain.

1 Steam the broccoli lightly for 5–6 minutes. Chop it finely.

2 Melt the butter, stir in the flour and cook over low heat for 2 minutes. Add the milk and bring to boiling point, stirring well to avoid lumps. Simmer for 2–3 minutes.

3 Preheat the oven to gas mark 5, 190°C (375°F), and line a 33×23cm (13×9in) Swiss roll tin with greaseproof paper.

4 Off the heat, beat the egg yolks into the sauce, one at a time. Season well, and mix in the broccoli.

5 Whisk the egg whites until stiff but not dry and gently fold them into the broccoli mixture.

6 Spread this over the prepared Swiss roll tin, and bake for 17–20 minutes.

7 Turn out onto a clean tea towel covered with a fresh sheet of greaseproof paper. Peel off the old sheet. Spread the filling over the roulade and roll it up, using the tea towel. Do not worry if it cracks slightly. Sprinkle with grated cheese and put back in oven for 5 minutes before serving garnished with tomato slices.

Basic vinaigrette

NUTRIENTS PER 90 ML
Protein Trace Fibre 0g
Polyunsaturated fats 6g Saturated fats 8g
Vitamins –
Minerals –

550 Calories

Ingredients
*60–90ml (4–6 tbsp) oil (olive or
sunflower or a mixture to taste)
15ml (1 tbsp) wine or cider vinegar
15ml (1 tbsp) lemon juice
1 large clove garlic, crushed
large pinch of mustard powder
salt and pepper*
Makes 90–120ml (6–8 tbsp)

Although in itself this vinaigrette dressing is not high in nutrients, combined with the ingredients of the mangetout and mushroom salad it will add the perfect finishing touch to the main course.

To vary this recipe, add a peeled and mashed avocado and blend until smooth. The result, more like a mayonnaise than a vinaigrette, is also good with a simple green or tomato salad, or with a coleslaw. Another alternative is to add 15–30ml (1–2 tbsp) soya flour and 5ml (1 tsp) honey and blend until smooth. This looks similar to egg mayonnaise. Both are useful recipes for those who prefer not to eat dairy products.

Mix all the ingredients together in a jar with a screw top and shake well.

Marinated oranges

NUTRIENTS PER PORTION
Protein 1g • Fibre 0g
Polyunsaturated fats 0g Saturated fats 0g
Vitamins C
Minerals –

90 Calories

Illustrated on page 217

Ingredients
*5 large oranges
1 lemon
10ml (2 tsp) honey
30ml (2 tbsp) Grand Marnier*
Serves 4

If you have not got any Grand Marnier in stock at home use Cointreau instead to add a full, rich flavour to the orange slices.

1 Peel four of the oranges, using a sharp knife to remove the pith. Cut into thin slices and place in a shallow dish.

2 Squeeze the juice from the remaining orange (save the peel) and the lemon and pour into a bowl. Add the honey and Grand Marnier and mix thoroughly. Pour over the orange slices.

3 Cut the zest of the squeezed orange into very fine julienne strips and sprinkle over the orange slices.

INDEX

Page numbers in italics refer to·illustrations

ACKNOWLEDGMENTS

Designer: Sue Hall
Editors: Sydney Francis, Mary Lambert
Typesetter: Bournetype, Bournemouth
Reproduction: Colourscan, Singapore

Dorling Kindersley
Managing editor: Jemima Dunne
Managing art editor: Derek Coombes
Editor: Julia Harris-Voss
Designer: Camilla Fox
Production: Helen Creeke

Photographic credits All photography by Philip Dowell except: pp 8/9 David Bradfield and p 42 Peter Myers